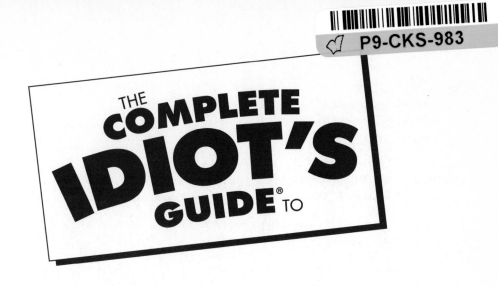

THE COMPLETE IDIOT'S GUIDE® TO

Economics

by Tom Gorman

ALPHA

A member of Penguin Group (USA) Inc.

ALPHA BOOKS

Published by the Penguin Group

Penguin Group (USA) Inc., 375 Hudson Street, New York, New York 10014, USA

Penguin Group (Canada), 90 Eglinton Avenue East, Suite 700, Toronto, Ontario M4P 2Y3, Canada (a division of Pearson Penguin Canada Inc.)

Penguin Books Ltd., 80 Strand, London WC2R 0RL, England

Penguin Ireland, 25 St. Stephen's Green, Dublin 2, Ireland (a division of Penguin Books Ltd.)

Penguin Group (Australia), 250 Camberwell Road, Camberwell, Victoria 3124, Australia (a division of Pearson Australia Group Pty. Ltd.)

Penguin Books India Pvt. Ltd., 11 Community Centre, Panchsheel Park, New Delhi—110 017, India

Penguin Group (NZ), 67 Apollo Drive, Rosedale, North Shore, Auckland 1311, New Zealand (a division of Pearson New Zealand Ltd.)

Penguin Books (South Africa) (Pty.) Ltd., 24 Sturdee Avenue, Rosebank, Johannesburg 2196, South Africa

Penguin Books Ltd., Registered Offices: 80 Strand, London WC2R 0RL, England

Copyright © 2003 by Tom Gorman

International Standard Book Number: 978-0-02-864492-9
Library of Congress Catalog Card Number: 2003104298

09   08   10

Interpretation of the printing code: The rightmost number of the first series of numbers is the year of the book's printing; the rightmost number of the second series of numbers is the number of the book's printing. For example, a printing code of 03-1 shows that the first printing occurred in 2003.

Printed in the United States of America

Note: This publication contains the opinions and ideas of its author. It is intended to provide helpful and informative material on the subject matter covered. It is sold with the understanding that the author and publisher are not engaged in rendering professional services in the book. If the reader requires personal assistance or advice, a competent professional should be consulted.

The author and publisher specifically disclaim any responsibility for any liability, loss, or risk, personal or otherwise, which is incurred as a consequence, directly or indirectly, of the use and application of any of the contents of this book.

Most Alpha books are available at special quantity discounts for bulk purchases for sales promotions, premiums, fund-raising, or educational use. Special books, or book excerpts, can also be created to fit specific needs.

For details, write: Special Markets; Alpha Books, 375 Hudson Street, New York, NY 10014.

Publisher: *Marie Butler-Knight*
Product Manager: *Phil Kitchel*
Senior Managing Editor: *Jennifer Chisholm*
Senior Acquisitions Editor: *Renee Wilmeth*
Development Editor: *Jennifer Moore*
Production Editor: *Billy Fields*
Copy Editor: *Sara Bosin*
Illustrator: *Chris Eliopoulos*
Cover/Book Designer: *Trina Wurst*
Indexer: *Angela Bess*
Layout/Proofreading: *Angela Boley, Mary Hunt, Ayanna Lacey*

Contents at a Glance

Contents

Foreword

Thirty years ago, television news rarely mentioned business and economics. The three major television networks were comfortable with that, and so were their viewers. Yes, the price of oil was widely reported, but only because of international developments like the 1973 oil embargo and the rise of OPEC. Data such as interest rates and the value of the dollar were rarely mentioned because, in general, the audience could not place the data in an economic context. Matters such as economic stagnation, inflation, and falling incomes were treated as purely political issues. Business and economics remained in the newsroom basement.

Back then, those of us who specialized in business news, especially business news on television, occupied a tiny niche market. The 1970s gradually changed that, but by the time we broke into the mainstream news, we faced another challenge: The viewing public still had very little knowledge of economics.

I was there, as the business news anchor, at the creation of CNN on June 1, 1980. The then-upstart network gave business news a high priority from Day One. We introduced coverage of economics to our audience, although I am sure some viewers thought we were speaking a foreign language. As one of the original interpreters of economics to a wide audience, I can tell you from experience: It was an uphill struggle. But we hung in there, and so did our audience … for a while.

The 1980s brought us that monster known as "The Deficit." Although it may run wild again, that beast has been tamed for some time. However, in the 1980s "The Deficit" came to dominate public policy. As a business news anchor, trying to explain—in thirty seconds, in front of a camera—the most important, yet most technical, economic issue of the decade … well, it wasn't a pretty picture. As a result, we dropped the subject and focused on rising stock prices, which made everyone feel good and required little in-depth knowledge.

By the mid-1990's the "New Economy" had arrived, with falling interest rates, full employment, and a roaring stock market, which people loved hearing about. Genuine interest soon developed, and the result was a new high for business and economic news. In one generation, we had gone from the basement to center stage. It was a great ride, but I only wish that the success of televised economic news had been matched by the audience's understanding of the subject. Television, with its demand for moving pictures and bare-boned scripts, makes a poor economics teacher.

However, *The Complete Idiot's Guide to Economics* makes an excellent economics teacher. Tom Gorman cuts through the jargon that economists enjoy using and makes abstract concepts concrete. He explains how the economy works and the parts played by consumers, businesses, and the government, and uses real-life examples to clarify any technical points. He helps you make sense of unemployment and inflation, taxes and deficits, and interest rates and Federal Reserve policy.

It's important stuff. Your economic life, and your understanding and control of it, dictate a big chunk of your lifestyle. Yet how many people understand why bond prices fall when interest rates rise? How many know what triggers a recession or kicks off an expansion? The economic news is now everywhere, available to all, but you still have to make sense of it. Tuning it out, or worse, misunderstanding it, can lead to business, career, and financial problems.

The Complete Idiot's Guide to Economics will help you understand economics, the economy, and the economic news. I only wish that this book had been available to viewers of my broadcasts for all those years when I tried to explain "the dismal science" in 30-second sound-bites!

—Stuart Varney

CNN Business News Anchor, 1980–2000

Introduction

Economics touches every part of our lives. Our jobs and livelihoods, our purchase and investment decisions, our choice of where and in what to live, even the way we vote— all depend to some extent on economics. The economy—the system that we as a society use to decide what to make and who gets what—represents a powerful force in our lives.

Yet few of us truly understand how our economy works. Oh, we have conventional wisdom of the type summed up in old sayings: The rich get richer and the poor get poorer. Money comes to money. The best things in life are free. There is even some truth to these sayings when you look at income patterns, returns on investment, and certain quality-of-life issues. But despite their truth, those old sayings don't provide enough information, insight, or inspiration to guide us in our economic lives. They are substitutes for understanding economics, a subject that many people find mysterious.

Economics is shrouded in mystery for several reasons, but I believe the main reason is that most people see the whole subject as way too complicated. Part of this has to do with language. Just like health care, auto repair, and other fields, economics has its own words for things. While words that describe economic activity may be unfamiliar, they are still just words. Those words all mean something, and once you understand what they mean, much of the mystery drops away.

Many people also think that economics is full of mathematics. While there can be a lot of numbers in economics, the most important aspects can be explained in plain English. Also, except in specialized areas such as economic forecasting, the arithmetic that does pop up is very basic.

Economics is a social science. Like the other social sciences, such as psychology, it explains human behavior. Economics explains people's behavior in the marketplace. Why do people buy what they buy? How do storekeepers decide what prices to charge? Why can't everyone have what they want? How do the owners of a business decide what to produce and how much to pay workers? What, if anything, can the government do to help poor people become better off? Economics answers these questions, and answers most of them without mathematics.

Sometimes it is economists who make economics seem complicated. Economists are the highly educated experts who study economics deeply, conduct research, formulate theories, and teach economics in colleges and universities. They also advise business and political leaders about the economy. Economists play an important role in society, but like all experts, they can handle the complexities of their subject because they create those complexities.

If you are a business person, professional, investor, or just a citizen with a vote you don't want to waste, *The Complete Idiot's Guide to Economics* will help you make better decisions in your business, personal, and public lives. If you are a student, this book will give you a clearer explanation of many economic concepts than textbooks or lectures often supply. No matter what roles you play in our economy—and we all play multiple roles, as workers, employers, buyers, sellers, lenders, borrowers, and so on—this book will explain that role and show you how to play it better.

This is not a book about economic theories, although it covers the major ones. It is a book about economic realities. So whenever possible, I will point out the effects of economics on businesses, consumers, lenders, borrowers, various segments of society, and our global neighbors. I will also, when appropriate, suggest steps you can take to protect yourself or benefit from economic realities.

Economics and politics often rub up against one another and, in a way, there's nothing wrong with that. Economics affects business, finance, government, and foreign policy, as well as what we have for dinner. Although economics can be fraught with politics, I have no political agenda in writing this book. When an author writing about economics has an ideological ax to grind or fails to stay politically neutral—for instance, by pointing out both management's and labor's view of an issue—then he's not just discussing economics. He's also presenting economic viewpoints.

Viewpoints are fine and, like everyone, I have mine. However, I want to give you a clear understanding of economics and leave you free to develop your own viewpoint. So I've kept my political beliefs out of this book.

Here's the Approach We'll Take:

Part 1, "The Big Picture," gives you an overview of economics, the U.S. economy, and some basic tools of economics. It also presents the concepts of supply and demand and shows you how prices are determined in the marketplace.

Part 2, "Capitalism at Work," examines the ways in which consumers and businesses make decisions, the dynamics of income and spending, and the expansions and recessions that constitute the business cycle.

Part 3, "The Government and the Economy," deals with the way income and wealth is distributed in the United States. It also looks at taxes, government spending, and fiscal policy, which is one of two ways the government tries to keep the economy stable and growing.

Part 4, "Money, the Banking System, and Monetary Policy," explains the roles that money, credit, and the Federal Reserve play in our economy. This section also explains monetary policy, which is the other way that the government tries to keep the economy stable and growing.

Part 5, "The Global Economy," takes you beyond our borders, on a tour of the international economy. Here we examine imports and exports, international trade policy, the foreign exchange system, and the issues facing developing nations.

Part 6, "Everyday Economics," wraps things up with a look at ways of gauging the effect of economic developments in your daily life and ways of understanding the impact that economic developments have on you and your business, job, and investments.

In the tradition of the *Complete Idiot's Guides* series, *The Complete Idiot's Guide to Economics* takes a complex subject and makes it clear and, I hope, fun to learn about. As you read this book, either straight through or when a part or chapter will help you understand something going on in the world (or in class), keep in mind that economics is affecting you every day, whether you know it or not. If you look around you and listen to the news, and watch what businesses and consumers and government officials do, you will see every aspect of economics that is covered in this book at work in the real world.

I will be pointing out some "instances of economics" in this book. Yet the real value of your reading will come when you see the workings of economics—supply and demand, expansion and recession, monetary and fiscal policy—in your daily life: in your paycheck, wallet, pocketbook, credit card statement, bank account, and investment portfolio.

Some "Economic Indicators"

Throughout this book, you will find the following features that will clarify certain points, add to your knowledge, and "keep it real."

 EconoTalk

These boxes explain economic concepts and technical terms in plain English.

The Real World

These sidebars show aspects of economics at work in history, business, and the news.

EconoTip

These notes warn you about potential points of confusion and help you apply the concepts and analytical tools to everyday life.

Acknowledgments

Thank you to everyone who helped make this book possible: Marie Butler-Knight, publisher at Alpha Books, and the entire editorial team (Renee Wilmeth, editor; Jennifer Moore, development editor; Sara Bosin, copy editor; Billy Fields, production editor; Trina Wurst, designer); Mike Snell, my agent; my wife Phyllis and my sons Danny and Matt; my professors and instructors at New York University's Stern School of Business; and my past employers and colleagues, particularly those at the economic forecasting and consulting firm DRI/McGraw-Hill (now Global Insight Inc.), where I worked as the managing editor from 1991 to 1996.

Trademarks

Part 1

The Big Picture

This first part of the book will introduce you to key concepts and tools, with an overview of economics and a look at the players in the U.S. economy—consumers, businesses, the government, and importers and exporters. You'll also learn how economists think about the economy.

For instance, economists often think in terms of markets. An economy contains thousands and thousands of markets. That would be pretty overwhelming if they didn't all work the same way. All markets operate by the law of supply and demand, and use prices to match supply and demand in a way that works for both buyers and sellers. So Part 1 will also show you how markets work, how prices behave, and how certain external forces can affect a market.

Let's get started.

Chapter 1

Who Gets What, and How?

In This Chapter

- ◆ Why economics matters
- ◆ How societies make decisions
- ◆ Major economic theories

Let's face it: If there's one fundamental principle guiding life on earth, it's scarcity. There simply aren't enough beachfront houses, luxury cars, and seats at the theater for everyone who wants one! And on a more serious note, there's not enough food, clothing, and medical care for everyone who needs it.

The entire discipline of economics—and all economic activity—arises from a scarcity of goods and services in comparison to human wants and needs. If there is not enough of something for everyone who wants or needs it, society faces a serious problem: How do we decide who gets that something and who goes without it?

Throughout history there have always been people who obtained what they wanted or needed by force. The barbarians who sacked Rome practiced this form of "economic activity," and in modern times it is practiced by armed robbers. But a society worthy of the name requires an orderly system of producing and distributing the necessities and luxuries of life.

Such a system is essential to a stable society. Economics is the study of systems of production and distribution—which are called economies—and of their fundamentals, dynamics, and results.

This chapter introduces the science of economics and examines various ways in which societies organize their economies. It also introduces several important economists and explains their ideas, which lead to major schools of economic thought.

What Is Economics and Who Cares?

Economics is the study, description, and analysis of the ways in which societies produce and distribute *goods and services*. Economics can be applied to ancient civilizations—the Greeks and Phoenicians had economies—and to modern societies at the national, state, and local levels. For instance, California has the largest economy of any state, while New York City has the largest of any U.S. city. Even a household has an economy (although this book does not cover "home economics"). Any system for deciding what is produced, how is it produced, and who gets to consume it, whether it is the system of an entire planet—as in the global economy—or a defined segment of society, is an economy and can be understood in economic terms.

An Inexact Science?

Economics is one of the social (as opposed to natural or physical) sciences, as are psychology and anthropology. Social sciences examine and explain human interaction. Because of this, the findings and knowledge produced by a social science generally cannot be as exact or predictable as those of a physical science, such as physics or chemistry.

EconoTalk

Economics is the study, description, and analysis of the ways in which a society produces and distributes goods and services. In economics, the term **goods and services** refers to everything that is produced in the economy—all products and services, including government "services," such as national defense and the prison system.

For instance, if you put water in a saucepan on a stove, you know with certainty that it will boil when it reaches 212° Fahrenheit. But if you are the governor of a state and you raise the state sales tax, you cannot be certain about the effect it will have or be able to answer any of the following basic questions: How much money will the tax raise? In order to avoid the tax, will people take more of their business across the state line? Will they shop more often on the Internet, where there is no sales tax (yet)? Will companies in the state experience lower sales and generate lower corporate income taxes as a result?

Economics deals with these kinds of questions, but it seldom comes up with totally precise explanations or correct predictions.

Why? Because human behavior in the economic realm is as complex and mysterious as it is in any other sphere of life.

It's Not Perfect, but It Helps!

The good news, however, is that economics can tell us the *likely* results of a sales tax. In addition, as a scientific discipline, economics provides extremely useful analytical tools and frameworks for understanding human behavior in the areas of getting and spending money, which (let's face it) occupies the majority of most people's waking hours.

Economics deals with fundamental, often life-or-death issues. That is why economics is important. Its challenge lies in its mysteries: We don't know when the next expansion or recession will arrive. We don't know if a federal tax cut will help the economy grow. We don't know which new technologies should be encouraged and which ones won't pan out. And, tragically, we don't know how to overcome poverty, hunger, crime, and other evils rooted in economic reality. But economics is the branch of the social sciences most concerned with these matters, and is it the one that's well equipped to help us deal with them.

Economics provides a framework for understanding government policies, business developments, and consumer behavior here and abroad. It provides a rich context for making decisions in your business, professional, and financial life. The economy is to business as the ocean is to fish. It is the environment in which business operates. The more you know about this environment, the better you will function as a manager, analyst, and decision-maker.

Will That Be Large or Small?

Economics has two main branches: macroeconomics and microeconomics.

Macroeconomics is what most people think of when they hear the word "economics." Macroeconomics—"macro" means "large"—focuses on the study of whole systems of production and distribution, that is, whole economies and large sectors of the economy. "Macro" (as it is often called by economists and students) also focuses on broad levels of economic activity, such as overall income and production in an economy. Finally, macroeconomics examines the relationships among the sectors of the economy.

The Real World

Economists and economics play an important role in addressing many of the world's most pressing problems. Many high-ranking public officials hold degrees in economics or, as in the case of Chairman of the Federal Reserve Alan Greenspan, are economists. The Council of Economic Advisors helps the president address economic issues.

Virtually every state, many cities, and some regions of the United States have established economic development agencies that create programs to maintain and improve the economic health of the area. Their goals include attracting and retaining businesses and jobs, fostering development of new technologies, and educating the area's workforce.

On a larger scale, U.S. and international organizations, such as the World Bank, build and implement programs to develop and stabilize economies of less developed nations around the world. The International Monetary Fund monitors national economies, trade activity, and the value of the world's various currencies.

Many people see economics as a theoretical "ivory tower" pursuit. That's far from the truth. All of the world's major investment and commercial banks—outfits seriously dedicated to making money—have staff economists monitoring the impact of consumer, business, and government decisions on the markets and on their customers.

We'll be talking about sectors of the economy in more detail in Chapter 2 but, broadly, most economies contain a public sector—local, state (or provincial), and federal governments—and a private sector, which includes consumers, businesses, and nonprofit and nongovernmental organizations.

EconoTalk

Macroeconomics focuses on whole economies and large sectors of economies and on broad levels of economic activity, such as overall income, and on relationships among the sectors of the economy.

Microeconomics focuses on individual economic entities, such as a single business or household, or on specific economic activities or phenomena, such as employment or prices.

Microeconomics, as the name indicates, concerns itself with smaller portions of the economy. Microeconomics focuses on individual economic entities, such as a single business or household, or on specific economic activities or phenomena, such as employment or prices. For example, labor economics—the study of labor markets and wages—falls within microeconomics.

One other aspect of economics warrants mention: econometrics. ("Metrics" is just another word for measures.) The discipline of econometrics uses statistical methods to analyze economic behavior and problems. Much of econometrics focuses on forecasting economic activity, such as next year's auto sales or interest rate levels, or when the next recession will begin. Forecasting is among the most challenging areas of economics, and economic forecasts are notoriously inaccurate. Then again, so are weather forecasts. Like most views of the future, economic forecasts should be used to describe different potential scenarios and their possible effects.

EconoTalk

Economic policies are measures that a government takes to help stabilize or grow its economy. Tools of economic policy include increasing or decreasing government spending and borrowing, adjusting certain interest rates, and increasing or decreasing taxes.

As a social science, economics has most of the characteristics of other sciences. Economists observe behavior and outcomes, systematically catalog those observations (by collecting data), and identify patterns and trends. Then they develop and test theories to explain the behavior, outcomes, patterns, and trends they have seen. Although economists can rarely test their theories in controlled experiments, they do seek practical applications of their theories. These usually take the form of *economic policies* implemented by local, state, and federal governments. Economic policy also affects major management decisions by large corporations and financial institutions. We'll discuss economic policies in greater depth in Parts 3 and 4.

For example, economists have formulated theories about the relationship between interest rates and the amount money businesses and consumers borrow. These theories help the government to develop policies that affect the ease with which people can borrow money, that is, use credit. The availability of credit affects the level of people's spending, which in turn affects the level of production, which affects the rate of economic growth.

The U.S. economy and even state and local economies cannot be completely controlled by the government or any other entity. They are too large and, as I mentioned, people's behavior is too complex to fully understand, let alone control. However, economic theory helps governments in their efforts to stabilize and grow their economies and temper the effects of bad economic conditions.

A Firm Base

Let's look at a few basic concepts that underlie the entire discipline of economics.

First, economics assumes that people make rational choices in the face of scarcity. It assumes that people can and will rationally decide what they want and what they are willing to do without. In some cases, this may seem odd. Are economists saying that people deliberately choose jobs with low pay? Are they saying that people choose poorly made products over high quality ones?

Well, in a way, yes, they are saying that. While individuals may face a limited range of choices or make bad choices, they do make choices. Economics aims to explain and predict people's choices and the ways in which various conditions affect their choices. Of necessity, economists must assume that people are making rational rather than irrational economic decisions.

Second, economics assumes that people have preferences that underlie their economic decisions. This concept resembles the idea of rational choice, but it focuses more on people's likes and dislikes and the trade-offs they are willing to make among these likes and dislikes. The assumption is that people know what they prefer and make choices that reflect these preferences.

Third, people's choices and preferences—their decisions—take the form of transactions in the marketplace. In these transactions they buy and sell labor, products, and services in exchange for money. Furthermore, these transactions collectively amount to economic activity. For example, someone who decides to work at a certain job in a certain place for a certain salary has engaged in a transaction. When we sum up all of the transactions that people in an economy have made regarding where they will work and for how much, the result is employment activity. That activity can be quantified, described, and studied.

Fourth, economic activity occurs in *markets*. A market is a place where goods and services and the factors of production—raw materials, labor, and plant and equipment—are bought and sold. Although most of us think of a market as a physical place, economists define markets more broadly. The market for financial securities, for example, is located not only on Wall Street but also in cyberspace where online brokerage services enable people to buy and sell securities. Economics delves deeply into markets—how they function and how people function within them.

EconoTalk

Markets are organized mechanisms or systems for exchanging money for goods and services (or in a barter system, goods and services for goods and services). They may be physical places, such as the New York Stock Exchange, or they may be located in cyberspace, like the international currency market. A market enables buyers and sellers to come together and engage in transactions.

Finally, some mechanism is required for a market to function properly. The mechanism used in most markets is the price mechanism, and prices are expressed in money. (Bet you were wondering when we would get around talking about money.) In all modern economies, money is recognized as the medium of exchange. A medium of exchange is something people within an economy have agreed to use as a standard of value. Certain Native American tribes reportedly used wampum, the purple parts of clamshells, as money. Other forms of money have included gold, furs, and huge round stones—all of which make about as much sense as using pieces of paper displaying pictures of deceased leaders. Essentially, money is anything that people agree to use as a medium of exchange on a large scale.

These concepts—people making rational choices and expressing preferences in marketplace transactions valued in money—are indeed basic. They form the basis of all that follows in economics. Keep these concepts in mind as we examine matters like the law of supply and demand in Chapter 3.

Getting Organized: Command, Market, and Mixed Economies

Not all economies are organized in the same way. The three major ways they can be organized are as a market economy, a command economy, or a mixed economy.

In a *market economy*, consumers and businesses decide what they want to produce and purchase in the marketplace. They make these decisions by "voting with their dollars." Producers decide what to produce given the demand they see in the marketplace in terms of their sales and the prices they get for their goods and services. In a pure market economy, also known as a *laissez-faire* economy (from the French "allow to do"), the government plays a very limited role in what is produced. The government does not direct, and may even lack the power to direct, the private sector to produce certain goods and services.

EconoTalk

In a **market economy,** the private-sector businesses and consumers decide what they will produce and purchase, with little government intervention. A **laissez-faire** economy is one in which the government plays a very limited role. In a **command economy,** also known as a planned economy, the government largely determines what is produced and in what amounts. In a **mixed economy** both market forces and government decisions determine which goods and services are produced and how they are distributed.

In a *command economy*, also known as a planned economy, the government largely determines what is produced and in what amounts. It directs producers to make and deliver goods and services in specified amounts. In practice, command economies are associated with socialism and communism, two closely related forms of government. Socialism and communism are characterized by collective ownership of the means of production and central planning functions that try to produce what people want and need, in the quantities and at the time required. The underlying philosophy of socialism is "from each according to his abilities, to each according to his needs."

In command economies, the people (in the form of the state) own the means of production. The state, which is seen to embody the will of the people, decides what will be produced according to a plan based upon what the state calculates to be people's need and desire for various goods and services. The state also plays an important role in determining how goods and services are distributed, that is, in deciding who gets how much of what.

In a *mixed economy* both market forces and government decisions determine which goods and services are produced and how they are distributed. In general, market forces prevail in mixed economies. The government does not direct the private sector to produce certain goods and services in certain quantities at certain times. However, the government's influence in the economy stems from the amount of money (raised in the form of taxes and borrowings from the private sector) that it spends and, through various forms of *welfare*, redistributes.

Today, the economies of most industrial countries are considered mixed economies. In Western European nations the government usually plays a larger role in the economy than in North America. Since the fall of the Soviet Union in 1991, the only two major planned economies are those of North Korea and the People's Republic of China. However, China has begun to incorporate some market mechanisms, such as competition, into its economy.

Although many people characterize the U.S. economy as a "free market economy," it is clearly a mixed economy. The federal government alone accounts for about 19 percent of the U.S. economy (depending on what forms of government spending are counted). Adding state and local governments brings the public sector share up to about 28 percent. With that kind of economic clout, government at various levels has a lot to say about what is produced in our society and who gets what. Nevertheless, the United States relies on markets to a larger degree than any other major industrial nation in the world, so from a relative standpoint, it is indeed a free market economy.

EconoTalk

Welfare refers to government efforts to provide for people's basic needs. Also known as public assistance, because it comes from the public sector, these efforts take the form of government sponsored work projects and, more commonly, payments made by the government to support basic needs of those who cannot afford them. The federal food stamp and Medicare programs are both forms of welfare.

EconoTip _____

As we will see, markets, like governments, can be inefficient in delivering some goods and services. They are considered most inefficient at delivering what are known as "public goods." Essentially, a public good is something that everyone wants, such as clean air or a well-educated populace, but no one wants to pay for. While the U.S. society is experimenting with market incentives to obtain these goods—for instance, tradable exemptions from emissions controls and school voucher programs—markets have a generally poor record of delivering public goods. Universal health care is arguably a good example of this.

Three Economists and Their Theories

The three most important economists were Adam Smith, Karl Marx, and John Maynard Keynes (pronounced *canes*). Each was a highly original thinker who developed economic theories that were put into practice and affected the world's economies for generations.

Adam Smith and His Invisible Hand of Capitalism

Adam Smith, a Scot and a philosopher who lived from 1723 to 1790, is considered the founder of modern economics. In Smith's time, philosophy was an all-encompassing study of human society in addition to an inquiry into the nature and meaning of existence. Deep examination of the world of business affairs led Smith to the conclusion that collectively the individuals in society, each acting in his or her own self-interest, manage to produce and purchase the goods and services that they as a society require. He called the mechanism by which this self-regulation occurs "the invisible hand," in his groundbreaking book, *The Wealth of Nations*, published in 1776, the year of America's Declaration of Independence.

While Smith couldn't prove the existence of this "hand" (it was, after all, invisible) he presented many instances of its working in society. Essentially, the butcher, the baker, and the candlestick maker individually go about their business. Each produces the amount of meat, bread, and candlesticks he judges to be correct. Each buys the amount of meat, bread, and candlesticks that his household needs. And all of this happens without their consulting one another or without all the king's men telling them how much to produce. In other words, it's the free market economy in action.

In making this discovery, Smith founded what is known as classical economics. The key doctrine of classical economics is that a *laissez-faire* attitude by government toward the marketplace will allow the "invisible hand" to guide everyone in their economic endeavors, create the greatest good for the greatest number of people, and generate economic growth. Smith also delved into the dynamics of the labor market, wealth accumulation, and productivity growth. His work gave generations of economists plenty to think about and expand upon.

Karl Marx: It's Exploitation!

Karl Marx, a German economist and political scientist who lived from 1818 to 1883, looked at capitalism from a more pessimistic and revolutionary viewpoint. Where Adam Smith saw harmony and growth, Marx saw instability, struggle, and decline. Marx believed that once the capitalist (the guy with the money and the organizational skills to build a factory) has set up the means of production, all value is created by the labor involved in producing whatever is being produced. In Marx's view, presented in his 1867 tome *Das Kapital* (*Capital*), a capitalist's profits come from exploiting labor—that is, from underpaying workers for the value that they are actually creating. For this reason, Marx couldn't abide the notion of a profit-oriented organization.

This situation of management exploiting labor underlies the class struggle that Marx saw at the heart of capitalism, and he predicted that that struggle would ultimately destroy capitalism. To Marx, class struggle is not only inherent in the system—because of the tension between capitalists and workers—but also intensifies over time. The struggle intensifies as businesses eventually become larger and larger, due to the inherent efficiency of large outfits and their ability to withstand the cyclical crises that plague the system. Ultimately, in Marx's view, society moves to a two-class system of a few wealthy capitalists and a mass of underpaid, underprivileged workers.

Marx predicted the fall of capitalism and movement of society toward communism, in which "the people" (that is, the workers) own the means of production and thus have no need to exploit labor for profit. Clearly, Marx's thinking had a tremendous impact on many societies, particularly on the USSR (Union of Soviet Socialist Republics) in the twentieth century.

In practice, however, two events have undermined Marx's theories. First, in socialist, centrally planned economies have proven far less efficient at producing and delivering goods and services—that is, at creating the greatest good for the greatest number of people—than capitalist systems. Second, workers' incomes have actually risen over time, which undercuts the theory that labor is exploited in the name of profit. If workers' incomes are rising, they are clearly sharing in the growth of the economy. In a very real sense, they are sharing in the profits.

While Marx's theories have been discredited, they are fascinating and worth knowing. They even say something about weaknesses in capitalism. For instance, large companies do enjoy certain advantages over small ones and can absorb or undercut them, as shown by examples as old as Standard Oil (now ExxonMobil) and General Motors and as recent as Microsoft and IBM, in high technology, and ConAgra and Dole in agriculture. In addition, as we will see in Chapter 11, income distribution in U.S.-style capitalism, which is a "purer," less-mixed form of capitalism than that of Europe, can *tend* to create a two-tier class system of "have's" and "have not's."

The Real World

Karl Marx was a true revolutionary and philosopher. Of Jewish descent but baptized and raised as a Lutheran, he coined the phrase, "Religion is the opiate of the people," thus contributing to the rise of "godless Communism."

Marx's philosophy was based on a materialistic conception of history. This was in sharp contrast to the popular idea that God was shaping human affairs. Essentially, Marx believed that the prevailing economic system at a given time determines the way people think. He also believed that history is a process of the evolution of economies, which proceed from pre-capitalism, to capitalism, to communism.

Even before he wrote *Capital*, Marx wrote *The Communist Manifesto* with his fellow philosopher Frederick Engels. Here, he posited the idea of a classless society. There was clearly more than a little idealism in Marx, despite his notorious irritability and arrogance.

Marx made his often meager living as a journalist. In 1849, after pretty much being thrown off the continent for revolutionary activities, he settled in London where he spent the rest of his life and is buried.

Keynes: The Government Should Help Out the Economy

John Maynard Keynes, a British economist and financial genius who lived from 1883 to 1946, also examined capitalism and came up with some extremely influential views. They were, however, quite different from those of Karl Marx and, for that matter, Adam Smith. In 1936, he published his *General Theory of Employment, Interest, and Money*. We will examine Keynes's theories later in this book. They mainly involve people's propensity to spend or to save their additional money as their incomes rise, and the effects of increases in spending on the economy as a whole.

The larger significance of Keynes's work lies in the view he put forth about the role of government in a capitalist economy. Keynes was writing during the Great Depression. We will look at the Great Depression in Chapter 10, but it's worth noting at this point that in the United States unemployment reached about 25 percent and millions of people had lost their life savings as well as their jobs. Moreover, there was no clear path out of the depression, which led people to seriously question whether Smith's invisible hand was still guiding things along. Was this worldwide collapse of economic activity the end of capitalism?

Keynes believed that there was only one way out, and that was for the government to start spending in order to put money into private-sector pockets and get demand for goods and services up and running again. As it turns out, President Franklin D. Roosevelt gave this remedy a try when he started a massive public works program to employ a portion of the idle workforce. However, the United States entry into World War II rendered this a less than pure experiment in government spending. The war effort boosted production to extremely high levels (to make guns, ammunition, planes, trucks, and other materiel) while simultaneously taking millions of men out of the civilian workforce and into uniform.

EconoTalk

Keynesian economics is an approach to economic policy that favors using the government's power to spend, tax, and borrow to keep the economy stable and growing. A Keynesian is an economist or other believer in Keynesian economics.

The validity and desirability of Keynes's prescription for a sluggish economy—using government spending to prime the pump—are still debated today. Again, we will look at the theory and practice of what came to be known as *Keynesian economics* later in this book.

Many other economists of note advanced theories and otherwise added to the body of knowledge in the science. We will look at their ideas as they arise in our examination of economics. However, Adam Smith, Karl Marx, and John Maynard Keynes (later Lord Keynes) are widely recognized as the most influential—Smith because he founded and formalized the science of economics, Marx because he challenged capitalism and had such a forceful impact on society and politics, and Keynes because he prompted new practices as well as new theories in the world of economic policy. Keynes also played a key role in the founding of the International Monetary Fund and in other political economic measures taken at the end of World War II.

The Dismal Science?

One other economist I want to mention at this point is Thomas Malthus, a British clergyman and professor who lived from 1766 to 1843. The Reverend Malthus developed the theory that orderly society was doomed because population growth would eventually outstrip the growth of the food supply. As a result, war, famine, and disease would periodically wipe out significant portions of the population in most countries.

He presented his theory, supported by mathematical proof, in 1798 in his widely circulated *Essay on the Principle of Population*. When the Scottish historian Thomas Carlyle read the piece, he pronounced economics "the dismal science," and the name has stuck. The idea behind Malthusian economics—that the scarcity or exhaustibility of resources breeds catastrophe—also caught on with quite a few people, and the idea has stuck. Many people today believe that overpopulation will eventually ruin the planet and that the finite nature of fossil fuel, and even timber, may lead to catastrophe.

They may have a point. However, optimistic economists point out that countervailing forces, such as ever increasing efficiency in food production, natural tendencies to limit population growth, and people's ability to develop substitutes for finite resources, nullify the Malthusian forecast.

Still, the "dismal science" tag has stuck. On the pessimistic side, there is no doubt that economics is the science of scarcity. Life can be dismal for people who don't have everything they want, and it is downright desperate for those who don't have everything they need.

Yet economics is also the science of plentitude. At its best, which is how it is practiced by most economists, the discipline aims to further our understanding of how to keep society stable and economies growing. That way, the proverbial pie continually grows larger and everyone has what they want and need, including productive work, basic necessities, some luxuries, and peace and prosperity. Given those aims, economics could more aptly be called the essential science.

The Least You Need to Know

- A stable society needs an orderly system of producing and distributing goods and services. Economics is the study of these systems, and of people's individual and collective behavior within those systems.

- Macroeconomics focuses on the study of whole systems of production and distribution—that is, whole economies—and large sectors within an economy. Microeconomics focuses on individual economic entities—such as a single business or household—or on specific economic activities or phenomena—such as employment or prices.

- Economics is based on certain assumptions. It assumes that people make rational choices and express preferences by engaging in transactions in the marketplace, which employs prices, valued in money, as its exchange mechanism.

♦ Basically, a nation's economy can be characterized as a market, command, or mixed economy, depending on the role the government plays in decisions about what is produced and how it is distributed.

♦ Adam Smith, Karl Marx, and John Maynard Keynes are history's most influential economists. Smith founded the science of economics and formulated the basic theory of capitalism. Marx challenged capitalism and had a wide impact on the political world. Keynes developed new practices and theories, the key one being the idea that government spending can stimulate the economy.

GDP and the Players Three

In This Chapter

- ◆ Major sectors of the U.S. economy
- ◆ The role of consumers, business, and government
- ◆ Drivers of economic growth

You may know the answer to the question, "How do you eat an elephant?"

"One bite at a time."

That's the approach you need to take when you are trying to understand the U.S. economy, which is the largest in the world. In this chapter, we start by carving this elephant into some fairly large parts, or sectors, as economists call them.

As we learn about these sectors, keep in mind that each one is made up of human beings. It is actual people in households, businesses, and government who decide how much of which goods and services to produce, what to purchase, and how much to pay for them. When dealing with trillions of dollars and entities like "government" and "business," it's easy to forget this fact. But when we lose sight of the people in the economy, we can also lose sight of the fact that we, and not some malevolent machine or faceless bureaucracy, *are* the economy. We have more control over our economic lives than we often realize.

All Together Now: C + I + G

Consumption by consumers, investment by businesses, and government spending are the three major parts of our economy and of most economies. (Foreign trade, conducted by exporters and importers, is the remaining sector, which I'll discuss soon.)

The size of a nation's economy is the total value of the spending on goods and services in the nation in a year. This spending occurs in the form of transactions within and between these three sectors. The flip side of this spending is production, because you can buy only what has been produced. So we can also measure an economy based on its production. Therefore, when you add up all of these transactions—and the value of foreign trade—the result is *gross domestic product*, or GDP. The formula for GDP is:

$$GDP = C + I + G + (Ex - Im)$$

The parts of the formula are simple:

C = total spending by consumers

I = total investment (spending on goods and services) by businesses

G = total spending by government (federal, state, and local)

(Ex – Im) = net exports (exports – imports)

C + I + G + (Ex – Im) currently equals over $10 trillion in the United States. That means the United States produces more than $10 trillion of goods and services within its borders *every year*.

EconoTalk

Gross Domestic Product is the sum of all spending on goods and services in a nation's economy in a year. The formula for GDP is: GDP = C + I + G + (Ex – Im), where "C" equals spending by consumers, "I" equals investment by businesses, "G" equals government spending and "(Ex – Im)" equals net exports, that is, the value of exports minus imports. Net exports may be negative.

You should know several things about GDP.

Spending by consumers, which economists call consumption or consumption expenditure, is by far the largest part of the U.S. GDP. It accounts for an average of about two-thirds of GDP in the United States. Also, consumption roughly equals household income, because people spend what they earn as income. (True, they also save some of it and they borrow to spend, but let's leave that aside for now.)

Business investment is the total amount of spending by businesses on plant and equipment, and it accounts for a little over 15 percent of total GDP. This might seem to be a relatively small portion of GDP for business, but it's an extremely important one. Businesses invest in productive equipment and that equipment typically creates jobs as well as goods and services. The wages and salaries that businesses pay to workers are not counted as businesses investment ("I"). That money is already counted in consumption ("C") because that is the money that households are spending. Investment ("I") includes only spending by businesses on goods and services, including raw materials, vehicles, offices and factories, and computers, furniture, and machinery.

Government spending on goods and services averages about 20 percent, or one fifth, of total GDP. The government takes in an amount equal to more than one fifth of GDP in taxes, but a portion of that money, equal to about 10 percent of GDP, goes to transfer payments rather than expenditures on goods and services. Transfer payments include Social Security, Medicare, unemployment insurance, welfare programs, and *subsidies*. These are not included in GDP because they are not payments for goods or services, but rather means of allocating money to achieve social ends.

EconoTalk

Subsidies are transfer payments to assist industries that benefit the public, but might not survive or remain stable if operated for profit without subsidies. Farm products and rail transportation are subsidized in most modern economies.

Net exports for the United States are close to zero or, oftentimes, a bit negative. Yes, the United States exports a tremendous amount of goods, but it imports even more.

So the composition of GDP breaks down roughly as follows:

Consumption	65%
Investment	15%
Government	20%
Net Exports	0
	100%

Each component of GDP is important. In this chapter, we examine the role and contribution of each component.

GDP Is "The Economy"

When people refer to "the economy" they are generally referring to GDP. If a newsperson says, "The economy grew by 3.5 percent last year," it means that GDP grew by 3.5 percent during the year (compared with the previous year's GDP). Incidentally, a growing economy characterizes an expansion, which is also known as a recovery. A contracting economy characterizes a recession. We will examine the cycle of recession and recovery—that is, the business cycle—in detail in Chapter 10. For now, it's important to know that a society benefits greatly from a stable, growing economy.

EconoTip

Economists also refer to GDP—total spending on goods and services—as total demand. In other words, the amount of goods and services accounted for in GDP is also the amount demanded by households, businesses, and the government.

A growing economy generates increasing amounts of jobs, incomes, and goods and services for its citizens. All of these are good things, of course. In a contracting economy, jobs and incomes are lost and the amount of goods and services produced shrinks. This puts people out of work, and means that there are fewer goods and services to go around. A stagnant economy—one that is neither growing nor contracting—isn't much better than one that's contracting. As the population grows, people need more jobs and more goods and services, and a stagnant economy doesn't produce them.

If you look at the formula for GDP, you'll see that if any one component increases, then the total GDP increases (assuming that the other components remain unchanged). For example:

- If consumer spending grows—if people buy more clothing and cars and homes—then the economy grows.

- If business investment grows—if companies invest in new buildings and equipment and buy more raw materials—then the economy grows.

- If government spending grows—if money is poured into the space program, defense, roads, and police forces—then the economy grows.

By the same token, if any one component of GDP decreases, then total GDP decreases unless another component of the GDP increases enough to make up for the loss.

Consumers: Buyers, Buyers Everywhere

As you have surely noticed, Americans are avid consumers. The advertising, credit card, banking, and retail industries—and the economy's ability to generate jobs—have created an environment in which people spend freely on the things they want and need. In contrast, the Japanese put a higher percentage of their incomes into savings, and both Asians and Europeans make much less use of credit cards. Consumer demand in the United States fuels continual economic growth.

EconoTip _____

You may have heard the term Gross National Product, or GNP. If so, you may be wondering why am I using GDP instead.

Economist now usually use GDP—gross domestic product—rather than GNP to measure the economy. Here's why: GDP includes all goods and services produced _within_ a nation's borders. GNP includes all goods and services produced _by_ a nation, including those produced overseas by that nation's companies. Given the number of foreign companies, such as car manufacturers, now operating in the United States, most economists see GDP as the better measure of economic activity in the country. U.S. companies have operations in foreign nations, but that does not create jobs or income here in the United States.

Aside from all of those slick advertisements and our appetite for goods and services, several more fundamental factors drive U.S. consumer spending. They also drive consumer spending in other nations. The most important of these are:

- Population growth and household formation

- Employment

- Incomes

- Interest rates and taxes

Let's examine each of these drivers individually.

> **The Real World**
>
> In the recession of 2001, the business news repeatedly pointed out that "the consumer" continued spending, despite concerns about job security and economic conditions. Indeed, consumer spending held up well during that period while business investment contracted. Businesses cut their spending because of worries over the growth prospects of the economy and downward pressure on profits.

Population Growth and Household Formation

The more consumers there are in an economy, the more goods and services the economy will consume (all other things being equal). A steady or sharp increase in the population in an economy will drive demand upward. This occurred in the post-World War II years, when returning servicemen married and started families. The individuals born during baby boom years of 1946 to 1965 have a well-documented record of consumption.

The post-World War II years were a time of high rates of household formation. When people (usually two) form a household, a whole series of purchases becomes necessary. First, there's the housing itself. Economists keep a close eye on housing starts—the number of single-family houses and multifamily dwellings on which construction began in a period—because a home is the largest purchase that most families ever make. Second, people then need to buy a huge number of items for the house or apartment—furniture, televisions, carpeting, appliances, pots, pans, dishes, and so on. Finally, in most households, sooner or later one plus one equals three, which brings us back to population growth.

Economists look at population growth, as well as the age patterns within the population, to gauge long-term economic growth. However, the growth rate of the population is a very long-term *indicator* of economic growth. Short-term indicators of economic growth include household formation and housing starts.

Let's Work: Employment

As we will see in Chapter 6, the more money people have, the more they spend. But to spend money you must make money, which is why employment and growth in employment are so important. Moreover, people need jobs not only so they can take care of their needs, but also to occupy themselves productively. High unemployment is associated with high crime and political instability, as well as with poverty.

Economists look at employment in several ways:

- ◆ **Employment** is the percentage of the workforce that is either employed or self-employed. This may also be the reported number of people employed (rather than or in addition to the rate). This is usually expressed as nonfarm employment, to focus the number on nonseasonal jobs, and excludes the armed services.

- ◆ **The unemployment rate** is the percentage of the workforce that is out of work but looking for work and willing to work. The unemployment rate is reported more commonly than employment because it is a bit more accurate because people file claims for unemployment insurance. As a smaller number it is also easier to comprehend changes in it.

- ◆ **New jobs** is (as you surely suspected) the number of new jobs generated by the economy in a period, usually a calendar quarter or year. The number of new jobs is commonly reported in the business news.

◆ **Jobs lost** is also just what it sounds like—the number of jobs eliminated in the economy in the period being considered. **Net new jobs** is the number of new jobs, minus the number of jobs lost. Jobs lost and net new jobs are also reported in the business news.

EconoTalk

Full employment occurs when every person in the economy who is willing and able to work has a job. In the United States, economists consider full employment to have been achieved when the unemployment rate falls to about 4 percent. That 4 percent is considered frictional unemployment— mainly people who just entered or re-entered the work force or who are between jobs.

These employment and job data all indicate the health of the economy. The larger the portion of the workforce that is employed, the better. A growing economy creates jobs, which is one reason that governments want to keep their economies growing. Political questions surround the government's role in ensuring *full employment*, and we will examine ways in which the government attempts to do that in Parts 3 and 4.

Income and Income Growth

Income is the total amount of money that households receive for supplying labor and capital in the economy: salaries, wages, bonuses, tips, benefits, interest, dividends, and so on. Rising incomes give people more money to spend and save. That increases demand and fuels economic growth.

Households can do only one of two things with their *disposable income*: spend it or save it. Whether they spend it or save it has a profound effect on the economy, and we'll examine that effect in Chapter 6. For now, it's enough to know that higher incomes (or lower taxes) put more money into people's pockets. When they spend it, they are increasing consumption—the "C" in the GDP formula. Yet even when they save it, they are fueling GDP growth. Some of that savings goes into bank accounts or investments that put money into the hands of businesses, which in turn invest that money and boost the "I" in the GDP formula.

EconoTalk

Disposable income is household income minus taxes. Disposable income is either spent, and thus boosts consumption, or is saved, which makes it available for investment by businesses.

Interest Rates and Taxes

The other main drivers of consumption are interest rates and taxes. U.S. consumers are the world's greatest users of credit. When interest rates are low, people will borrow and spend more money. This is particularly true with regard to rates on home mortgages and auto loans. When lower taxes increase people's disposable income, they dispose of it either by spending it and boosting consumption or by saving it, which makes it available for investment. Higher taxes, which nobody ever wants, take money away from households and thus lower consumption expenditure. Yet higher taxes do not *necessarily* reduce GDP. If the government purchases goods and services with all the money raised through higher taxes, then total demand and GDP remain unchanged.

I mention interest rates and taxes together because they are two of the three major levers that the federal government uses to implement economic policy. The other lever is government spending, and we will cover them all in Parts 3 and 4.

Let's turn to the role of business investment in the economy.

Investment: Business Buys as Well as Sells

The word investment can mean several things: a purchase of stock by an individual investor, a college student's "investment in herself" in the form of tuition, a company's investment in a new factory or a new fleet of trucks. Only the last of these would be counted in investment in the formula for GDP. The other two would be counted in "C" as consumption.

EconoTip

Keep in mind that wages and salaries paid by companies are not included in investment. Doing so would double count wages and salaries in GDP, because that money is already included in consumption expenditures.

By definition, a capitalist economy is one in which people in the private sector can raise capital, invest it in a business, produce goods and services, and attempt to sell them in the market at a profit. Several forces drive business investment, and the most important of these are:

- Interest rates and taxes
- Availability of capital
- Availability of opportunities

Interest Rates and Taxes, Again

Why would interest rates and taxes be listed first for business investment but last for consumption? Because, compared with consumption, business investment is more sensitive to interest rates and taxes. Of course, people are people, and people are making a decision to spend money whether they are part of a household or a business. However, people making business investment decisions usually (but not always) make them in a more disciplined and analytical manner than people making household spending decisions.

A business analyzes the amount of money it will earn on a new factory or piece of equipment and expresses it as a percentage of the money invested. That percentage is the investment's *rate of return*. The managers of the business compare the rate of return on an investment with the interest rate they will have to pay on the money that will finance the investment. If the rate of return on the investment is lower than the interest rate they must pay, the managers will not make the investment. For example, if a piece of equipment that costs $10,000 a year to lease and operate will produce goods that can be sold for a profit of $1,000, then the rate of return on the investment is 10 percent. ($1,000÷$10,000 = 10 percent) If the business pays an interest rate of, say, 7 percent on the money for the investment, then the investment would probably be considered attractive.

EconoTalk

The **rate of return** on an investment is the amount of profit earned on the investment—that is, the amount of money earned after subtracting the expenses from the revenue brought in by the investment—expressed as a percentage of the investment.

Lower interest rates mean that more (lower return) projects become attractive to businesses, and therefore they will make more investments. For instance, projects with a rate of return of 12 percent are attractive to a company that only has to pay 8 percent interest. But at an interest rate of 12 percent, the investment is not worth pursuing.

Taxes on business, such as the corporate income tax and the capital gains tax, also affect business investment. This is a politically charged issue. Those who favor taxes (or higher taxes) on business believe a business benefits from government services, such as national defense, and should therefore pay its "fair share" of the cost. Those who favor no taxes (or lower taxes) on business believe that everyone who works for or invests in a business already pays personal income taxes. They also believe that taxes discourage business investment by taking money away from businesses and lowering the amount of money—the return—that the company realizes on an investment.

Although lower taxes can boost business investment, other factors, particularly interest rates, are usually more important drivers than taxes.

Availability of Capital

The availability of investment capital—that is, money—drives interest rates, but for the sake of clarity I discuss it separately from interest rates. Investment capital comes from households, through the banking system and the financial markets. People save their money in banks, buy insurance policies, and invest in stocks, bonds, and vehicles such as 401(k) accounts and mutual funds. A good portion of that money goes to businesses that invest it in plant and equipment.

As I mentioned earlier, U.S. households have a relatively low savings rate. They spend a larger portion of their income than consumers in most other industrial nations. But the U.S. economy is so stable and productive that many foreign financial institutions, which channel the savings of foreign households into investments, quite willingly invest in the United States. This foreign investment increases the supply of capital in the states beyond what it would be if U.S. businesses relied solely on the savings of U.S. citizens.

EconoTalk

Budget deficits occur when a government of a nation, state, or city spends more than it acquires in tax revenue during the period under consideration. The government borrows money from households and businesses to cover the spending that is not covered by taxes. A **budget surplus** occurs when the government takes in more tax money than it spends in a period.

The government, however, also borrows money from households through the financial markets to finance *budget deficits*. When the government borrows truly large sums of money relative to the available capital, a phenomenon known as "crowding out" occurs. Crowding out refers to the fact that the government can borrow enough funds to crowd businesses out of the market for investment capital. In other words, if the government borrows enough money, it can curtail the availability of funds to other borrowers.

Available Opportunities

The major determinant of business investment may be the one least subject to economic analysis: the number of good investment opportunities that businesses have to choose from. It's true that lower interest rates can make low-return investments more attractive. It's also true that lower taxes and good availability of capital can spur investment. However, unless businesses see good opportunities, they will hold onto their cash or distribute it to their stockholders as dividends.

The business cycle of expansion and recession affects the number of opportunities for better or worse. Business formation—the number of businesses being established in a period—also contributes to or detracts from the level of business investment.

For instance, business investment remained relatively low throughout 2001 and 2002. As mentioned earlier, consumers did their part to hold the economy up. They continued to spend. But businesses saw few opportunities, particularly relative to all the opportunities they saw (or thought they saw) during the "e-business revolution" of the 1990s. Also, during the 1990s, they had invested heavily in productive capital, especially information technology, and needed time integrate it into their operations.

During 2001 and 2002, interest rates remained at 30-year lows. However, when business didn't see opportunities, they certainly weren't about to invest.

Government: He's Your Uncle, Not Your Dad

As we've seen, the U.S. government—"Uncle Sam"—spends money on goods and services, thus boosting GDP. The government also makes transfer payments, which are not counted in the government's contribution to GDP. Transfer payments can, however, contribute to consumption expenditure if they wind up in the hands of households who will spend that money, which they often do. But that's part of "C," and we are now discussing "G."

The government's money comes from only two sources: taxes and borrowing. The government levies taxes on and borrows funds from the private sector. This is true of government at the federal, state, and local levels. (Yes, government agencies do charge fees, for instance at national and state parks, and states and cities assess fines for criminal and traffic violations. Technically, these are not taxes, but economists lump them in with tax revenue.)

The role of the government in an economy is large and complex, and there are various views of how the government should play it. In most modern, capitalist economies, however, the role of the government is to create and maintain conditions that will ensure a stable, orderly (but free) society.

The most basic of these conditions are a sound currency, low unemployment, and sustained economic growth. A sound currency maintains its buying power, because the economy undergoes minimal *inflation*. We'll talk about inflation in Chapter 3.

EconoTalk

Inflation refers to price increases that erode the value of currency.

The government uses economic policy to help ensure a sound currency, low unemployment, and sustained growth. Economic policy falls into two broad areas: fiscal policy and monetary policy. Fiscal policy, which we take up in Part 3, has to do with budgetary matters, such as taxes, spending, and borrowing. Monetary policy, covered in Part 4, has to do with interest rates and the amount of money in the economy.

In their effect on economic growth, the government's policies are as important as its actual purchases of goods and services. Those policies determine not only government spending, but also taxes or borrowing; and spending, taxes, and borrowing all profoundly affect the economy.

Imports and Exports

When a country exports goods, it sells them to a foreign market, that is, to consumers, businesses, or governments in another country. Those exports bring money into the country, which increases the exporting nation's GDP. When a country imports goods, it buys them from foreign producers. The money spent on imports leaves the economy, and that decreases the importing nation's GDP.

Net exports can be either positive or negative. When exports are greater than imports, net exports are positive. When exports are lower than imports, net exports are negative. If a nation exports, say, $100 billion dollars worth of goods and imports $80 billion, it has net exports of $20 billion. That amount gets added to the country's GDP. If a nation exports $80 billion of goods and imports $100 billion, it has net exports of minus $20 billion, and that amount is subtracted from the nation's GDP.

Conceivably, net exports could be zero, with exports equal to imports and in fact this does occasionally happen in the United States.

EconoTalk

Protectionism refers to government policies designed to restrict imports from coming into the nation. A **tariff**, also called a duty, is a tax on imports as they come into the country. **Free trade** means international trade that is unrestricted by tariffs or other forms of protectionism.

If net exports are positive, the nation has a positive balance of trade. If they are negative, the nation has a negative trade balance. Virtually every nation in the world wants its economy to be bigger rather than smaller. That means that no nation wants a negative trade balance.

Because no nation wants a negative trade balance, some countries try to protect their own markets. This policy, called (logically enough) *protectionism*, uses barriers to keep out imports. These barriers include high *tariffs*—taxes or surcharges on imported goods—and strict rules about what products can be imported.

The Real World

A nation's balance of trade is calculated for a country in relation to the rest of the world, and in relation to other individual nations. It can even be calculated for a specific industry.

For example, the United States usually has a negative balance of trade with the rest of the world. That means the United States imports more than it exports.

The United States also has a negative balance of trade with Japan. The United States imports more from Japan than it exports to Japan. However, the United States exports more fruits, grain, and vegetables to Japan than it imports from Japan. So the United States has a positive agricultural trade balance with Japan.

Despite some nations' attempts at protectionism, *free trade*—trade unencumbered by barriers—has recently been the dominant trend for most countries. Economists usually favor free trade because it tends to give consumers the greatest choice of products at the lowest prices. That occurs because some nations are better at producing certain products than others.

Part 5 covers trade policy and the drivers of international trade in detail. In general, however, the more goods a nation exports, the better for that nation's GDP.

It All Adds Up

The U.S. economy is a $10 trillion system of production and consumption, but it can be broken down and analyzed. The major players—consumers, businesses, and government—constantly interact with one another. Each interaction, whether it is a purchase or sale, investment or paycheck, tax or loan, constitutes a transaction and a form of economic activity.

It is that economic activity—and the millions of decisions that underlie that activity—that add up to our economy. The same is true of the economies of other nations, although some of them depend on exports and imports far more than the U.S. economy. Economics is the study of the interactions of these various players in the economy, and of the motivation behind and the effects of the decisions that drive these interactions.

The Least You Need to Know

◆ Consumption by consumers, investment by businesses, government spending, and foreign trade all add up to the economy, which is measured by gross domestic product, or GDP.

- The formula for GDP is C + I + G + (Ex − Im). "C" is consumption. "B" is business investment. "G" is government spending on goods and services and does not include transfer payments. "(Ex − Im)" is exports minus imports, or net exports, which may be either positive or negative.

- The most important forces driving consumption are population growth and household formation, employment, incomes, interest rates, and taxes.

- The most important forces driving business investment are interest rates, availability of capital, and availability of investment opportunities.

- Government spending accounts for almost 20 percent of GDP, but government economic policies also play a large role in the economy.

- Exports increase GDP, while imports decrease GDP. Therefore most nations want their exports to be higher than their imports, and many use some form of protectionism to try to ensure that this occurs.

Chapter 3

The Economist's Toolbox

In This Chapter

- ◆ Understanding economic data
- ◆ How to read charts and graphs
- ◆ Pitfalls to avoid in the economic news

Virtually all aspects of economic activity can be measured, and most of them are. As you've seen, consumer spending, business investment, government expenditures, exports, and imports are all counted. So are the number of houses under construction, automobiles sold, people looking for work, and people who already have work. Economists monitor the levels of income, debt, and prices, and even the way consumers feel about the future of the economy.

All of this information helps people understand the economy, including people who are not economists and don't want to become one. For instance, say you want to buy a house and need a mortgage, but you would be happy to keep your present house for another six to twelve months if it would benefit you financially. If you have a good idea of the direction in which interest rates are moving, you can better decide whether to buy that house now or nine months from now. To have a good idea of interest rate movements, however, you must understand the current level of interest rates, recent levels of rates, and the forces that affect rates.

Even then, you might be wrong. Heaven knows the interest rate forecasts of highly paid economists are often incorrect. (In fairness, they are trying to be quite precise, and they usually do get the direction of interest rate movements right.) However, if you understand interest rates—or whatever economic activity might affect you or your business—you will be right more often than wrong.

This chapter introduces some concepts and tools that economists use to deal with the information involved in following economic developments. These concepts and tools will help you more easily understand the rest of this book, and more quickly grasp the economic and business news. That way, you will improve your ability to form sound opinions and use economic information in making decisions.

Numbers Please: Economic Data

In this book and in the business press, you will read economic data. Often these data are called economic indicators because they indicate the level of activity or future activity in some area of the economy. I will explain economic data and indicators as they arise in this book, but first I want to introduce you to some tools that economists use to organize and present data. These tools—various types of tables and charts—portray relationships between data more clearly. They help you understand the nature and degree of the economic activity that the data represent.

Reading Tables

Much of the economic data you will encounter will be presented in tables. To orient you to tables of economic data, we're going to work with actual GDP data. Table 3.1 shows annual Gross Domestic Product for the years 1990 to 2001 in two different ways and with two different growth rates.

Table 3.1   Gross Domestic Production (1990–2001)

(1)	(2)	(3)	(4)	(5)
Year	GDP in Billions of Nominal Dollars	Percent Change Based on Nominal Dollars	GDP in Billions of Real Dollars*	Percent Change Based on Real Dollars*
1990	5,803	5.7	6,708	1.8
1991	5,986	3.2	6,676	-0.5
1992	6,300	5.6	6,880	3.0

(1)	(2) GDP in Billions of Nominal Dollars	(3) Percent Change Based on Nominal Dollars	(4) GDP in Billions of Real Dollars*	(5) Percent Change Based on Real Dollars*
Year				
1993	6,642	5.1	7,063	2.7
1994	7,054	6.2	7,348	4.0
1995	7,401	4.9	7,544	2.7
1996	7,813	5.6	7,813	3.6
1997	8,318	6.5	8,160	4.4
1998	8,781	5.6	8,509	4.3
1999	9,274	5.6	8,859	4.1
2000	9,825	5.9	9,191	3.8
2001	10,082	2.6	9,215	0.3

*1996 dollars
Source: Bureau of Economic Analysis

Now, there are a lot of numbers here and some unfamiliar terms in the column headings, so let's take this piece by piece.

The title of the table indicates that it covers Gross Domestic Product for a twelve-year period from 1990 to 2001. (These are all actual values from the Bureau of Economic Analysis website, which I'll tell you about at the end of this chapter.) I've numbered the Columns 1 through 5 for easy reference as I walk you through the table. The column headings describe the data in the column.

Taking each column in its turn, Column 1 indicates the year for the data in that row. (So far, so good.) The other columns require a bit more explanation.

> **EconoTip**
>
> When you look at a table, be sure to read the title of the table and all the headings for the columns and rows carefully. It's easy for many people to plunge into the numbers without really reading the words, but it's the words that tell you what numbers you are looking at.

Nominal vs. Real Dollars

Column 2 is GDP in billions of *nominal dollars*. These dollar values are expressed in billions, meaning that you should imagine that each dollar figure in the table is followed by nine (yes, nine) zeros. So GDP for 2001 is $10,082,000,000,000, or ten trillion, eighty-two billion dollars. Another way of writing this would be $10.082 trillion.

Nominal dollars, also known as current dollars, are dollar values that have *not* been adjusted for inflation. They are dollars counted the way everyone counted them in the year they correspond to, with the effect of inflation included. Again, we will learn about inflation in Part 3, but you know that inflation causes money to lose its value. If the general rate of inflation is 3 percent a year, then the average item that cost $100 on January 1 of that year would cost $103 by December 31. The price is "inflated" because the dollar lost some of its value, that is, some of its purchasing power.

Economists want to be able to look at what's going on in the economy without the effect of inflation. They want to know that GDP or exports or incomes are really growing, not just being inflated by a dollar that is losing its value. So, to get rid of the effect of inflation, they convert current dollars into *real dollars*, which are also known as inflation-adjusted dollars. In Table 3.1 they do this by converting all of the values in Column 2 into the 1996 dollar values you see in Column 4. I won't bother you with the calculations economists use to do this, but they do it. Also, they could have pegged the real value to the value of the dollar in another year, for instance 1985. The key thing is to convert the value of GDP across all years to the value of the currency in one base year. That way, you are comparing year-to-year growth in real GDP, not nominal GDP.

To see the results of their calculations, let's jump over to Column 4. In Column 4, GDP is valued in billions of *real dollars*. As a result, we see that some of the value of our $10 trillion economy is indeed due to inflation. In fact, the real, inflation-adjusted value of the 2001 GDP in 1996 dollars is "only" $9.2 trillion.

So now when you hear a newscaster say, "Real GDP grew by 2.5 percent last year," you'll know what it means. In fact, GDP growth rates reported in the business news usually are based on real, inflation-adjusted values.

EconoTalk _____

Values expressed in **nominal dollars,** also known as current dollars, have not been adjusted for the effect of inflation. They are values reported in the dollars of each year being examined. Values expressed in **real dollars,** also known as inflation-adjusted dollars, are free of the effect of inflation. Economists use real dollars in many analyses because they want to understand economic activity without distortions introduced by inflation. For instance, if nominal incomes are rising, but real incomes are falling, consumers are actually worse off even though they are making "more money."

The use of 1996 as the base year for converting nominal to real dollars creates an issue that will help you understand the nature of real dollars. You may have noticed that in the year 1996—and only in the year 1996—GDP has the same value in both nominal and real dollars: $7.813 trillion. Before the year 1996, the real dollar values for GDP are higher than the nominal dollar values. After 1996, the real dollar values are lower. That's because *after* 1996, the conversion from nominal to real dollars deflates the nominal GDP number. However, *before* 1996, the nominal values inflate GDP to the value of the dollar in 1996, which was higher. (This would not have occurred if real dollars valued in a base year before 1990 had been used.) Comparing the nominal and real values of GDP in any given year doesn't really do all that much for us.

What does this say about real dollars? It says that they are best used when comparing a value from one period to the next. Knowing that in 1991 GDP grew by 3.1 percent in nominal terms but *fell* by 0.5 percent in real terms tells me a lot. It tells me there was a recession going on—a fact that would escape me if all I had to work with were current dollars. But knowing that the value of GDP in 1991 was $5.986 trillion in 1991 dollars and $6.676 trillion in 1996 dollars doesn't do me much good at all.

Keep on Growing

Columns 3 and 5 tell us about GDP growth. The point of using real, rather than nominal, dollars becomes really clear when you look at growth over the years. For instance, in 2001 nominal GDP grew by 2.6 percent. But real GDP grew by a paltry 0.3 percent, a little over zero. The rate of growth of real GDP is telling a much more accurate story than the rate of growth for nominal GDP.

The Real World

The year 1991 in Table 3.1 is revealing. As Column 3 shows, nominal GDP grew by 3.2 percent in 1991. But, as Column 5 shows, real GDP *contracted* by 0.5 percent. That was the year of the so-called "Bush recession" (named, perhaps unfairly, for George W.'s father).

President Bush believed that the nation was not in recession and was criticized for that belief. Then-candidate Bill Clinton's team ran their campaign on economic issues, famously hanging a sign in their offices saying, "It's the economy, stupid!" to keep themselves on message.

Perhaps President Bush was looking at the growth of nominal GDP. Actually, whatever data he was looking at was in a pretty raw form. It takes several months, sometimes a couple of quarters, to finalize the economic data for a quarter, and that was part of Bush's problem. In fact, the 1991 recession was fairly mild, especially next to the 2 percent contraction—in real GDP—that President Reagan weathered in 1982. But the economy was sluggish, Bush found the criticism hard to handle, and the Clinton team made the most of it.

Here's another interesting way of looking at GDP growth. (It's a good idea to refer to Table 3.1 during this discussion.) Nominal GDP grew from just over $5.8 trillion back in 1990 to nearly $10.1 trillion in 2001. That means that GDP grew by a total of 74 percent in the 11 years from 1990 to 2001—in nominal terms (10,082 − 5803 = 4,279 and 4,279÷5803 = .737 or 74%). However, real GDP grew by only 37 percent in the same period (9,215 − 6,708 = 2,507 and 2,507÷6,708 = .373 or 37%). That's half the rate of nominal growth!

EconoTip _____

Over the long term, meaning 20 years and longer, U.S. GDP grows at an average of about 3 percent in real terms. It's interesting that even in 1990 to 2001, a period characterized by tremendous advances in technology, healthy levels of consumer spending and business investment, relatively low inflation, and good management of the economy by the government, real GDP still grew at an average rate of about 2.85 percent.

One factor in this is that the U.S. economy is so large, even if newsworthy growth occurs in various areas, as it did in high technology or Las Vegas, there are still large, older, slower-growing industries and regions that offset that growth. Also, some of the growth in the 1990s was, in a way, *not real*, as we will see in Part 2.

While tables are kept in a handy place in the economist's toolbox, charts are every bit as important.

How to Construct and Read a Chart

If one picture is worth a thousand words, one chart may be worth a thousand numbers. It's certainly the only way to deal with a thousand numbers. Charts or graphs enable economists to see things they are always looking for: trends in data and economic activity, and relationships between two or more economic concepts or activities.

A chart almost always consists of two lines, each called an axis, one horizontal and one vertical. (Some charts feature one horizontal and two vertical axes, but we won't get into them here.) A point is plotted on a chart by using the axes as coordinates that define the spot where the point goes.

For example, the following chart relates the quantity of baloney sold to the price of baloney at a (fictitious) supermarket chain. The manager of the chain has only four pieces of data: When the price of baloney is $3, they sell 2,000 pounds per month, and when the price is $1.50, they sell 7,000 pounds per month.

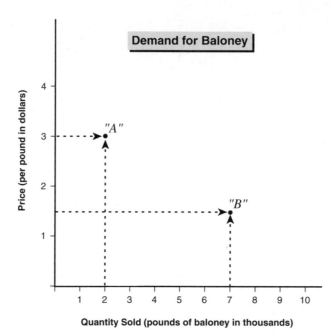

Figure 3.1

You plot a point on this chart by going along the vertical (price) axis to find the $3 mark and along the horizontal (quantity) axis to find the 2,000 pound mark. Those are your coordinates for the first point to be plotted, which I've labeled point "A." You do the same for the next two pieces of data, the price of $1.50 and the quantity of 7,000 pounds. Those coordinates yield point "B."

Notice that charts should be properly labeled, as this one is. The title of the chart, "Demand for Baloney," is clear, and each axis is labeled for the data that it represents. Also, the measure—whether it is dollars or pounds of baloney—is mentioned in parentheses. To understand a chart, you must have this information.

Now the two points on a chart can be connected, like in Figure 3.2.

When we connect two or more data points, the result is a curve. Figure 3.2 relates the price of baloney to the quantity sold—it tells us about the demand for baloney at these prices. Even if they are not actually curved, they are called curves. Some of the curves in this book would normally be drawn as actual curves, but I have generally used straight lines to keep the data simple and the explanations clear.

Economists also call a curve like this—in which two variables are related—a *function*. That's because the quantity of baloney sold—the demand for baloney—is a function of its price. The two *variables* in the function are price and quantity. Of course, other variables may affect the demand for baloney, such as the time of year or the price of ham. But those are left out of this function so that the economist can isolate the relationship between price and quantity.

Figure 3.2

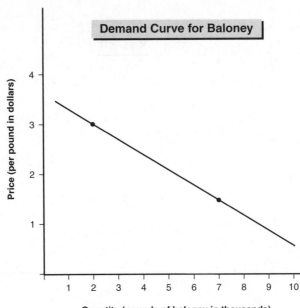

EconoTalk

A **function** is a curve or a mathematical formula (usually both) that expresses the relationship between two facts, which are known as **variables**. In a function, the variables are usually numbers. Of course, the political climate or a war could be a variable as well, but to find its way into a function, it would have to be expressed as a number, which economists can do.

Incidentally, the relationship between the price of baloney and the demand for it is *inverse*. That means that the higher the price, the lower the quantity sold, and the lower the price, the higher the quantity sold. Variables can also be in a *positive* relationship, meaning that as one variable increases, the other increases, and as one decreases, the other decreases.

Figure 3.3, "Household Income and Spending on Clothing" depicts a positive relationship between two variables.

This chart needs no numbers to illustrate the positive relationship between income and spending on clothing: the higher the income the higher the amount spent on clothing, the lower the income, the lower the amount spent on clothing.

Two more points about charts are important.

First, when economists, managers, or analysts plot data points on a chart, those points don't line up so that you can connect the dots and have a nice smooth curve in the way I do here. For instance consider the following set of data points, which, again, relate spending on clothing to annual household income.

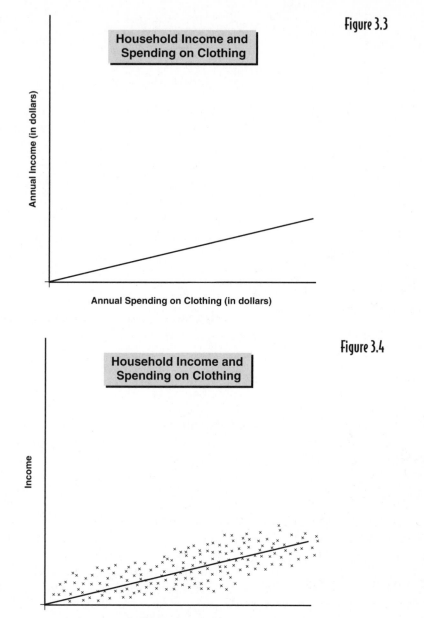

Figure 3.3

Figure 3.4

The points all over the lower part of this chart resemble the kind of pattern that often results when the data on two related variables are plotted on a chart. This is called a *scatter diagram*, for the obvious reason that the data points are scattered over the

EconoTalk

The relationship between two related variables may be **positive** or **inverse**. In a positive relationship, as one variable increases, the other increases, and as one decreases, the other decreases. In an inverse relationship, when one variable increases the other decreases, and when one decreases, the other increases.

EconoTalk

A **scatter diagram** shows the various data points plotted onto a chart. If the variables are related, the plotted points on a chart will tend to cluster into a pattern. The **line of best fit** is a line plotted through a scatter diagram that represents the relationship between the two variables.

chart. Data points that represent variables that are related will cluster into a pattern, but they certainly won't fall neatly into a line or curve.

Then what's that curve doing in there?

That curve is called the *line of best fit*. This is a line that is plotted through a set of data so that the relationship between the two variables becomes clearer. The line of best fit is calculated mathematically by computer in such a way that the distances between all of the variables and the line is minimized. In other words, the line of best fit is the line that is as close as possible to all of the data points. (That's why it's called the line of best fit—it's the line that best fits into the pattern of the data points on the chart.)

Again we will be dealing with simple curves in this book. However, I want you to know that in reality, the data, the curves, and the functions are not always that simple.

Finally, what happens in situations where there is no relationship between two variables?

Suppose you were to plot average annual temperature in the United States over the past 50 years against each year's growth in real GDP. You might wind up with a chart that looked very much like the one in Figure 3.5.

Here there is no relationship between the variables, and no meaningful line of best fit or function to be developed. There is no discernable pattern to help us relate GDP growth to average temperature.

GDP growth and average temperature might, however, be related variables when considering the GDP of a single state. (Yes, each state has its own GDP.) For instance, unusually warm years might hurt the GDP of a state such as Vermont or Idaho, where ski resorts bring in significant sums of money from other states.

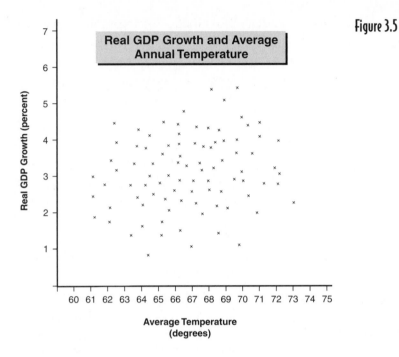

Figure 3.5

Real GDP Growth and Average Annual Temperature

Charting GDP

In addition to helping us clarify relationships between variables, charts give us a way to visually depict trends over time by relating a value on one axis, usually the vertical, to a point in time, usually on the horizontal axis.

For example, let's return to the nominal and real GDP data we examined earlier and look at the trend in GDP over that 12-year period. Trends are best seen in line charts, which plot the values of a variable over time.

EconoTip

It is up to the economist, analyst, or manager reviewing the data to think through relationships and their meaning when considering various data. No computer—or any other tool—can do that for us.

Figure 3.6 is a line chart of the values for nominal and real GDP from Table 3.1. The solid line represents nominal GDP, and the dotted line represents real GDP.

The chart is saying that annual GDP grew significantly in both nominal and real terms. The chart shows that nominal GDP grew faster than real GDP because the solid (nominal GDP) line is steeper than the dotted (real GDP) line.

Line charts are widely used in the investment profession to track the performance of various stocks. In finance, they are used to track sales, expenses, and other numbers.

In economics, they are used mainly to see the trend of a variable such as GDP, income, and specific types of spending and production over time.

Figure 3.6

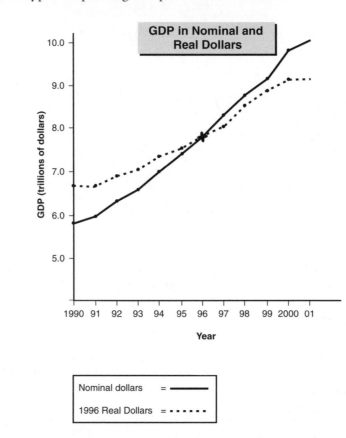

Also with a line chart and its underlying mathematical function, economists try to forecast the future performance of GDP, income, spending, production, and other variables. The mathematical functions—called equations—that represent the line are quite complex and not covered in this book. But essentially, in economic forecasting and econometrics, which I mentioned in Chapter 1, an economist plots a line that represents the relationship among multiple variables and attempts to gauge the future path of that line, and thus the future value of whatever is being forecasted.

A bar chart is another tool that helps us make comparisons between variables over time. For example, again, going back to Table 3.1, the bar chart in Figure 3.7 shows both the growth rates for both real and nominal GDP from 1990 to 2001.

The chart clearly shows that real GDP growth was substantially less than nominal growth, especially in the years 1990, 1991, and 2001, when real growth was less than half of nominal growth.

In economics, in business, and in this book, tables and charts are the two main tools for organizing, presenting, and analyzing data.

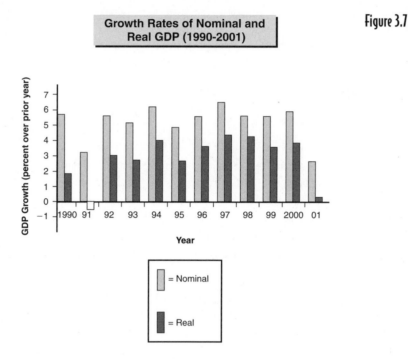

Growth Rates of Nominal and Real GDP (1990-2001)

Figure 3.7

Watch Out!

When you are considering economic data and other numbers, for example financial data, watch out for the following ways of misinterpreting information.

Correlation Is Not Causality

Just because two variables seem related, one is not necessarily causing the other to occur. For example, suppose in our earlier example of the average U.S. temperature and growth in GDP, we found that the higher the average temperature, the higher the growth rate in GDP.

It would be premature to assume that the higher average temperatures were causing the higher growth, simply because high temperature and high growth were correlated.

EconoTip

An old joke may help you remember that correlation is not causality. Jimmy keeps whistling all the time. Jane asks him why. He says, "It keeps the elephants away." Jane says, "But there are no elephants around here." Jimmy says, "See? It's working."

(Correlated is a mathematical term meaning that two variables move together, in an inverse or positive relationship, in a consistent manner.)

A causal relationship between high temperature and high nationwide economic growth could conceivably exist. However you would need to do further analysis—of variables such as farm production, travel expenditures, and so on—to determine that.

Don't Play with Percentages

Growth rates and values expressed as percentages should be handled, and listened to, carefully.

First, when you or anyone else expresses a value—such as the dollar amount of the federal budget deficit for this year—as a percentage of another value, such as GDP, be sure that 1. it is clear what that other value is and 2. there is a logical relationship between the two values. For instance, if the budget deficit is expressed as a percentage of GDP, what year GDP are we talking about? Last year's? This year's forecasted GDP? Or what? (For that matter, which year's budget deficit are we talking about?)

And if the budget deficit is being expressed as a percentage of GDP, is that a valid way of expressing it? It may be and, indeed, it sometimes is expressed that way. Yet, the usual intention in expressing the budget deficit as a percentage of GDP—or for that matter in expressing anything as a percentage of GDP—is to make it appear small. After all, nothing is larger than GDP.

Second, be careful of growth rates. For example, suppose someone says, "Incomes in the highest (or lowest) one-fifth of the population have grown 5 percent."

EconoTalk

Growth rates for part of the year are usually **annualized**. A newsperson might say, "The economy grew at an annual rate of 4 percent during the first quarter of this year." That means that if the economy kept growing at the rate that it grew in the first quarter, it will be 4 percent larger than the economy (meaning real GDP) of the previous year.

The first issue is, of course, are we talking about nominal or real income? If it's nominal, it might not be really real.

The second issue is the period being considered. Are we talking about the rate of income growth in the first quarter of this year compared with that of the first quarter of last year? Or are we comparing that of the most recent full year with the year before that? Or are we comparing the rate of income growth in the first quarter of this year with the rate for all of last year?

If that last situation is the case, then be sure that the first quarter growth rate has been *annualized*, meaning multiplied by four (because there are four quarters in the year). To annualize a rate of growth, you simply multiply the actual, numerical rate of growth by the appropriate number—twelve for a monthly rate, four for quarterly rate, and two for a six-month rate.

Also be careful when dealing with the growth rate of any value that is expressed as a percentage. Potential confusion surrounds a statement like, "Unemployment increased by 2 percent last year." If the unemployment *rate* rose from 4 percent to 6 percent, then the correct way to say that is, "The unemployment rate increased by 2 percentage points." That way you are clearly saying that unemployment rose from .04 (four one-hundredths, or 4 percent) of the workforce to .06 (six one-hundredths, or 6 percent) of the workforce.

A Few Final Points

Finally, think critically when you hear the following statements:

"The rate of growth is falling."

This means that growth is still positive, not negative. Politicians of both parties are fond of pointing out that they are cutting the rate of growth in spending in Washington. Yet government spending keeps growing. Clearly, a lower rate of growth still generates growth. Only an actual reduction in the *level* of spending will reduce spending.

"Average (income, spending, production, etc.) is (higher, lower, etc.) than last year's."

In most situations, economists use the median rather than the average to summarize a set of values. That's because the average—also known as the mean—is more subject to being raised or lowered by extremely high or low values among the data.

Let's define our terms. The *mean* is calculated by adding up each value in a set of data and dividing the total by the number of values. Suppose we have the following figures for household income for seven households:

Household	Income ($)
A	94,000
B	41,000
C	40,000
D	39,000
E	38,000
F	37,000
G	37,000

The average household income is about $46,600 (which equals the total of the seven incomes, $326,000, divided by 7). The mean is not representative of the level of income among these seven households. It is well above six of the seven incomes. That, of course, is because the mean is being pulled up by the income of $94,000.

The *median* is the central value—the value in the center when all of the values are arrayed from highest to lowest or lowest to highest. In our example here, the median value of $39,000 is far more representative of the level of income of most of the households in the group.

Although I have obviously constructed this sample to make the point about the median being preferable to the mean, the fact is that, in economics, income figures (among many others) usually are reported, presented, and analyzed as median values rather than averages. Beware of averages when you hear them quoted, and use them carefully when you do use them.

"Holding everything else constant."

Actually there is nothing wrong with using this phrase, which is used often by economists and throughout this book. It indicates that you are going to be isolating the effect of a change in one variable, such as interest rates, on another variable, such as borrowing. The phrase—which is often rendered in the Latin, *ceteris paribus* and which also can be translated as "holding all else equal"—means that the analysis assumes that nothing changes except the variable being analyzed.

Economists know that this is not the way things work in the real world, and you should, too. But for the purposes of understanding a single variable, it is a useful and widely used convention.

The Least You Need to Know

- Data is the lifeblood of the economics profession—and of anyone who wants to understand and keep up with economic developments. Tables and charts are the two main tools for handling economic data.

- The distinction between nominal and real growth in GDP, incomes, spending, production, or other aspects of economic activity is a crucial one. Nominal dollars are dollars as they were valued in the year they relate to. Real dollars are dollars valued in a base year, chosen by the economist or analyst, in order to eliminate the effect of inflation.

- Be aware that the way economic information is presented and discussed can affect your understanding of economic events.

Supply, Demand, and the Invisible Hand

In This Chapter

- ◆ The dynamics of supply and demand
- ◆ How free markets function
- ◆ What makes a monopoly

Transactions—payments of money in return for goods and services—occur because various consumers, businesses, and government agencies have various wants and needs. In Chapter 2, you learned that these transactions all add up to gross domestic product, or GDP. Economists also refer to GDP as total demand. Economists not only analyze total demand; they also analyze demand for specific goods and services. The demand for a specific item depends on many factors, including its uses and importance, the size and age of the population, the prevailing fashions and tastes, and, of course, its price.

In a market economy, if there is demand for something there will surely be people willing to supply it. In that sense, supply is the flip side of demand. Economists think and talk in terms of the supply of cars and housing, the supply of labor and materials, and so on. The supply of a product or service depends on many things including the resources and productive capacity devoted to producing it and, again, its price.

In a market economy, the interaction of demand—wants and needs—and supply—resources and productive capacity—largely determine what is produced and how it is allocated.

This chapter examines the dynamics of supply and demand and the interaction of these two essential market forces. It also shows how these forces determine prices in a market.

Demand: Wants, Needs, and Red Meat

In a market economy, everything has a price, and buyers—those with the demand—always want the price to be lower. Meanwhile, sellers—those with the supply—want the price to be higher.

In general, the lower the price of a given product or service, the greater the quantity people will be willing to buy. The higher the price of the product or service, the lower the quantity that people will be willing to buy. People buy more hamburgers than caviar, more costume jewelry than diamonds, more Chevrolets than BMWs.

Let's assume that a large supermarket chain sells beef (a fairly safe assumption). Let's further assume that it has experimented with various prices and has gathered the following data, here arranged into what economists call a *demand schedule*.

Table 4.1 The Demand Schedule

Price per pound	Pounds of beef sold
5.00	20,000
4.00	40,000
3.00	60,000
2.00	80,000
1.00	100,000

The demand schedule shows the quantity of a product that people will buy (demand) at a series of specific prices. *Holding all other things equal*, the lower the price, the greater the quantity of beef people will buy. Conversely, the higher the price, the lower the quantity of beef people will buy.

I emphasize "holding all other things equal" for two reasons:

First, we are assuming that the price of beef is rising or falling and that the prices of all other goods are not. That is, we are assuming that the price of beef is rising or falling *relative* to the price of other goods. We make this assumption because if, say, the price of chicken were rising or falling, this might not be the demand schedule for beef. (I'll explain why in a moment.)

Second, we are assuming that no factors other than price are affecting demand. There have been no reports of Mad Cow disease in Kansas, which would surely lower demand for beef. There are no new scientific studies telling us to eat more beef because it is rich in iron and makes us healthier, which would increase demand. Assuming that all other things remain equal may be unrealistic (actually, it *is* unrealistic), but it lets us analyze the effect of price on demand.

EconoTalk

A **demand schedule** shows the quantity of a product that people will buy (or demand) at a series of specific prices. A demand curve shows the same information in graphic form.

If we plot the data—prices and quantities—from the demand schedule on a chart, we get a picture of the demand for beef as shown in Figure 4.1. The demand curve slopes downward because as the price increases, the quantity of beef demanded decreases. A downward sloping demand curve holds true for most—but not all—types of products and services. There's an inverse relationship between price and demand: The higher the price, the lower the quantity demanded. The lower the price, the higher the quantity demanded.

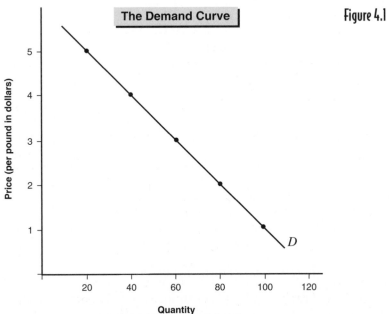

The Demand Curve

Figure 4.1

It may seem obvious that people will buy more of a product when the price decreases and less when the price increases. However, they do so for two reasons. First, many people who never buy a product because it is too expensive will buy it if the price falls far enough. For instance, many seafood lovers never buy lobster because it's just out of their price range. If the price of lobster fell substantially, they would start buying it. Second, many people who already buy a product will buy more of it if the price decreases. If the price of lobster fell substantially, lobster lovers would buy it more often.

Demand Change!

Okay, let's stop holding everything else equal. Aside from movements in prices, what factors might cause a change in the demand for a product such as beef?

Overall demand can change, moving upward or downward, because of changes in:

- Preferences
- Population
- Prices of other goods and services
- Incomes
- Perceptions of future prices

Preferences

In Chapter 1, I mentioned that people express their preferences in the transactions they enter into. Some people like beef and some don't. Moreover, people's preferences can, and usually do, change over time. For instance, demand for beef can increase or decrease because of social trends—say, toward or away from steakhouse dining or vegetarianism—and health concerns—beef is high in cholesterol, but also rich in iron.

Population

In Chapter 2, I noted that population growth affects consumption (consumer demand). That's also true for the demand for a specific product. Imagine that Argentina's economy collapses (which it did in 2002) and hundreds of thousands of Argentines immigrate to the United States (which they did not). The people of Argentina are great beef eaters, and a huge number of Argentines entering the U.S.

population could conceivably increase the demand for beef. Usually, however, population growth occurs slowly over time, exerting gentle, long-term pressure on demand.

The Real World

When a product or brand appeals only to older people in the population, the manufacturer often becomes concerned over the future demand for his wares. He knows demand is slowly shifting downward. For instance, the average age of Cadillac and Lincoln buyers is over 55. Those brands are working hard to develop products that appeal to younger buyers. Similarly, so-called "brown liquors," such as bourbon and scotch, are consumed more by older people, while young adults favor "white liquors," such as vodka and rum. Therefore makers of bourbon (Jim Beam) and scotch (Dewars) are using advertising to appeal to young adults. Producers hate it when demand for their product dies off.

The more important reasons for a change in demand, however, involve factors other than preferences or population. Key among these is the price of other goods and people's incomes.

Prices of Other Goods

If the price of beef remained the same while the price of chicken fell dramatically, what do you think the effect on the demand for beef would be?

Demand for beef would *decrease*.

Why? Because chicken is a *substitute* for beef. A substitute is a product or service that people use *in place of* another product or service. When shoppers in supermarkets see that that the price of chicken has plummeted while the price of beef has stayed the same, they'll substitute chicken for beef in their diets. They may not eliminate beef, but they will certainly start eating more chicken and less beef. This would also happen at fast-food restaurants—more Kentucky Fried Chicken and fewer Big Macs would be sold. Other examples of substitutes include rice and potatoes, bus rides and subway rides, and (to the horror of the music industry) compact discs and music shared over the Internet.

Sometimes the price of a *complement* to a product can affect demand for the product. A complement is a product or service that people use *with* another product or service. For example, if the price of hamburger rolls were to increase

EconoTalk

A **substitute** is a product or service that people use in place of another product or service. A **complement** is a product or service that people use with another product or service.

dramatically, we could expect demand for hamburger meat to decrease. Other examples of complements include DVD players and DVD disks, turkey and stuffing, rods and reels, gin and vermouth.

The Real World

The world of information and entertainment technology provides many examples of economic reality. This is because most of us are familiar with these technologies, but also because the technologies and the markets for them change so fast. It's the economic equivalent of the geneticist studying fruit flies because a new generation comes along every three days.

For instance, a large market for an entertainment product cannot really develop until the product falls to a price where people will use it as a substitute for another product. Expensive substitutes are not going to find a large market. For instance, premium cable television, CD players, and cellular phone service all had to reach prices where people felt the products were reasonable substitutes for movie tickets, records or audio tapes, and land-line phone service.

Similarly, complementary high-tech products must reach "popular" prices before a large market can develop. Software, personal computers, and digital cameras are an example of (three-way) complementary products. In the early 1990s, PhotoShop—software that allows you to load and manipulate photos on a personal computer—was an expensive tool for graphic designers and artists but is now more reasonably priced. Also, digital cameras, once wildly expensive, have come down in price. Today, many households own a computer *and* the software *and* a digital camera, because the prices of these complementary products have fallen to more affordable levels.

Income

Changes in income can also change overall demand for a product or service. As people's incomes rise, they demand more goods and services. They also demand better goods and services—the "good things in life."

Most people still rate beef among those "good" things, and indeed more beef is consumed in wealthy nations than in poorer nations. Similarly, when people's incomes fall, they demand fewer goods and services—and fewer of the "good things in life." Therefore, if incomes increase, we would expect demand for beef to increase. If people's incomes were to decrease, we would also expect a decrease in the demand for beef.

Incidentally, this assumes that beef is among what economists call *normal goods*. Normal goods are those for which demand increases as incomes rise, which includes many products and services. Products and services that see decreased demand when incomes rise are called *inferior goods*. Porgies—a bland, bony, but inexpensive fish—are a good example of such a product. Subway rides are such a service. As incomes rise, people substitute salmon for porgies and taxi rides for subway rides.

> **EconoTalk**
>
> **Normal goods** are those for which demand increases as people's incomes increase. **Inferior goods** are those for which demand decreases as income increases.

Perception of Future Prices

One other factor can shift demand for a product: the price people expect to pay for it in the future. If people suddenly learned that beef prices were going to double next month, they would probably stock up their freezers with steaks, roasts, and hamburgers this month. People buy and hoard products when they believe sharp price increases lay ahead.

Notice that this factor does not affect services as much. You might have dental work done or have your house painted right now, if you knew the price of those services was going to increase soon. But you could not have two haircuts or make two visits to your doctor now in the hope of not needing another one in the near future.

Back to the Curve

A change in overall demand represents a *shift* in demand, upward or downward. That means that one or more of the factors I just discussed can cause the entire demand curve to shift to the right (upward) or to the left (downward), as shown in Figure 4.2.

A shift in demand is different from a change in the quantity demanded because of a change in the price. If the supermarket chain lowers the price of beef from $4 to $3 and sees its sales increase from 40,000 to 60,000 pounds, the price change caused a change in the quantity demanded. That change represents movement *along the demand curve*, that is, along the curve D, the middle curve of the three curves in Figure 4.2.

A shift in demand occurs when the whole relationship between price and quantity changes. The new demand schedule provides the values that correspond to all three demand curves in Figure 4.2.

Figure 4.2

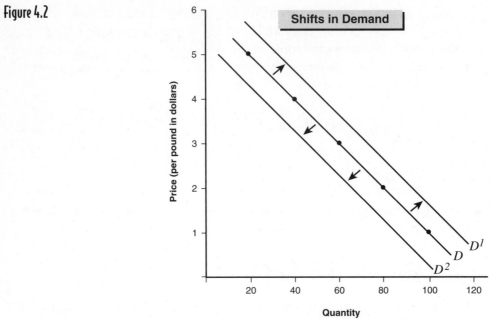

D^1 = upward shift in demand (increase)
D^2 = downward shift in demand (decrease)

Table 4.2   Shifts in Demand

	Old Demand	New Higher	New Lower
		Demand Schedule (D1)	Demand Schedule (D2)
	Schedule (D)		
Price per pound	*Pounds of beef*	*Pounds of beef*	*Pounds of beef*
5.00	20,000	30,000	10,000
4.00	40,000	50,000	30,000
3.00	60,000	70,000	50,000
2.00	80,000	90,000	70,000
1.00	100,000	110,000	90,000

The whole relationship between price and quantity changes when a shift in demand occurs. For example, the new, higher demand curve shows that at the $3 price, people will now buy 70,000 pounds of beef. Perhaps the price of chicken has increased to the point where people figure they may as well buy beef. Or maybe incomes in the region have increased to the point where people now have more money to spend on beef. If that's the case, at the $3 price—and at any price along the new demand curve—they will buy more of it.

Similarly, along the new, lower demand curve, people collectively will buy only 50,000, rather than 60,000, pounds of beef at $3. This type of shift also usually occurs for one of the reasons I just discussed. For instance, the price of chicken may have fallen sharply or people's incomes may have decreased due to layoffs in the region.

As I mentioned at the start of this chapter, when there is demand for a product in a market economy someone will supply it. Let's move to the other side of the transaction and examine the dynamics of supply.

Supply: You Want It, We Got It

Just as there is a quantity that consumers will demand at a given price, there is a quantity that producers will supply at a given price. The demand schedule depicts the relationship between the price of a good and the quantity consumers will buy. Similarly, the supply schedule depicts the relationship between the price of a good and the quantity that producers will make.

As you may imagine, the relationship between price and quantity supplied differs from that between price and the quantity demanded. Table 4.3 below depicts this relationship.

Table 4.3   The Supply Schedule

Price per pound	Pounds of beef produced
5.00	120,000
4.00	90,000
3.00	60,000
2.00	30,000
1.00	0

The supply schedule shows the quantity of a product that producers will produce (supply) at a series of specific prices. Holding all other things constant, the higher the price, the greater the quantity of beef producers will supply, and the lower the price, the lower the quantity of beef people will supply.

Notice the positive relationship between price and quantity supplied: the higher the price, the higher the quantity supplied. This stands in contrast to the inverse relationship between price and quantity demanded. When the data are plotted on a chart, they generate a very different curve.

Figure 4.3

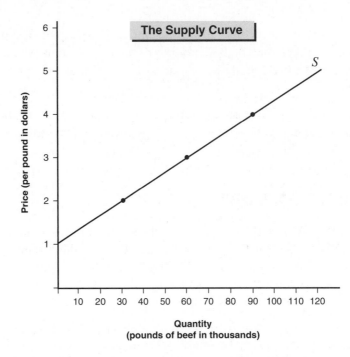

The supply curve depicts the quantities that producers will make at a series of given prices. As you can see, the quantities supplied at the various prices generally differ from those that consumers are willing to purchase at those prices. We'll see how this is resolved later in this chapter.

The supply curve can apply to a single supplier or to all suppliers as a whole, and it holds true for virtually every product or service produced for profit in a market economy. Also in "holding all other things constant," the supply schedule and supply curve leave certain realities out of the analysis in order to focus solely on price. Those other things can change the overall relationship between price and quantity supplied, so let's look at them just as we did for demand.

Change Supply!

A change in the overall quantity supplied can occur because of changes in any of the following areas:

- ◆ Capacity and technology
- ◆ Cost structure
- ◆ Prices of substitutes and complements
- ◆ Perceptions of future prices

Capacity and Technology

From time to time you may have heard that there is "too much capacity" in an industry. This has been the case in the telecommunications industry in the first years of the 2000s. So much fiber optic cable, so many cellular systems, and so many factories for making telecommunications equipment were put in place in the 1990s that the industry's ability to supply telecommunications services and equipment has outstripped demand.

When overcapacity occurs in an industry, the entire supply of that industry's product increases. When that happens, producers are willing to deliver a greater quantity of goods and services for the same price. Why shouldn't they? They have more capacity than they can use, so they may as well use as much as they can, at any price (well, almost any price).

An increase in supply also occurs if there are numerous producers for a product or service. Some observers of the business scene have argued that the telecommunications industry has too many providers, which contributed to the overcapacity. Indeed, a large number of producers in any industry adds capacity, which causes supply to increase. Finally, technological developments can lead to a shift in supply. Returning to our beef example, suppose the industry develops better methods of feeding cattle or controlling disease. Or suppose more efficient processing and shipping technologies come along. Under those circumstances, the quantity supplied for a given price would increase.

The converse of these factors also holds true. Too little capacity, a paucity of producers, or lack of technological innovation will decrease the supply.

> **The Real World**
>
> Shifts in supply and demand usually occur over a long time. For example, the U.S. steel industry did not keep pace with technological developments in steel making in the 1970s and much of the 1980s. The industry suffered, and then began to recover in the late 1980s and 1990s by building more efficient, technologically updated "mini-mills," which replaced many of the industry's older, larger, inefficient steel mills.

Cost Structure

If the cost of any factor of production—labor, raw materials, equipment—decreases, the quantity that producers are willing (and able) to supply at a given price increases. Producers with lower costs will always be able to supply more of a product at a given price than those with higher costs. Therefore, a decrease in producers' costs will increase the supply.

Conversely, if production costs increase, the quantity supplied at a given price will decrease. Higher costs mean that producers will have to produce less to be able sell a product at a given price. If you're thinking, "Why don't they just raise their prices when their costs go up?" you're asking a good question. Essentially, consumers will resist the higher prices, and may move to substitutes, do without the product, or buy from a more efficient producer.

Prices of Substitutes and Complements

A producer sees substitutes and complements differently than consumers do. To a producer, a substitute is another product he can make instead. Suppose a major meat producer can devote feed, feedlots, transportation, and other resources to raising either cattle or sheep. That makes cattle and sheep *substitutes in production*.

 EconoTalk

Substitutes in production are two or more products or services that a producer can make or deliver in place of one another. For instance, a farmer may be able to grow either corn or soybeans, a manufacturer may be able to produce either men's or women's clothing, or an arena may be able to host either sports events or concerts. A producer or service provider who can supply substitutes in production has the flexibility to offer whichever good is in greater demand.

If the meat producer has the flexibility to choose to raise cattle or sheep, and the price of lamb rises dramatically, what do you think she will do? She will devote more resources to raising sheep and fewer to raising cattle. In general, if the price of a substitute in production (lamb) rises relative to its related product (beef), then the supply of the related product (beef) will decrease. If a producer can produce either of two products, she's going to produce the one that fetches the higher price.

The reverse is also true. If the price of a substitute in production falls, then the supply of the related product will increase. If the price of lamb nosedives, the outfit will devote fewer resources to sheep and more to cattle. As a result, the supply of beef will increase.

Complements in production are products that are created along with one another. Cowhide and beef are complements in production. (Wool, of course, can be obtained by shearing sheep, rather than slaughtering the poor things.) If the price of a complement (cowhide) rises, so will the supply of the related product (beef).

Why? If the cattle producer makes more money off the cowhide, he can afford to sell the beef at a lower price. If he increases his cowhide production when its price rises, his supply of beef is going to automatically increase as well. That means more beef will be available at a given price, which increases the supply of beef. Conversely, if the price of cowhide falls far enough, so might the supply of beef.

EconoTalk

Complements in production are products created with one another. Often one is a by-product of another, that is, a product created in the course of making another product. For instance, certain lubricants and other petroleum products are by-products of making gasoline from crude oil.

Perception of Future Prices

Finally, if a producer believes she can get a better price in the future, she will hold off production or delivery and sell when the price has risen. Thus if higher prices for beef are expected four months from now, producers will decrease the quantity they are now supplying. Conversely, if producers can get a better price now than they can expect in four months, they will produce more now, which increases the supply.

Notice that the effect of perceptions of future prices on supply are the opposite of their effect on demand. Higher prices in the future increase current demand, but decrease current supply. Lower prices in the future decrease current demand, but increase current supply. Stated another way, higher prices in the future shift demand into the present and supply into the future. Lower prices in the future shift demand into the future and supply into the present.

As Figure 4.4 shows, if supply increases for any reason, the supply curve shifts to the right because producers are willing to supply more beef at a given price. Conversely, if supply decreases, the supply curve shifts to the left because producers will supply less beef at a given price.

Thus the dynamics of supply and demand tend to work at cross-purposes. But that's why we have markets, where these forces working at cross-purposes start working together. Let's turn to the market and see what happens—especially to prices—when demand and supply interact.

Figure 4.4

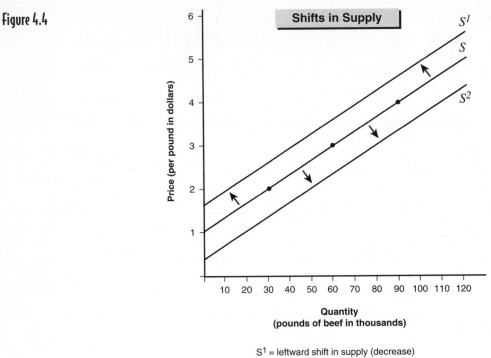

S¹ = leftward shift in supply (decrease)
S² = rightward shift in supply (increase)

EconoTip

Think of the supply curve as shifting to the left (for increased supply) or to the right (for decreased supply) rather than thinking of the curve shifting "up" or "down." It's potentially confusing because an "upward" movement of the curve—to the left—actually depicts a decrease in supply and a "downward" movement—to the right—is signaling an increase. Instead think, rightward is an increase in supply and leftward is a decrease.

Equilibrium: Mr. Demand, Meet Mr. Supply

The beauty of the market is that the competing motivations of consumers and producers interact to arrive at a price and quantity for a product that's determined by impersonal market forces. You've heard the expression "market price" (or seen it written on menus next to the word "lobster"). The market price for a product is the price at which the quantity demanded is equal to the quantity supplied. Figure 4.5 shows how this occurs.

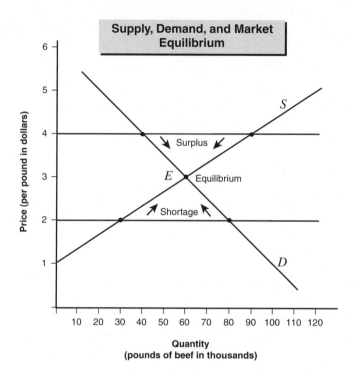

Supply, Demand, and Market Equilibrium

Figure 4.5

Price (per pound in dollars) / Quantity (pounds of beef in thousands)

The arrows along the supply and demand curves in this chart indicate the pressures at work in the market for beef (or any market for that matter). To understand how the price and quantity reach the equilibrium point, let's first examine the area above that point. Above the equilibrium point—say, at the $4 price where I have drawn a line—producers would be supplying more beef (90,000 pounds) than consumers would be demanding (40,000 pounds). That price results in a surplus of beef on the market—supply would be greater than demand because consumers won't buy enough of it at the $4 price.

If supply is greater than demand, then there are meat lockers full of unsold beef across a region. What are the suppliers of that beef going to do? They will cut the price until consumers start buying it. In this way, a surplus of a product puts downward pressure on its price.

It also puts downward pressure on supply. If beef is not selling briskly—if there's a surplus of it on the market—what are producers going to do? They are going to raise fewer cattle. They'll shift the resources to raising sheep or maybe hogs. Maybe some ranchers will get out of the business. Whatever it takes, that surplus quantity of beef will be taken off the market for the simple reason that consumers don't want to buy that quantity of beef at the price suppliers want for it. The excess supply will dwindle until the quantity supplied equals the quantity demanded—at a price both consumers and producers can live with, in this case $3 a pound.

So surplus quantity puts downward pressure on the prices and the supply of the product. That pressure is exerted by market forces until the quantity supplied equals the quantity demanded.

Let's turn to the area *below* the equilibrium point. There we have a shortage of beef. The market is demanding more beef (80,000 pounds) than the quantity that producers are supplying (30,000 pounds). That results in a shortage, which puts upward pressure on prices.

How? When sellers see that they are constantly running out of beef before the next delivery, they know they can raise the price of the stuff. Consumers, in effect, are bidding up the price. When the price starts increasing (from the $2 mark), producers start producing more beef. They send their cattle to market sooner, and they move resources away from raising sheep and into raising cattle. If it's a long-term trend, more people may take up cattle ranching.

Again, whatever it takes, that shortage of beef will disappear as the price rises and the higher prices bring more beef to market. How much more beef will come to market? Enough to bring the quantity supplied equal to the quantity demanded—in this case, 60,000 pounds—again, at a price both consumers and producers can live with.

Market Forces Are the Invisible Hand

The market forces described here, working through the price mechanism, are the essence of Adam Smith's "invisible hand" (see Chapter 1). The beauty of a market is that supply and demand come into balance without central planning, mandates, boycotts, raids, or wars, as each consumer and producer responds to the price of the product. The price sums up, contains, and channels the forces of the market—the motives and desires of consumers and producers.

This is not to say that markets do away with pain and loss for consumers and producers. Market forces generate tremendous amounts of pain and loss. People go without beef, suffer protein deficiencies, and even go hungry. They see people eating sirloin steak and prime rib and feel terrible that they can't afford it. Producers get stuck with beef they can't sell. Some meat may be sold at a loss or go to waste. Some ranchers and meat wholesalers go out of business and lose their livelihoods.

Markets can be inefficient and even cruel. However, the pain and loss that occur in the market arise largely from decisions—good and bad decisions—made freely by consumers and producers. Therefore, most Americans prefer the inefficiencies and cruelties of the market to those of a command economy.

What About Shifts in Demand or Supply?

Finally, let's return to those overall shifts in demand or supply. What effect do they have?

Essentially, they shift the equilibrium point up or down. Two pictures will be worth 2,000 words. First, let's look at the effect of a shift in demand as illustrated in Figure 4.6.

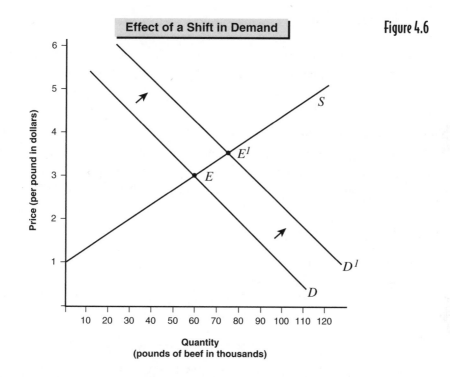

Effect of a Shift in Demand

Figure 4.6

As the chart shows, an increase in demand raises the quantity demanded at a given price. This results in a new, higher market price, and producers will be more than happy to supply that higher quantity, which is 75,000 pounds, at that higher market price, which is $3.50. Thus, when demand shifts upward, the equilibrium point rises.

To see the effect of a decrease in demand, simply reverse the situation and pretend that the curves in the chart are reversed (that D is the new curve and D¹ is the original one). A shift to lower demand decreases the quantity demanded at a given price. Producers will (not quite so happily) meet that lower demand at a new, lower market price. This generates a new, lower equilibrium point.

Turning to a shift in supply, as depicted in Figure 4.7, an increase in supply—which shifts the curve to the right—lowers the market price to $2.50 and raises quantity supplied from 60,000 to 70,000. That is why overcapacity or numerous competitors in an industry will cause the price to decrease. There's more supply than people demand.

 Figure 4.7

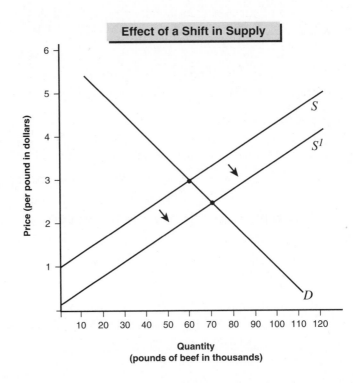

However, a decrease in supply—which shifts the curve to the left—has the opposite effect, as you can see by pretending that S^1 is the original curve and S is the new one. The decrease in supply *increases* the market price. That's because demand now exceeds the quantity supplied, and in that circumstance consumers bid up the price.

It's Not Just a Good Idea, It's The Law

All of this boils down to the law of supply and demand. The greater the demand for a given supply of a product, the higher the market price. The lower the demand, the lower the price. Likewise, the greater the supply of a product given a certain level of demand, the lower the price of that product. The lower the supply—the scarcer it is—the higher the price.

You knew that was the case. But now you know why. You also understand how markets work, how market forces are channeled into prices, and what can cause overall demand or supply for a product to shift.

The Least You Need to Know

- A demand schedule and demand curve for a product show the quantity of the product that consumers will purchase at a range of prices.

- Overall demand for a product can shift upward or downward because of changes in preferences, population, prices of related products, incomes, and consumers' perceptions of future prices.

- A supply schedule and supply curve for a product show the quantity of the product that producers will make available at a range of prices.

- The overall supply of a product can shift upward or downward because of changes in productive capacity or technology, producers' costs, prices of related goods, and producers' perceptions of future prices.

- Market dynamics move the price and quantity of a product to an equilibrium point. At that point, producers are supplying the quantity that consumers are demanding (and vice versa) at a price both parties can live with.

- While markets represent an orderly and efficient way of determining how much of which goods and services are produced for whom, they are neither painless nor perfect for all goods and services.

Look at These Prices!

In This Chapter

- ◆ Factors that affect prices
- ◆ All about elasticity
- ◆ How a sales tax affects supply and demand
- ◆ The effects of rent control and a minimum wage

As the saying goes, "Everything has a price." The question for anyone trying to understand our economy is, "Why that particular price?"

In Chapter 4 we saw how supply and demand interact in the market so that the "right" amount of goods and services is produced. Chapter 4 also introduced the price mechanism and its role in determining supply and demand. In this chapter, we learn how the consumer's need for a product affects demand and how market interventions, such as sales taxes and rent control, affect supply, demand, and prices.

Let's Stretch: Elasticity of Demand

Anyone who has set foot in a discount store knows that some sellers try to increase the quantity of goods they sell by lowering their prices. From what we saw about supply and demand, that should work. However, in reality, it may or it may not. Moreover, the seller may or may not bring in more money even if he does sell more goods at the lower price.

If a seller reduces his prices, will demand always increase? (Never say "always" in economics.) The more important question is, "How much should he reduce his prices?" In other words, how much will demand rise in response to a price reduction?

The answers to these questions depend on the buyer's situation and his need or desire for the product, as well as on the seller's situation. That is, the answers depend on the *elasticity of demand* for the product or service.

Don't be alarmed by the technical term "elasticity." It's really a snap. (Sorry, I couldn't resist.) Elasticity of demand refers to the change in demand for a product or service that occurs when its price changes. Specifically, it is the degree to which an increase or decrease in price will change the quantity demanded.

First, I'll discuss the three degrees of elasticity—unitary elasticity, elasticity, and inelasticity. Then we'll look at the factors that contribute to the elasticity of demand of a product.

EconoTalk

Elasticity of demand refers to the change in demand for a good or service that occurs in response to a change in its price. Specifically, it is the degree to which an increase or decrease in price will change the quantity demanded. It is a way economists have of nailing down the relationship between price and demand more precisely.

If you drive a car, you need gasoline. If the price of gasoline was cut in half starting next week, would you start buying twice as many gallons of it per week? If the price rose by 100 percent, would you buy half as much per week? Let's say that, in both cases, you would.

Let's put some numbers to this example. We'll start with gasoline at $1.50 per gallon and with you using 100 gallons a week. (Ever think of shortening your commute?) This example will show how changes in the price affect your demand and flow through to affect the revenue that the gas station receives from you. Revenue, also known as total sales, equals price multiplied by quantity, that is: $R = P \times Q$.

Table 5.1 shows the changes in price, quantity, and revenue in the example I'm presenting here.

Table 5.1   Unitary Elasticity of Demand for Gasoline

	P	×	Q	=	R
Original situation	$1.50	×	100 gals.	=	$150
Price drops 50%	$0.75	×	200 gals.	=	$150
Price doubles	$3.00	×	50 gals.	=	$150

In this admittedly fanciful example, your demand for gasoline is characterized by *unitary elasticity*. Unitary elasticity occurs when the quantity of a product demanded changes in response to price changes in a way that leaves total revenue the same. Here, regardless of price increase or decrease, revenue remains at $150.

With unitary elasticity, the percentage *increase* in price calls forth an offsetting *decrease* in demand. If the seller doubles his price, he sells half as much. Similarly, a percentage *decrease* in price calls forth an offsetting *increase* in demand. If he halves his price, he sells twice as much. Either way, the seller brings in the same revenue. (His profit— the amount he makes after subtracting his costs from his revenue—may vary, but that's another story, told in Chapter 8.)

The unitary elasticity relationship is depicted in Figure 5.1.

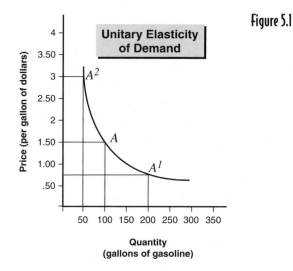

Figure 5.1

Figure 5.1 is saying that when the price decreases from $1.50 (point "A") to $.075 (point "A¹"), total revenue equals $150 in both cases (200 gallons at 75¢ a gallon equals $150).

EconoTalk

Unitary elasticity occurs when the quantity of a product demanded changes in response to price changes in a way that leaves total revenue the same. **Elasticity** occurs when a reduction in price increases the quantity demanded so that the seller's revenue increases. **Inelasticity** occurs when a reduction in price increases the quantity demanded by more than zero but less than unity. (Unity refers to the proportional change in quantity sold and revenue that occurs under unitary elasticity.)

This chart is also saying that the price increase from $1.50 to $3.00 leaves revenue unchanged, because the demand for gasoline falls to 50 gallons (50 gallons at $3.00 a gallon equals $150).

When a producer or seller faces unitary elasticity of demand, she can't increase revenue by increasing or decreasing her price. Why? Because the quantity demanded will exactly offset the effect of any change in price. However, that is rarely the case in the real world.

Selling More by Charging Less

Sticking with our gasoline example, suppose that in response to a 50 percent decrease in the price of gasoline you tripled your gasoline purchases to 300 gallons a week. What would be the effect on the service station's revenue? The second line in the table below provides the answer: a sharp increase in revenue.

Similarly, let's suppose that if the price of gasoline doubled, you would use only one-third as much. This would generate revenue of $75, as shown in the third line of the table. (Incidentally, I am using numbers that illustrate the type of elasticity I am discussing. In reality, elasticity is "all over the place" both for any given individual and for groups that use a product. Also, elasticity can be greater in response to a price increase than to a price reduction, or vice versa.)

	P	×	Q	=	R
Original situation	$1.50	×	100 gals.	=	$150
Price drops 50%	$0.75	×	300 gals.	=	$225
Price doubles	$3.00	×	25 gals.	=	$75

Here your demand for gasoline is characterized by *elasticity* of demand. In contrast to unitary elasticity, elastic demand occurs when a reduction in price *increases* the quantity demanded so that the seller's revenue *increases*. This is the way things "should" work for most businesses: The seller can sell more by cutting his price—and it's worth it to the seller.

As the table also shows, however, this cuts both ways: The seller will lose revenue if he increases his price. With elastic demand, an increase in the price calls forth a decrease in the quantity demanded which decreases the seller's revenue.

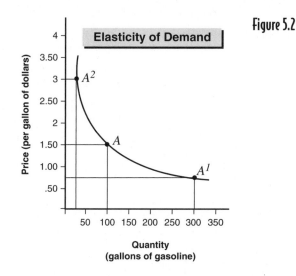

Figure 5.2

Figure 5.2 demonstrates that a decrease in price increases demand by more than unity. At the $0.75 price, demand increases to 300 gallons, bringing revenue up to $225 (which is equal to $0.75 × 300). With elasticity—as opposed to unitary elasticity or inelasticity—decreasing the price increases revenue. Also, the area of the rectangle formed by connecting the $0.75 price point with point "A¹" and point "A¹" with the 300 gallon mark is clearly larger than the area of the rectangle formed by connecting the $1.50 price point with point "A" and the 100 gallon mark. That, too, represents the higher revenue resulting from the price decrease.

The elasticity of demand chart also demonstrates that, with elasticity, a price increase will decrease demand to the point where revenue also decreases. At the $3.00 price, demand falls to just 25 gallons and revenue drops to $75.

EconoTip

A change in price may result in only a small increase in demand and revenue. The examples I'm choosing here use round numbers and simple relationships for the sake of clarity. But many producers face markets in which a price decrease of 10 percent may increase revenue by only 2 percent. This may or may not be a profitable decision for the producer. It depends on his costs. However, when a price reduction increases both the quantity demanded and revenue, it is, by definition, a case of elasticity of demand.

Are there situations in which a price change will cause the quantity demanded to drop to zero? Yes. Economists call this *infinite elasticity*. Cases of infinite elasticity are rare and usually confined to a single locale or a special situation.

For instance, the Internet has created an environment in which many users feel that everything on the web should be "free." Now it's not really free, because they've paid their Internet service provider for access to the web. But they feel they should not have to pay one penny more for information, music, or pictures pulled from websites. For some web users, this is a matter of principle, and they will not pay at all for something they believe should be free. Therefore, if a fee is requested as they are browsing a site, their demand for that site's offerings is zero. In such a situation, a price cut (let alone a price increase) is impossible because the price the buyer will pay is zero.

Figure 5.3 portrays infinite elasticity.

Figure 5.3

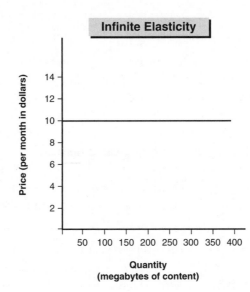

Figure 5.3 depicts the situation for our highly principled Internet browser. He will pay $10 a month to his Internet service provider for access to the web. But he will not pay a penny more for any web-based content. Regardless of the price, if there is a price beyond the $10 access charge, his demand for web-based content is zero. It is also saying that there is no real relationship between price and quantity demanded.

Inelastic Demand: No Price Cuts Here

Some sellers learn, to their dismay, that a price decrease does not increase revenue. For instance, say our service station reduces his price by 50 percent, but you increase your gasoline usage by only 20 percent.

Table 5.2   Inelastic Demand for Gasoline

	P	×	Q	=	R
Original situation	$1.50	×	100 gals.	=	$150
Price drops 50%	$0.75	×	120 gals.	=	$90
Price doubles	$300	×	80 gals.	=	$240

The result here is lower revenue, and an instance of inelastic demand. In general, inelastic demand occurs when a price decrease calls forth an increase in quantity that results in a *decrease* in revenue. In other words, price goes down, quantity goes up, but revenue still goes down.

This means that the effect on quantity demanded is less than unity but greater than zero.

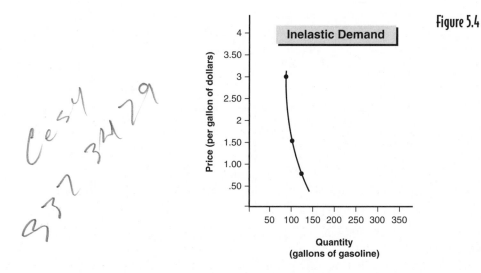

Figure 5.4

This chart depicts inelasticity of demand, meaning a decrease in price increases demand but not by enough to raise revenue. Inelasticity basically means that people demand a certain quantity of the product and are not going to change that demand very much because of price decreases. They'll change it a bit, but not by much.

However, this also cuts both ways. Inelasticity also means that demand will not decrease very much in the face of a price increase. Therefore, a seller of a product with inelastic demand can raise prices and people will generally pay the increase. They can't really reduce their consumption all that much. As the chart shows, a doubling of the price calls forth a mere 20 percent decrease in demand. This boosts the gas station's revenue to $240, well above the $150 brought in before the price decrease.

However, although consumers cannot reduce their consumption much in the short run, as we'll see later in this chapter, they can reduce their demand for almost any product in the long run.

Zero elasticity, or what economists call perfect inelasticity, occurs when a price change has no effect on the quantity demanded. Certain medicines and health care services face perfectly inelastic demand (or close to it). For instance, people with AIDS require certain medicines and people with kidney disease require access to a dialysis machine regardless of the cost. Figure 5.4 depicts inelastic demand, while Figure 5.5 depicts zero elasticity, also called *perfect inelasticity* (the quantity remains the same, regardless of price).

Figure 5.5

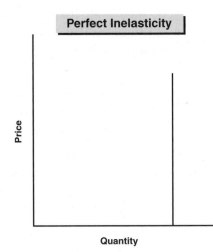

Perfect, or zero, elasticity means that no matter how the price changes, the quantity demanded remains the same. The consumer needs this amount of the product, regardless of how expensive or inexpensive it is.

What Determines Elasticity?

Either consciously or subconsciously, the issue of elasticity surfaces for consumers and producers in many everyday, real-world situations. Let's examine some of these situations and the main factors that determine the degree of elasticity of demand. These factors are:

◆ Availability of substitutes

◆ Short-run versus long-run

◆ Percentage of income spent on the product

Availability of Substitutes

Overall demand for gasoline—at least in the United States—is generally considered relatively inelastic. Americans own cars and trucks, and the country is large and laced with highways. Americans need gasoline because there are few substitutes for it. In fact, the only real substitutes are public transportation, which is not always available, and the electric car, which is still a relatively new technology.

However, any individual consumer's demand for gasoline can be elastic or inelastic, depending on their access to a substitute. Suppose the price of gasoline were to double over the next two months. If you commute from a suburb into New York City or another city with good public transportation, you could start taking the bus or train to work and dramatically reduce your demand for gasoline. Your demand for gasoline is relatively elastic.

On the other hand, if you commute from your home in one suburb to an office campus in a distant suburb, your transportation options may be quite limited. You need gasoline, and therefore your demand for it is relatively inelastic.

If there are few substitutes for a product, the demand for it is relatively inelastic. That means that the price can change, but the quantity demanded doesn't change very much in response.

Short-Run Versus Long-Run

The long-run and a short-run demand for many goods and services can differ substantially, and that affects elasticity.

In our gasoline example, a driver whose demand for gas is inelastic in the short-run may have elastic demand in the long run. She may find a job or start a business closer to home, or start a home-based business. She might buy a more fuel efficient car, or—in an instance of substitution—buy an electric car when her vehicle needs replacement.

For most products and services, long-run demand is far more elastic than short-run demand. As a fossil fuel with a finite supply, gasoline itself will be unavailable in the long run. Over the long run, people can make any of a number of adjustments that will alter their demand for a good.

In the short run, however, inelasticity tends to prevail, relative to the long run.

The Real World

The oil embargo of the early 1970s showed inelasticity of U.S. demand for gasoline in action. The embargo dramatically curtailed the supply of gasoline in the United States. As you would reason from the law of supply and demand, the price also increased dramatically. However, consumers' need for gasoline did not decrease very dramatically. Indeed, they not only paid the higher prices, but also waited in extremely long lines for the privilege of paying them.

In the longer run, however, as the 1970s progressed, consumers decided to reduce their demand for gas in the face of the higher prices. They began demanding smaller, more fuel efficient cars. Japanese auto makers, who were already making small cars for their island nation, were ready to meet that demand. Doing so actually helped manufacturers such as Toyota, Nissan, and Honda to establish themselves in the U.S. market. Soon U.S. auto manufacturers also began making smaller cars.

Presently, demand for gasoline seems relatively inelastic once more. The effect of the higher prices has been absorbed because people's incomes have grown over time while gasoline prices have remained high, but stable. However, the U.S. automobile fleet is without a doubt less fuel efficient than that of the 1970s due to the popularity of minivans and sport utility vehicles. If gasoline prices were to skyrocket and remain high, people would be stuck with gas-guzzlers for the time it would take for auto makers to retool their factories and begin producing smaller cars again.

Percentage of Income

The higher the percentage of income that a product or service consumes, the higher the elasticity. The lower the percentage of income, the lower the elasticity. For example, if the price of Tic Tacs goes up by 10 percent I doubt that many consumers of the mints would alter their demand for them. It's partly because the percentage increase would occur on a small base price relative to other common purchases, such as food, clothing, and gasoline. But it's also because the money spent on mints is a tiny percentage of most people's incomes.

Demand for items purchased with a small percentage of people's incomes is fairly inelastic. Price changes don't have a big effect on the quantity demanded. By that same token, cutting the price would probably do little to stimulate demand.

Things that people spend a higher percentage of their incomes on, such as cars, have higher elasticity of demand. People will consistently seek out the best deal on a new car or buy a used car because the price represents a relatively high percentage of most people's incomes. Some people never buy a new car, only used ones. Meanwhile, few people are shopping for the best deal on Tic Tacs (or are willing to accept used ones).

 **EconoTip**

If you produce or sell anything, or work for an outfit that does, you should have some idea of the elasticity of demand for your product or service. When the economy takes a downturn and people cut back their spending, can they cut back on your product or service? If you work for a hospital or a liquor store, you have little to worry about. People who need medical services or a drink aren't worried about what it costs—their demand is relatively inelastic.

On the other hand, if you work in a travel agency or fine restaurant, you may want to keep a Plan B handy. In general, inessentials or highly discretionary expenses have a higher elasticity of demand. If people can do without something, when times get tough they will.

Elasticity is worth knowing about because, first, it explains a lot of consumer behavior and, second, it lays the groundwork for understanding other aspects of consumer purchase decisions, as you will see in Chapter 6.

Tinkering with Markets

Up to now we have been examining the way markets operate when they are left to their own devices. However, markets are rarely left to their own devices. External measures are often introduced into a market, often by the government, sometimes by business. These *interventions* can affect the price of a product or service, the quantity demanded, and the behavior of producers and consumers. The rest of this chapter examines some of these measures—specifically, sales taxes, rent controls, and the minimum wage—and their effect on supply and demand.

Please note that I intend only to show the effects of these measures on the market purely from the economic standpoint. I am neither addressing nor judging the social impact or political aspects of these measures.

A Sales Tax Is a Price Increase

Sales taxes are levied by all states (except New Hampshire) and many cities as a way of raising revenue. Each individual state or city decides the amount of sales tax to charge, usually a small percentage—around or less than 5 percent—of the purchase price.

EconoTalk

Interventions in the market consist of steps by the government (price controls), businesses (monopolies), or even consumers (boycotts or trade unions) that affect the price, quantity, demand, supply, or some other aspect of the market. In general, however, the term market intervention refers to government actions. The parties doing the intervening generally believe that they are doing so for a good reason.

The term "sales tax" refers to a general tax on purchases. In some jurisdictions certain items, such as food or clothing, are exempt from sales tax. Also, the term "sales tax" does not usually apply to taxes on specific goods. For instance, taxes on gasoline and so-called "sin taxes" on cigarettes and alcoholic beverages are called gasoline and cigarette taxes and so on. Despite their titles, they are a form of sales tax and have the same general effect.

That effect is to increase the price of the item being purchased. As you know by now, the law of supply and demand dictates that if the price increases, the quantity demanded decreases. As Figure 5.6 shows, that is exactly what happens when a sales tax is levied.

Here we return to our Chapter 4 example of the market for beef. Figure 5.6 shows that the equilibrium price without the sales tax is $3 a pound. At that price, consumers demand 60,000 pounds of beef. The chart assumes a sales tax of $1 per pound of beef (don't laugh, cigarette taxes are often well over $1 a pack). The tax raises the price, but notice that overall demand for beef—the demand curve—*does not shift*. Instead, demand decreases along the existing demand curve to 40,000 pounds.

The price increase does, however, shift the supply curve. The shift reflects the new reality imposed by the "higher price" under the sales tax. Supply curve S^T in the chart shows that, given the decreased demand due to the higher price, suppliers are willing to supply less beef at all price levels. Therefore, the new equilibrium point (E^T) stands at a price of $4 (equal to $3 plus the $1 tax) and a quantity of 40,000 pounds.

As a result of the tax, the producers supply and consumers demand 20,000 fewer pounds of beef. In effect, the tax on beef takes 20,000 pounds of beef off the market. These dynamics hold true for most sales taxes on most products. There are arguments for and against sales taxes and "sin taxes," but without question, they alter the prices and quantities that would prevail in the market if they were absent. However, they do raise tax revenues.

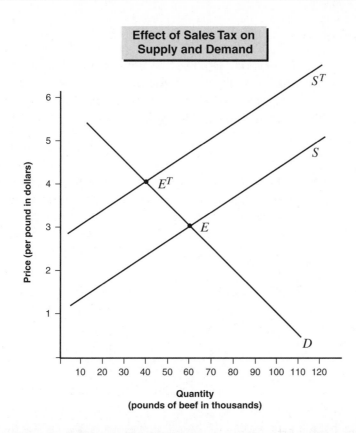

Effect of Sales Tax on Supply and Demand

Figure 5.6

Price (per pound in dollars) vs. Quantity (pounds of beef in thousands)

The Real World

In 2002, New York City raised its cigarette tax to the point where cigarettes cost about $7.00 a pack. Mayor Michael Bloomberg, a zealous former smoker, made no bones about his goal of encouraging people to quit. Smokers felt that they were being singled out as easy targets in a city where many evils prevail. They also feel they are being asked to shoulder an unfair share of the city's tax burden.

Whatever your views on smoking, the situation highlights issues of both elasticity and sales taxes (which are generally related). Historically, those who levied cigarette taxes counted on fairly inelastic demand for cigarettes. The product is habit-forming, and those with the habit were generally not deterred by cost.

Until recently, that is. The skyrocketing cost of cigarettes, due to manufacturers' price hikes as well as higher taxes, has encouraged many people to quit. High costs especially deter teenagers, who often avoid the habit due to the expense. And you know why: Cigarettes consume a higher percentage of a teenager's income than an adult's income.

Rent Controls

Some communities employ rent controls to make affordable housing available to people without enough income to otherwise live in the community. In general, rent controls keep the price of rental units below the market price. Indeed, that is their goal, because at the market price there's not enough housing for people with lower incomes.

EconoTalk

A **price ceiling** is a government-mandated maximum price that a seller can charge for a product or service. A **price floor** is a government-mandated minimum price that a seller can charge. Rent control is an example of a price ceiling, while a minimum wage is in effect a floor on the price of labor.

If you consider the relationship between price and quantity in a free market, you'll realize that over time the effect of rent control will be to limit the amount of housing available in the community. Why? Because if the *price ceiling* is below the market price (that is, the price at the equilibrium point), then the quantity of housing will be kept below the point that buyers would demand in a free market. Figure 5.7 illustrates this.

Figure 5.7

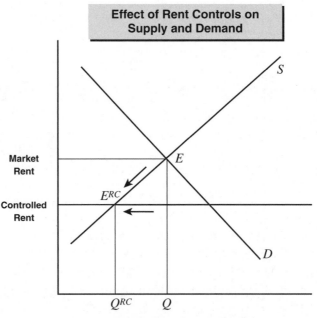

Effect of Rent Controls on Supply and Demand

The price ceiling imposed by rent control creates a shortage of housing and leads to some renters being unable to find apartments. In Figure 5.7, the shortage is the difference between the "imposed equilibrium quantity" of Q^{RC} and the market equilibrium quantity of Q.

In practice, rent controls do limit construction of new rental units in the long run, as has been seen in New York and other cities. New Yorkers lucky enough to live in rent-controlled apartments love the system. But, over time, landlords found that the costs of buying or constructing and maintaining a building outpaced the rent increases permitted under the controls. That made owning an apartment building a bad business proposition and led landlords to abandon buildings. A two-tier system developed, in which people with rent-controlled apartments paid rents well below market rates and those in decontrolled apartments or new buildings not subject to rent control had to pay market-rate rents well above what they would have been in a free market.

Again, the social value of making affordable housing available to lower income people is left out of this analysis. Yet the danger in rent controls (as opposed to other means of helping people afford housing, such as welfare payments to raise their incomes) is that a city can wind up with two levels of housing—very inexpensive and very expensive. This tends to squeeze middle income people out of the city. This also occurred to an extent in New York, although other factors ranging from decaying schools to rising crime also played a role in the movement of middle class people out of the city.

The Minimum Wage

While rent control sets a ceiling on the cost of housing, the minimum wage sets a floor under the price of labor. Minimum wage legislation aims to provide every worker with a "living wage," meaning an hourly rate that covers the cost of life's necessities.

Whether the current minimum wage does that is open to debate. Working a 40-hour week, at the current U.S. minimum wage of $5.15, a worker would earn $206 a week, or about $10,700 a year. According to the U.S. Census Bureau, the *poverty threshold* for one person is currently a little over $9,000 a year. For a household of two people the threshold is $11,600. Therefore, the minimum wage keeps a single person just above the official definition

EconoTalk

The **poverty threshold** (sometimes called "the poverty line") is the level of annual household income, adjusted for household size, which officially defines poverty. A household that earns an income below the threshold is "officially" poor, and eligible for certain types of public assistance. The U.S. Census Bureau updates these data every year to reflect changes in incomes and price levels.

of poverty. It fails to do the same for a household of two with one breadwinner, let alone a household with one or more children and a full-time homemaker.

All of this aside, an economist would analyze the effect of a minimum wage on the labor market as depicted in Figure 5.8.

 Figure 5.8

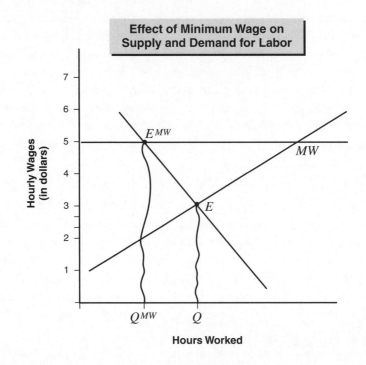

If the minimum wage is set above the wage that would otherwise prevail in the free market, then the wage floor will generate unemployment. Figure 5.8 shows why.

The line labeled MW at the $5.00 wage level represents the minimum wage, while the free market wage stands at $3.00. The minimum wage creates an "imposed equilibrium point" (E^{MW}) at which the quantity of labor demanded (Q^{MW}) stands well below the quantity that employers would demand (Q) at the free market wage of $3.00. This generates a surplus of labor (that is, idle workers) equal to Q minus Q^{MW}. Workers who are lucky (or skilled) enough to land a job at the minimum wage are happy. However, many of those who cannot command the minimum wage are unemployed.

The Wages of Control

Thus in the case of rent control and the minimum wage, government intervention in free markets distorts the dynamics of supply and demand. In the case of rent control, a city winds up with too little housing, or with a two-tier system. In the two-tier system, some lucky people enjoy apartments at below-market rates, while others are paying inflated rates for a scarcer number of "free market" apartments.

In the case of the minimum wage, some workers are idle because the government is, in effect requiring them to demand a wage that employers are not willing to pay. This may have the unintended consequence of actually putting less money into the workers' pockets.

There are good arguments for and against rent control and the minimum wage. Here, however, the goal is to examine their "pure" effect on supply and demand. To do this, we are leaving social aims and other factors, such as welfare payments and differences in the cost of living around the nation, out of the discussion for the moment.

The Price You Gotta Pay

This chapter extends the exploration of supply and demand that began in Chapter 4. As we've seen, several factors, including elasticity and government intervention in the market, can affect the demand and supply for a product or service.

In Part 2, we examine more of the workings of the market and the behavior of consumers and producers.

The Least You Need to Know

- Elasticity of demand refers to the change in demand that occurs in response to a change in price. Specifically, it is the degree to which an increase or decrease in price will change the quantity demanded.

- Unitary elasticity occurs when the quantity of a product demanded changes in response to price changes in a way that leaves total revenue the same. Elasticity occurs when a reduction in price increases the quantity demanded so that the seller's revenue increases. Inelasticity occurs when a reduction in price increases the quantity demanded by more than zero but less than unity.

- Elasticity can be affected by the availability of substitute goods or services, the percentage of income spent on the good or service, and whether the short term or long term is being considered.

- Interventions in the market consist of steps by the government (sales taxes), businesses (monopolies), or consumers (boycotts or trade unions) that affect the price, quantity, demand, supply, or some other aspect of the market. Those who intervene usually believe that they are doing so for a good reason.

◆ A sales tax has the effect of increasing the price and lowering both the supply of and demand for whatever it applies to.

◆ Rent controls seek to ensure that housing is available to people in a community who may otherwise be unable to afford it. However, rent control can limit the overall supply of housing or inflate the price of decontrolled or uncontrolled housing, or both.

◆ A minimum wage aims to provide workers with a "living wage." Yet if the minimum wage is set too high above the market rate, it can add to unemployment because the quantity of labor that employers demand at the minimum wage is below the quantity they would demand at the (lower) free market rate.

Part 2

Capitalism at Work

Buyers and sellers have different—even opposite—needs and motivations that must be resolved in markets. In this part, we unscrew the top of the consumer's head and find out how he or she makes buying decisions.

Most consumers are also sellers—of their labor. Everyone who works for a living (or who plans to) should understand the dynamics of the labor market. This market has seen more than its share of turmoil, and we explore ways in which labor and management have tried to handle their differences. Speaking of management, we also examine businesses in this part. Production decisions are every bit as difficult as buying decisions, and there is usually a lot more riding on them. Therefore, we see what goes into making these decisions profitable.

Part 2 closes with an introduction to the business cycle. This cycle of economic expansions and recessions affects almost every manager, business owner, worker, investor, and consumer in the nation. The more you know about the business cycle, the better prepared you'll be to cope with it.

Chapter 6

Buyer Be Where? Consumer Behavior

In This Chapter

◆ How consumers make purchase decisions

◆ The true value of goods and services

◆ Why water is very valuable, but very cheap

◆ What makes consumers better off

To understand the U.S. economy, you must understand consumers. Consumers drive the growth of the economy, as well as its character. They drive its growth because consumption by households represents two-thirds of GDP. They drive the character of the economy—which is that of a "consumer society"—because of their wealth and buying behavior. The high levels of wealth, together with a low savings rate and high use of credit, mean that Americans tend to buy what they want when they want it. This flows through to producers, who are always scrambling to produce more goods and services for this voracious market.

This is not to ignore the many U.S. households that cannot afford to buy what they want when they want it. Nor is it to say that every American is always on a buying binge. It is to say that, relative to other nations, the United States produces and consumes a broader array of goods and services in larger quantities. This is also why many foreign producers want to establish themselves in the U.S. market.

This chapter reveals the economic forces underlying consumer behavior. It also examines how consumers maximize their happiness in this land where the pursuit of happiness (but not happiness itself) is constitutionally guaranteed.

What's the Use? Demand and Utility

The entire demand curve for a product—let's stick with beef—is actually the sum of all consumers' demand for the product. If you could determine every single consumer's demand for beef, that is, the quantity that each would buy at various prices, and add up the quantities at each price, you would have the total demand for beef.

In other words, you would add them up horizontally, as shown in Figure 6.1.

As Figure 6.1 shows, total demand is the sum of what individual consumers demand at various prices. Here, at $2 per pound, these two fictitious consumers, Jim and Diane, demand a total of 3 pounds of beef. Jim wants 2 pounds, and Diane wants 1 pound.

Obviously there are more than two people in the market for beef. But no one (not even an economist) is going to survey all consumers on their demand for beef at different prices. Thus the demand curve for a good or service theoretically represents total demand. That curve is—also theoretically—the sum of the demand of all the individuals in the market for that good or service.

I'm bringing this up because I want to focus on individual consumers for a while and show how they think and behave. Focusing on individual consumers (and thinking about your own buying behavior) is a good way to understand what drives buying behavior.

You Want *Another* One?

One key driver of buying behavior is *utility*. Utility is the reason you buy something. It is the value or benefit you get from buying a good or service. Utility varies from consumer to consumer. A pickup truck has no utility for people who would never buy one. But a pickup truck has a huge amount of utility for people who couldn't get along without one.

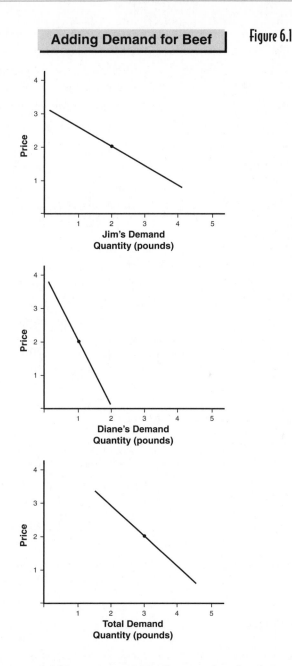

Adding Demand for Beef   Figure 6.1

The utility of a pickup truck also varies among the people who do own one. Some people buy one because they need it to make a living. Others buy one to haul their firewood and dogs around. And others never haul anything. They buy a pickup truck because they think it makes them look cool.

Whatever the benefit or enjoyment you get from buying a product, that is its utility.

EconoTalk

Utility is the value, benefit, or enjoyment that a person receives in buying a product. **Marginal utility** is the value, benefit, or enjoyment a person receives from buying each additional unit of the product. **Diminishing marginal utility** means that the utility (the benefit or enjoyment) of consuming the last additional unit of a good is less than that of the previous unit consumed.

Marginal utility is the benefit you get from buying each additional unit of the good. For instance, most individuals who own a pickup truck own just one. If they bought a second one, do you think it would give them the same benefit as the first one? Would it have the same utility?

How about beef? If you went to a restaurant and had a steak dinner tonight and then went out to a steakhouse again tomorrow night, would you enjoy tomorrow's steak as much as tonight's? What if you went to a steakhouse the night after that?

The answer to all these questions is generally no. You can only drive one car (or, for that matter, one pickup truck) at a time. You can only eat so many steaks before you want a can of tuna fish. In fact, almost all products and services are characterized by *diminishing marginal utility*. The "utility," that is, the benefit and enjoyment you derive from the last unit consumed is less than that of the one previously consumed. Sooner (for pickup trucks) or later (for hamburgers) the benefit and enjoyment of the last unit consumed will be less than that of the unit before that.

Figure 6.2 depicts diminishing marginal utility.

Figure 6.2

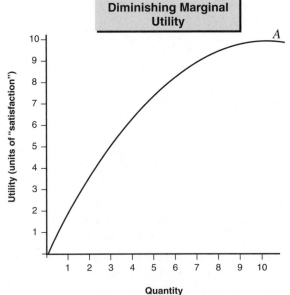

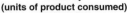

Each additional unit of a product consumed provides less utility than the previous one consumed. Note that until point "A" *total* utility is increasing. But it is increasing at a decreasing rate.

Now what does this have to do with buying behavior?

Just this: Each consumer is on a limited income or has a limited amount of wealth. (Remember scarcity? It applies to money, big time.) Each consumer spends his money with the aim of maximizing the overall benefit and enjoyment he can get for that expenditure. Therefore, each consumer will be best off if he spends his income so that the marginal utility of every product or service is in exact proportion to its price.

In other words, to maximize your well being—the total utility you get from your purchases—the last dollar you spend on beef should bring you the same marginal utility as the last dollar you spend on anything else. Moreover, this has to be the case for everything else you buy.

Why? If you're not getting the same marginal utility on the last dollar you spend on each product you buy, then you would shift your spending around so that you did. Why would you spend money on something when something else would make you happier, that is, have more marginal utility?

This is called the *law of equal marginal utilities per dollar*. It says that a consumer will buy each product she wants until the marginal utility per dollar spent on it equals that of any other product she buys.

> **EconoTalk**
>
> The **law of equal marginal utilities per dollar** states that a consumer will buy each product she wants until the marginal utility per dollar spent on it is exactly the same as it is for any other product she buys.

> **EconoTip**
>
> It may be useful to picture a "market basket" of all the goods and services you buy in the average month with your average monthly income. This should include not just the products that would fit into a market basket, but also your housing, electricity, gasoline, entertainment—all the goods and services you buy.
>
> Ask yourself these questions: Why do I buy these things? Why do I buy this particular mix of products and services? Am I allocating my expenditures in proportion to the marginal utility I derive from these products and services? Or could I be happier if I bought less of something and more of something else?

Think about this the next time you go to the supermarket or mall: Every consumer out there is struggling to reach a point that economists call consumer equilibrium. That's the point where the consumer is maximizing the total utility he obtains from his total spending. With so many choices, no wonder we're all going crazy!

The Price of Utility

What could have more utility than water? You can drink it, bath in it, swim in it, sprinkle your lawn with it, wash your car with it, and you would die without it. Yet water is one of the cheapest products you can buy—in the United States, that is, not on the planet Dune. Also I'm discussing the water that comes out of your faucet and showerhead, not the water that comes in bottles labeled Evian.

Water has tremendous utility and value. Yet its price is low. How can that be? This question stumped Adam Smith (of "invisible hand" fame) who you learned about in Chapter 1. He wondered why water, one of life's essentials, was cheap while diamonds, which you cannot drink or bath in, are expensive. He never did figure it out.

However, later economists did. The answer is partly that water is plentiful, especially in comparison to diamonds. Water is also easy to produce and deliver, once reservoirs and pipelines are in place. Diamonds are tough to produce and deliver (requiring the services of diamond miners and diamond cutters). But the real economic issue is the total utility versus the marginal utility of water and diamonds.

The *total* utility of water is high, but its *marginal* utility is low. Water is so plentiful and we use so much of it, that an extra glass of it or an extra minute in the shower has a tiny bit of extra utility. Diamonds are scarce, and we use very few of them. Since most people buy one diamond, or at most a few, in our lifetimes, the marginal utility—the benefit and satisfaction—of, say, an engagement ring, is huge.

And that is the answer to Adam's Smith question about the price of water: The marginal utility—the utility obtained from the last unit consumed—and not the total utility determines the price of something. In general, the price of a good falls until it reflects the utility of the last unit sold. Why? Because if the price were any higher, then that last unit cannot be sold. Sellers want to sell as much as they can of whatever they sell, so they set their prices to clear out their inventory.

The Consumer's Surplus

Incidentally, because market prices are driven by marginal utility—the utility of the last unit sold—the earlier units we purchase are actually worth more to us than the last. This means that we get more utility than we are paying for from the earlier units we purchase. We're paying a price set by the utility of the last pound of beef for the first pound and second pound and third pound we buy. Economists refer to this "extra utility" as a surplus—more accurately, as *the consumer surplus*.

The Real World

The theory of utility has been criticized. For one thing, utility really cannot be measured. In Figure 6.2, I labeled the vertical axis "units of satisfaction" and economists do that, too, but it's a theoretical concept. Of course, utility and marginal utility make sense: We buy things that benefit us, and that benefit does diminish as we consume more of the thing. But that benefit cannot be precisely measured.

Another criticism is that people don't walk around thinking about the benefit they will derive from spending another dollar on another pound of beef or another gallon of gas. So, say the critics, can marginal utility make a difference in buying behavior?

Economists acknowledge that these objections have some validity. However, regardless of whether utility can be measured or whether people think about it, people buy things that they want and they cannot have everything that they want. Therefore, they buy the things that give them the greatest satisfaction. They buy them until they are satisfied with the amount they have. And they buy a mix of goods that somehow maximizes their overall satisfaction. This is, after all, rational behavior, and economics assumes that people behave rationally.

Consumers would actually be willing to pay more for the first and perhaps the second and third pound of beef than they are actually being charged. The difference between what a consumer would pay and what she does pay is the consumer surplus. For example, suppose that Diane would actually pay $7 for her first pound of beef, $6 for her second pound, $5 for her third pound, and $4 for her fourth pound—and that the price of beef is $4.

If Diane buys four pounds of beef, she pays the store $16 (for four pounds at $4 a pound). However, Diane is receiving $22 worth of beef. That's because she would have been willing to pay $7 for the first pound, $6 for the second, $5 for the third, and $4 for the fourth, and $7 + $6 + $5 + $4 = $22. In this situation, Diane's consumer surplus equals $6. That's the difference between the total utility she derives from the purchase and the actual purchase price. Again, that price is set by the market at the value of the marginal utility of beef.

This is depicted visually in Figure 6.3. Diane pays $16, which is represented by the square under the line labeled "Market Price," because four pounds (the quantity on the horizontal axis) times $4 (the market price on vertical axis) equals $16. The $6 is represented by the shaded areas above the line labeled "Market Price." Although this whole situation still relies on the concept of utility and marginal utility, it has the advantage of expressing the concept in dollars instead of "units of utility."

Figure 6.3

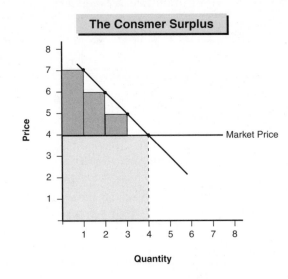

To grasp the impact of the consumer surplus on the larger economy, consider the fact that we are all Diane when we are shopping. We would *all* pay more for the things we really need and want. If you had a raging headache, what would you pay for your first aspirin and then your second? During a gasoline shortage, what would you pay for your first gallon, your second, and so on? Certainly, for both the aspirin and the gasoline, you would pay substantially more than the market price set by the value of the last unit sold. But you don't have to pay that, because the market prices goods and services based on their marginal utility, not total utility.

The Real World

You might think of the total utility of an item as the *value* of the item to the consumer. If you had a raging headache, and you were stuck in a place that sold aspirins in those little envelopes stapled to the cardboard displays, you would probably pay $2 or $3— that is, the price of a bottle of aspirins—just for two of them. Isn't getting rid of a headache worth $2 or $3 to you?

By the way, a monopoly basically operates by getting its customers to pay for the total utility of the product or service rather than setting the price based on marginal utility. The monopolist can get away with this because he faces no competition and controls the supply. He can therefore make the product artificially scarce.

In a way, a newsstand selling aspirins in little envelopes for an outrageous price is acting like a monopolist. If there were a nearby drugstore, where aspirins are sold at a range of prices and sizes, he wouldn't get away with it.

So consumers are out to maximize their total utility, given their budgets. And prices are set by marginal utility, rather than total utility. So far, so good. Now let's delve more deeply into the complex mind of the consumer.

Milk and/or Cookies

Let's consider the complex mind of a seven-year-old consumer. His name is Jimmy, and he only buys two things: milk and cookies. Jimmy loves milk and cookies. He loves milk and cookies so much that he will buy them in almost any combination. But he wants them both. He finds milk with no cookies to be insufferably dull. He finds cookies with no milk to be insufferably dry. But beyond that, Jimmy is indifferent to most combinations of milk and cookies. Over the course of his week in school, he'll find equal satisfaction among the following combinations of glasses of milk and cookies:

Indifference Combinations

	Milk	Cookies
A	2	12
B	4	6
C	6	4
D	8	3

These are called indifference combinations because Jimmy is indifferent regarding which combination he gets. He would derive equal enjoyment (that is, utility and benefit) from any of these combinations of milk and cookies.

Like so many things in economics, these indifference combinations can be plotted to on a curve, as shown in Figure 6.4.

Jimmy will derive equal satisfaction anywhere along this curve, not just at the combinations in the small table of indifference combinations. Why? Because Jimmy is willing to trade off cookies for milk and milk for cookies in the proportions shown in his indifference combinations and anywhere along his *indifference curve*. This is called an indifference curve because all

EconoTalk

An **indifference curve** shows a series of combinations of purchases of two goods that are all equally acceptable to the consumer. The consumer is "indifferent" in the sense that he would be equally happy with any of the combinations plotted on the curve.

the combinations are equally satisfactory to Jimmy. He would be indifferent about which combination he actually received.

Figure 6.4

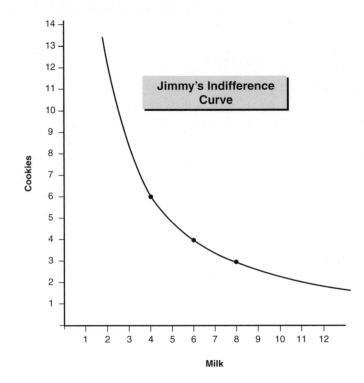

Jimmy's Indifference Curve

Consumers—all of us—are willing to trade off one good for another. We do it every day, don't we? We all buy some things instead of others.

That's the case with Jimmy. However, at different points on the indifference curve, he will make tradeoffs in different proportions of each good. For instance, when Jimmy has four glasses of milk and six cookies, he will give up two cookies to get another two glasses of milk. Say he makes that trade and winds up with four cookies and six glasses of milk. At that point, he will only give up one cookie for two glasses of milk. Why? Because at that point he has plenty of milk, but is starting to run low on cookies. In fact, from this point on, he will need more and more milk to separate him from each remaining cookie.

EconoTalk

The **marginal rate of substitution** is the rate at which a consumer will trade one good for another as one becomes scarcer to her and the other becomes more plentiful. In general, as a good becomes scarcer, a consumer will trade it only for increasingly greater amounts of the more plentiful good.

This illustrates an important concept: the *marginal rate of substitution*, also known as the substitution ratio, changes along the curve. (This, for the geometrically inclined—no pun intended—means that the slope of the curve is changing.) The various points on the indifference curve show the marginal rate of substitution between two goods for a consumer. This ratio changes along the indifference curve. It changes as the proportion of the two goods to one another changes. The less you have of a good relative to another good, the less you want to trade it off. For many goods, you may reach a point were you simply won't trade it off.

For instance, Jimmy will not trade every last drop of milk for a cookie or trade his last bite of cookie for more milk. He holds onto his cookies as they become scarce and milk becomes plentiful. Likewise, he holds onto his milk as it becomes scarce and cookies become plentiful. This is why the indifference curve flattens out at each end. The curve eventually becomes vertical for cookies and horizontal for milk, because Jimmy does not want all milk and no cookies (too dull), nor does he want all cookies and no milk (too dry).

In econospeak, this means that, to Jimmy, the marginal utility of milk increases as milk becomes scarce and cookies become plentiful (and his mouth fills with dry crumbs). And it means that the marginal utility of cookies increases as they become scarce and milk becomes plentiful (and Jimmy longs for variety in his life). In general, the more you have of something, the lower the marginal utility of each additional unit you receive. After our study of marginal utility earlier in this chapter, that should make complete sense. (Want to buy a bucket of water??)

EconoTip

An indifference curve is also called an equal utility contour. (It's a contour as well as a curve, you see.) It's an equal utility contour because the curve (or contour, if you must) depicts a series of points where the relative marginal utilities of the two goods—in this case milk and cookies—are equal for the consumer—in this case Jimmy.

More (Or Less) Cookies and Milk

Believe it or not, the indifference curve in Figure 6.4 is just one of many that I could have drawn for Jimmy. That's because there are many other combinations of milk and cookies that will satisfy the boy, as shown in Figure 6.5.

For instance, along curve I^2 Jimmy would be as happy to have four cookies and four glasses of milk and as he would be to have two cookies and seven glasses of milk. However—and this is important—no combination along curve I^2 would make Jimmy as happy as any combination on the original curve I^1 (which is the original curve in Figure 6.4). Of course, that's because at any point on curve I^1, Jimmy has more cookies *and* more milk, in various combinations.

Figure 6.5

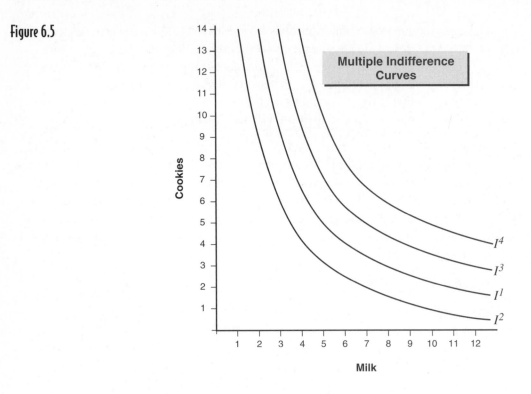

Similarly, Jimmy would be happier with any combination on curve I^3 than he would be on curve I^1 and even happier with any combination on curve 1^4.

Please file these thoughts where you can get at them easily, because we'll be coming back to them soon. First, though, we need to examine Jimmy's financial situation.

That Awful Thing Called a Budget

There's no such thing as free milk and cookies (or a free lunch). At Jimmy's school, cookies cost 50¢ each, and milk costs 75¢ a glass. Jimmy's on a meal plan, so his lunch is paid for in advance. But he foots his own cookie-and-milk bill, out of a cookie-and-milk allowance of $6 a week. Jimmy can spend that $6 allowance on cookies and milk, in any combination he chooses.

Figure 6.6 illustrates the possible ways in which Jimmy could spend that money.

If he wanted to, which he doesn't, Jimmy could allocate his whole cookie-and-milk budget to cookies—and buy 12 of them at 50¢ each—or to milk—and buy 8 glasses at 75¢ each. Those two points, and all the points between them—that entire line on Figure 6.6—is called the *budget line*. It's also known as the *consumption possibility line*.

That's the perfect name because that line shows all the possible combinations of cookies and milk that Jimmy could consume with his $6.

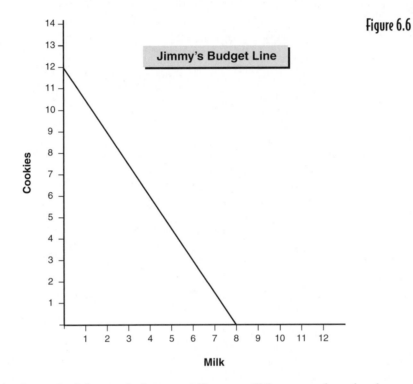

Jimmy's Budget Line

Figure 6.6

At the end of the week, however, Jimmy will have purchased only one combination of cookies and milk. Which combination do you think he will buy?

He'll buy the combination of cookies and milk that will give him the greatest total utility. To find that combination we could wrack our brains running a bunch of numbers but, because we have charted Jimmy's indifference curves and his budget line, there's a much easier way. It is shown in Figure 6.7.

In Figure 6.7, we lay Jimmy's consumption possibility line on top of his multiple indifference curves. This clearly reveals the cookie-and-milk combination that will give Jimmy the greatest utility given his budget or, as economists say, the biggest bang for the buck: six cookies and four glasses of milk. This point rests on the

EconoTalk

The **budget line** or con-sumption **possibility line** shows the range of combinations of two goods that a consumer can afford, given his budget. The consumer's **optimal equilibrium point** is the point on the highest indifference curve that the budget line just touches. That is the com-bination of purchases in which the marginal utility of each dollar spent on the two goods is equal.

highest indifference curve that Jimmy's budget will carry him to, and it is called the *optimal equilibrium point*. At this point, the marginal utility of the last dollar spent on each product is equal.

Figure 6.7

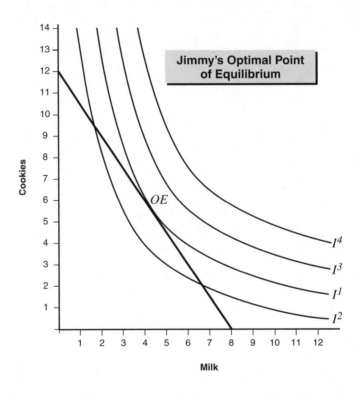

What About Changes?

Changes in the price of products and services (such as cookies and milk) and in the consumer's income (or allowance) will change these pictures and the underlying situations.

An *increase* in the price of either cookies or milk will change the budget line. If the price of cookies increases, Jimmy will be able to afford fewer than 12 of them on his $6 allowance. That will cause the budget line to pivot downward and place the optimal equilibrium point in Figure 6.7 out of reach. An increase in the price of milk will have a similar effect. Moreover, an increase in the price of both cookies and milk will shift the entire budget line lower. In all of these cases, Jimmy winds up on a lower indifference curve and at a lower optimal equilibrium point.

A *decrease* in the price of either cookies or milk, or both, will have the opposite effect, and will move Jimmy to a higher indifference curve and a higher equilibrium point.

Changes in income have similar effects. An increase in income moves the entire budget line—that is, the consumption possibility line—higher. A decrease in income moves the entire budget line lower. When the line moves higher, the consumer winds up on a higher indifference curve and at a higher equilibrium point. When the line moves lower, the consumer is on a lower indifference curve and at a lower equilibrium point.

EconoTip

The cookies and milk example simplifies an extremely complex situation in which a consumer, facing a vast number of choices, attempts to optimize the marginal utility of her expenditures. The theory of marginal utility and consumer equilibrium is, admittedly, theory. However, something very much like this process goes on in consumer behavior.

A shopper doesn't go to the store and buy 40 pounds of beef and no potatoes, even if she and her family really enjoy beef. At a certain point, the marginal utility of beef will diminish, particularly if the shopper has no potatoes in the house. Think of the entire market basket of goods and services you buy. Isn't there a subconscious analysis of marginal utility going on in your buying behavior?

There are, of course, other drivers of consumer behavior. We will examine some of them in Chapter 7. Yet the mechanism of choice plays out along the lines of utility, marginal utility, and consumer equilibrium—whether the consumer knows it or not.

The Least You Need to Know

- Total demand for a product is the sum of all consumers' demand for the product.

- Utility is the value, benefit, or enjoyment that a person receives in buying a product. Marginal utility is the value, benefit, or enjoyment a person receives from consuming each additional unit of the product. After a point, marginal utility diminishes with each additional unit consumed.

- In general, the price of a good falls until it reflects the utility of the last unit sold. If the price were any higher, then that last unit could not be sold. In this way, the consumer derives more benefit from the first units of a product she bought, because the product is actually priced at its marginal utility.

- Indifference curves show a series of combinations of purchases (of two goods) that are all equally acceptable to the consumer. The consumer is "indifferent" in the sense that he would be equally happy with any combination of goods plotted on the curve.

♦ The budget line or consumption possibility line shows the range of combinations of two goods that a consumer can afford, given his budget. The point on the highest indifference curve that the budget line just touches is the consumer's optimal equilibrium point. That is the combination of purchases that he can afford that will make him happiest. That is also where the marginal utility of each dollar spent on the goods is equalized.

♦ Changes in prices and income affect a consumer's well being. Lower prices or higher income will leave the consumer better off, while higher prices or lower income will leave her worse off. Here, better and worse off are defined as points on higher or lower indifference curves. On higher curves, the consumer has more goods; on lower curves, she has fewer goods.

Pluses and Minuses: Income, Outgo, and Investment

In This Chapter

◆ Sources of income

◆ Propensity to spend and to save

◆ The consumption function

◆ The multiplier effect

In Chapter 6, we examined consumers' buying behavior based upon their individual wants and needs. In this chapter, we look at consumers on a larger scale, as a driving force in the economy.

It's well worth doing. Consumers' choices about how much of their income to spend and to save affects the growth of the economy and, over time, its size. That's because, as you recall, the savings of households are channeled into businesses' investment in productive capital, which determines the long-term ability of an economy to produce goods and services.

Where Income Comes From

Households receive income in exchange for providing businesses with the factors of production—the essential things needed to produce goods and services. Economists define the *factors of production* as land, labor, and capital. Land is self-explanatory, and includes not only farmland but all land devoted to factories, offices, terminals, and other commercial purposes. Labor refers to all human effort aimed at producing something or performing a service for payment.

The term capital requires more explanation. Economists define capital as any product created to make more products. Capital includes factories and equipment, computers and tools, vehicles and roads—the entire productive infrastructure and its individual components. Interestingly, economists do not include financial capital in their definition of capital, only productive capital.

EconoTalk

The **factors of production** are land, labor, and capital. Capital refers to productive plant and equipment—any tangible thing that is created in order to create another product. Plant and equipment are also called capital goods, meaning goods that produce other goods.

There is one other "factor." In a capitalist system, an entrepreneur organizes the factors of production into a business to produce a product or service, sell and deliver it to customers, and, in the process, earn a profit for herself and her investors. This entrepreneurial function is essential to a developed economy because the factors of production do not organize themselves. (They couldn't, even if they tried.)

The process of capital formation generates capital goods. Capital formation—building productive capacity—is an essential step in developing an economy that can produce goods and services beyond farm and handmade products. Capital formation is also called investment and is the "I" in C + I + G you learned about in Chapter 2. As you will see in Part 5, capital formation is a crucial issue for the developing economies of the world, which face the challenge of attracting financial capital and then channeling it into productive capital.

Each factor of production receives a specific kind of payment, although it's all money. Landlords, who provide the land, receive *rent*. Workers receive *wages* (or salaries). Capitalists, who provide the productive capital (or more accurately, the money that finances that capital), receive *interest*. And entrepreneurs, who organize the factors of production, receive *profit*.

I've italicized these terms because each one has a specific meaning: Each relates to the factor being provided and paid for in the production process. Economists use these four types of income—rent, wages, interest, and profits—to calculate a figure for national income.

It All Adds Up

National income is the total rent, wages, interest, and profits paid to the factors of production in a year. The following are the figures for the years 1990 and 2001.

Table 7.1   National Income (in billions)

	1990	2001
Wages & Salaries	$3,351	$5,875
Rent	430	865
Interest	452	650
Profits	409	732
National Income	$4,642	$8,122

Source: Bureau of Economic Analysis, National Income and Product Accounts

Figure 7.1 shows how these payments and the factors of production relate to one another and flow through the economy.

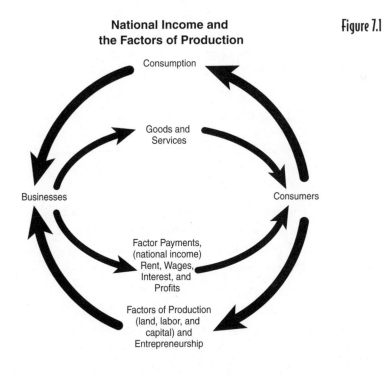

National Income and the Factors of Production

Consumption

Goods and Services

Businesses

Consumers

Factor Payments, (national income) Rent, Wages, Interest, and Profits

Factors of Production (land, labor, and capital) and Entrepreneurship

Figure 7.1

EconoTalk

National income is the total rent, wages, interest, and profits paid to households for providing the factors of production in a quarter or a year.

In the lower half of the diagram, consumers (households) provide the factors of production to businesses, which make factor payments to consumers in return. In the top half, consumers pay businesses and receive goods and services in return. The diagram shows a circular relationship between consumers and businesses because that's what it is. Businesses pay consumers to produce goods and services, and consumers pay businesses for those goods and services. Is this a great system, or what?

Propensity to Save and to Consume

Disposable income is what's left after taxes, and there are only two things a consumer can do with that income—spend it or save it. Either way, that income is being recycled into the economy. It either becomes part of consumption—the "C" in C + I + G—or it becomes part of investment—the "I" in C + I + G.

Up to now in this book, I have spent a good deal of time discussing demand. We will discuss it again, even in this chapter. First let's focus on the investment aspect of GDP. Investment in capital goods does not simply represent a boost to GDP in the year it is made. It represents a boost to the economy in the years ahead. Remember, investment in capital goods expands our economy's productive capacity.

When people save part of their income, they forgo current consumption for later consumption. The saver engages in this act of delayed gratification for his own good, not to provide money for businesses to invest. He wants to make an expensive purchase in several months or years, or wants to have money for retirement. The problems of a businesses searching for money to finance capital goods are the furthest things from his mind.

Businesses are equally unconcerned about the saver's situation. They also don't give a thought to the larger economy and the issue of raising "I" in the GDP formula. They are interested in growing. They are concerned about latching onto (or developing) a new technology, building a new factory or office, or getting a new product out to market.

You'll recall that the impersonal dynamics of supply and demand work themselves out in the market through the price mechanism to bring consumers and producers to an equilibrium point. Similarly, the dynamics of saving and investment are resolved in the market, by interest rates (the price of money) and by unemployment and income levels. Too little savings will boost interest rates. A surplus of savings will cause interest rates to fall. Too little investment will generate unemployment. Too much investment can cause inflation, thus eroding the purchasing power of income.

Let's look more deeply into those dynamics.

Spend or Save?

As you may imagine, people with high incomes save more money than people with low incomes. The poor don't save at all, while families in the higher income brackets do most of the saving.

Many economists, financial planners, and public officials have expressed concern in recent years that the U.S. personal savings rate—the amount of disposable income that an individual saves instead of spends—has plummeted over the past 30 years. Indeed the overall personal savings rate fell from 8.2 percent in the 1970s to 6.7 percent in the 1980s and to about 3 percent in the 1990s.

The Real World

Those concerned about the savings rate usually worry more about the long-term well-being of the savers (actually, the nonsavers) than the pool of funds that can be invested. While the U.S. personal savings rate is undoubtedly low, both historically and compared with other nations' (notably Japan's and Germany's), two things should be kept in mind.

First, the savings rate does not include or count the appreciation of financial securities or home values. Many nonsavers have a good deal of wealth in those forms. While unrealized appreciation (or a "paper gain") is not the same as money in the bank, it is a form of wealth. Second, as a large, stable, prosperous economy, the United States attracts more foreign investment capital than any other nation in the world. That provides investment capital for businesses even if the U.S. savings rate is low.

So, overall, we can infer that Americans today have a lower propensity to save and, therefore, a higher propensity to consume than they did in the 1970s. The *average propensity to save* is equal to the savings rate. It is the amount saved in a period divided by disposable income in a period. Similarly, the *average propensity to consume* is consumption expenditure in a period divided by disposable income in the period.

The average propensity to save rises as income rises. This is true for a single household and for the population as a whole. By that same token, the average propensity to spend decreases as income rises. At the lowest levels of income, savings are negative, meaning that people borrow to make ends meet. As income rises, people generally save an increasingly larger fraction of their income.

However, as is so often the case in economics, it is the *marginal* propensity to consume and the *marginal* propensity to save that are often more important than the averages. The marginal propensity to consume is the percentage of another dollar of disposable income that a person, household, or population will spend. The marginal propensity to save is the percentage of that dollar that will be saved. As we will see when we look at government fiscal policy in Part 3, the marginal propensity to consume and to spend—and the values of these propensities at various income levels—have serious implications for economic policy.

To understand the propensity to consume or save, let's focus on one household, that of the Hobstweedles. Below is the Hobstweedles' average propensity to consume and to save and their marginal propensity to consume and to save.

Table 7.2   Average and Marginal Propensity to Consume and to Spend (for one hypothetical family)

(1) Disposable Income	(2) Amount Spent	(3) Amount Saved	(4) Average Propensity to Consume	(5) Average Propensity to Save	(6) Marginal Prop. To Consume	(7) Marginal Prop. To Save
$10,000	$11,000	$- 1,000	1.10	–.10	—	—
20,000	20,000	0	1.00	0	.90	—
30,000	28,500	1,500	.95	.05	.85	.15
40,000	36,000	4,000	.90	.10	.75	.25
50,000	42,500	7,500	.85	.15	.65	.35
60,000	48,500	11,500	.81	.19	.60	.40
70,000	54,000	16,000	.77	.23	.55	.45
80,000	59,000	21,000	.74	.26	.50	.50

As I walk you through this table, I'll refer to the columns by number.

The first three columns are straightforward. Column 1 is disposable income, that is, the Hobstweedles' household income after taxes over the years as their careers progressed and their salaries rose. Column 2 is the dollar amount of disposable income that they spent each year. Column 3 is the amount of disposable income that they saved each year.

Notice that in the first year, their disposable income was $10,000 and they borrowed another $1,000 to spend. In that year, they realized what economists call a "dissavings" of $1,000. The following year, they earned $20,000 after taxes and spent the whole amount. That, incidentally, means that $20,000 is their break-even point—the level of disposable income at which they neither save nor borrow. After that break-even point, they start saving a portion of their disposable income every year.

So much for the dollar amounts.

Column 4 is the percentage (expressed as a decimal value) of total disposable income spent that year. It is calculated by dividing the value in Column 2 by the value in Column 1. Column 5 is the percentage of disposable income (again, expressed as a decimal) that the Hobstweedles saved that year. This value is calculated by dividing the value in Column 3 by the one in Column 1.

In the first year, the 110 percent average propensity to spend indicates that the Hobstweedles spent 10 percent more than they earned. That amount is offset by the negative 10 percent propensity to save.

As income rises, the average propensity to consume *decreases* and the average propensity to save *increases*. This is the case for most people. Households with rising incomes save more money than lower income households, and not just because they make more money. They also save a higher percentage of their income than lower income households.

Once again we come to the issue of what happens at the margin of an economic phenomenon. In economics, the term marginal usually means "one additional" or "an added amount," The marginal propensity to consume—which is listed for various income levels in Column 6—refers to the percentage of *additional* income that is spent. Marginal propensity to consume is calculated by dividing the *increase* in consumption over the previous level of consumption (in Column 2) by the *increase* in income over the previous level (in Column 1).

In our table, the increase in consumption varies from one level to the next. For instance, at the $40,000 income level, the increase in consumption is $7,500 over the previous year. This $7,500 equals the $36,000 in consumption at the $40,000 level minus the $28,500 spent the previous year. The increase in income is always $10,000 in Column 1. So we divide $7,500 by $10,000 and get the .75 propensity to consume shown in Column 6.

The marginal propensity to consume is the answer to the question, If a person receives one more dollar of income, how much of it does he spend? In Table 7.2, I have used the income increments of $10,000 to make the example clear and a bit more realistic. (No one really thinks in terms of an extra dollar of income—except economists.)

As the table shows, the marginal propensity to consume decreases as income increases. Moreover—and this point is key—as income reaches higher levels, the marginal propensity to consume is usually lower than the average propensity to consume. The reason for that is simple. As income rises, more of that additional income is saved, and less is spent. In other words, people spend more of the $10,000 they earn between $20,000 and $30,000 than they do of the $10,000 they earn between $50,000 and $60,000.

The flip side of the marginal propensity to consume is the marginal propensity to save. The marginal propensity to save—in Column 7—is the percentage of *additional* income that is saved. It is calculated by dividing the *increase* in savings over the previous year's savings (in Column 3) by the increase in income over the previous year's income (in Column 1). As income rises, people save a larger percentage of the added income than they saved when they were making less. Therefore, as income rises, the marginal propensity to save rises.

For the Hobstweedles, the marginal propensity to save rises all the way to 50 percent at the $80,000 level of household income.

The Consumption Function

Plotting some of the values in Table 7.2 will give us a clearer picture of how consumption and savings relate to disposable income.

Figure 7.2 plots the values for consumption (on the vertical axis) as a function of disposable income (on the horizontal axis). The curved line on the chart represents the amount spent from Column 2 at the various levels of disposable income in Column 1.

What about the line on the chart at a 45-degree angle? That line shows what would happen if consumption and disposable income were always equal. That is, it shows what would happen if all disposable income were spent. Thus the line shows that consumption is $10,000 at disposable income of $10,000, $20,000 at income of $20,000, $30,000 at income of $30,000, and so on. If that's what the 45-degree line shows, then a line showing any deviation from the 45-degree line will represent consumption that is either above or below disposable income.

That is exactly the case here. For the Hobstweedles, consumption is $20,000 at disposable income of $20,000. That is called the break-even point for them, and I have therefore labeled it BE. The break-even point is the point where consumption and disposable income are equal—all disposable income is spent.

At any point on the consumption function to the *left* of the break-even point, the situation of dissavings exists. If the household is spending in excess of its disposable income, then they must be borrowing. Likewise, at any point to the right of the break-even point, there are savings. If the household is spending less than it brings home in income, then they are saving the difference.

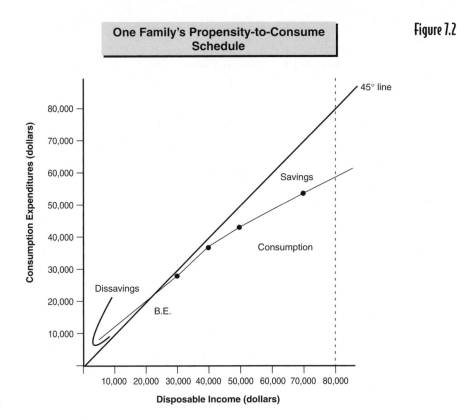

One Family's Propensity-to-Consume Schedule

Figure 7.2

In addition, a vertical line drawn upward from any point on the disposable income axis (as I have drawn at $80,000) will show the area under the consumption function to represent consumption expenditures and the area between the consumption function and the 45-degree line to represent the amount saved.

The Real World

The consumption function, and this discussion of propensities to consume and save, implies that income is the main driver of spending and saving behavior. Income is one of the most important factors, if not the most important. However, other factors affect a family's or nation's spending and saving behavior. Cultural norms, for example, play an important role at both the household and national levels.

Having lived in both New York City and New England, I believe that cultural norms in New York predispose people to spend more freely than they do in New England. Many New Yorkers strive to present themselves to others in a fashionable, even impressive, manner. That costs money—money that could be saved instead.

New Englanders tend to place more value in the old Yankee habit of thrift, and generally devote less attention (and less money) to fashion.

The Savings Function

If there is a consumption function, there must be a savings function. There is, and we will examine it briefly, because it is basically the mirror image of the consumption function.

The savings function for the Hobstweedle household is shown in Figure 7.3. The curve is plotted from the values for disposable income and savings in Table 7.2.

Figure 7.3

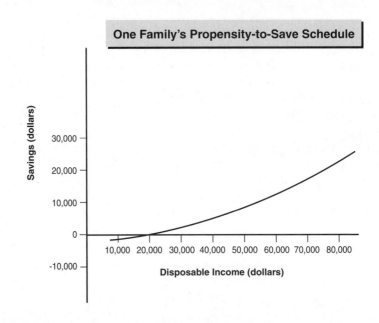

Figure 7.3 shows the dollar amounts that our sample family saves as their disposable income rises. As income rises, savings increase at an increasing rate. That is why the line curves gently upward.

Notice, too, that savings is less than zero at the $10,000 income level, due to the dis-saving I discussed earlier. At $20,000, savings is zero, and thereafter, savings increase as income increases.

Meanwhile, At the National Level

The real issue for economic policy is not what the Hobstweedles will do with added income, but rather what large segments of the population or the entire population will do with it.

In other words, we need a consumption function for the whole United States. Table 7.3 shows the values we need in order to plot the function.

Table 7.3   Disposable Income, Consumption, and Personal Saving (in billions of current dollars)

	1990	1991	1992	1993	1994	1995
Disposable Income	4,294	4,475	4,755	4,935	5,165	5,423
Less: Consumption	3,959	4,103	4,341	4,584	4,850	5,120
Equals: Saving	335	372	414	351	315	302
Saving Rate	7.8%	8.3%	8.7%	7.1%	6.1%	5.6%

Table 7.3   (continued)

	1996	1997	1998	1999	2000	2001
Disposable Income	5,678	5,968	6,356	6,627	7,120	7,393
Less: Consumption	5,406	5,715	6,054	6,453	6,919	7,224
Equals: Saving	272	253	302	174	202	170
Saving Rate	4.8%	4.2%	4.7%	2.6%	2.8%	2.3%

Source: Bureau of Economic Analysis, National Income and Product Accounts Tables (Values may be off by one due to rounding error.)

Note that the saving rate fell from 7.8 percent of disposable income in 1990 to 2.3 percent in 2001. For Americans, the 1990s were not exactly the Age of Thrift.

Figure 7.4 shows the relationship between actual U.S. disposable income and consumption for the 12 years from 1990 through 2001. It is called a consumption function because it shows consumption *as a function of* disposable income. I have drawn a line of best fit (which you learned about in Chapter 3) through the 12 data points for the 12 years to serve as the consumption function.

The area between the consumption function and the horizontal axis for disposable income represents total consumption. The area between the consumption function and the 45-degree line represents savings. With the consumption function approaching the 45-degree line, the chart clearly shows that savings decreased steadily over the period.

Figure 7.4

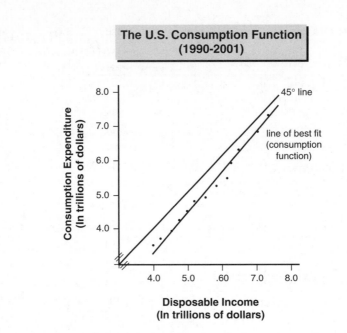

The U.S. Consumption Function
(1990-2001)

The Importance of Investment

Up to now, I have discussed consumers and households, consumer demand, savings by households, and so on. I've focused heavily on the "C"—consumption—in C + I + G. Now, however, we must shift the focus to investment—the "I" in our GDP formula—in order to understand more fully how the economy really works.

You'll recall that consumption represents about two-thirds of GDP—that's a significant portion of the economy. However, in a very real sense, investment determines economic growth, particularly long-term economic growth. First, keep in mind that economists define investment as investment in productive capacity by businesses. This includes building and expanding factories and offices and purchases of equipment and vehicles. It also includes one other item: increases in inventories of goods to be sold. While inventories are obviously not productive capacity, they are the product of that capacity. Therefore they represent a store of wealth that will be delivered to consumers.

Productive capacity is a store of wealth, too. A machine is not simply a machine. It is a device that converts raw material into saleable, usable products. It also requires an operator—and a repairman, a manager, a laborer to pack the products into boxes, a salesperson to sell them, a driver to deliver them to customers, a customer service person to explain how to use them, and ... you get the idea.

Most of the income that households get to dispose of comes from businesses. When businesses invest in plant and equipment, they create employment and incomes. When they stop investing in plant and equipment, they diminish employment and incomes.

To an economist, consumer demand is more or less a given. Who doesn't want a new car, new kitchen, new clothes, and vacations, restaurant meals, and plasma screen TVs? The problem is all of these things cost money—disposable income—and income comes from employment, and employment, by and large, comes from businesses. If they're not investing in productive capacity, businesses sure aren't going to need more employees.

In that sense, consumption demand is *not* a driver of the economy. It is a given. True, it fluctuates a bit, but economists have no trouble forecasting consumption. Investment is another story. It's a much longer-term decision, and one that is made with much more deliberation than the decision to eat out tonight or buy a new sofa. It depends on profits, which are often reinvested in productive capacity, and it depends on interest rates. But most of all, it depends on expectations and estimates of the future, and often the distant future at that: It can take as long as three to five years to build a factory and get it up and running.

In addition, business investment decisions are made independently of the spending-versus-saving decisions made by households. That means that the amount of investment that businesses want to do may not match the amount of saving that households want to do. That, too, has implications for the economy.

EconoTip

When an investor purchases shares of stock that have already been issued, the money does not go to the company that issued the stocks. Instead, the money goes to the party that was holding the stock. Only new shares of stock sold by a company raise money for the company to use for expansion.

Mismatches Between Savings and Investment

When businesses want to invest more or less than households want to save, or households want to save more or less than businesses want to invest, we have disequilibrium. As you saw in the case of supply and demand for goods and services, when disequilibrium occurs, economic forces push buyers and sellers toward a point of equilibrium.

A similar situation prevails when it comes to savings and investment. Figure 7.5 depicts the situation.

Figure 7.5

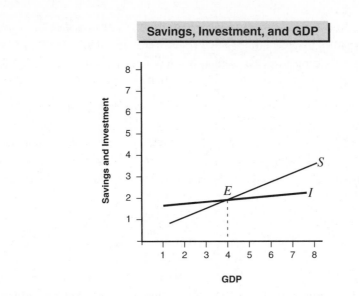

Savings, Investment, and GDP

Notice that in Figure 7.5 both lines—S, representing savings—and I, representing investment—slope upward (as you go to the right). This indicates the positive relationship between savings and GDP growth and investment and GDP growth. Both savings and investment increase as GDP increases. Similarly, GDP increases as savings and investment increase. So we do not have a downward sloping demand curve for investment in this situation.

But we do have a mismatch between savings and investment. At levels of GDP to the right of the equilibrium point ("E"), savings are greater than investment. Households are saving more than businesses want to invest. What forces will move the economy toward equilibrium GDP?

If households are saving more than businesses want to invest, then they are not spending their money. Consumers are "sitting on their wallets" or banking their money instead of spending it. This means that inventories of goods will pile up, and businesses will reduce production. Workers will be laid off, and machines will stand idle. Investment—expansion of productive capacity—will stop when people aren't buying the goods already being produced. When the layoffs occur, income will start to fall, and, so will savings. As a result, GDP will contract—it will move to the left, toward the equilibrium level.

Conversely, at levels of GDP to the left of the equilibrium point ("E"), households are saving less than businesses want to invest. That means they are also spending freely. They are buying more goods and services than businesses can produce with their current productive capacity. No wonder businesses want to invest in more factories and equipment!

If people are buying more than businesses can produce, businesses will sell off their inventories and step up production. They will hire new workers, put current workers on overtime, and leave no machine idle. This will increase incomes and, as we have seen, when incomes increase, savings increase thanks to the increasing marginal propensity to save. This stepped-up production also increases GDP, which will move to the right, toward the equilibrium point.

Equilibrium GDP tends to remain elusive. In fact, that's the way (uh-huh, uh-huh) we like it. Because in a capitalist, growth-oriented society, we always want GDP moving to the right, the direction in which it gets larger. We want business to be always adding workers and capacity so that the economy keeps growing. Does this mean that we can make this happen by spending instead of saving? To an extent, it does, and that is part of the secret of our continual economic growth. But saving must also occur if business is to have funds to invest. There must also be profitable opportunities if businesses are to decide to invest.

As important as consumer spending is to our economy, investment is equally important. In the next and final section of this chapter, I want to show you one more reason that this is so.

Multiplicity: How Investment Flows Through the Economy

In the previous section, you learned that an increase in investment causes an increase in employment and income, and that a decrease in investment causes a decrease in employment and income.

What I didn't tell you is that the effect of a dollar increase or decrease in investment is actually greater than one dollar. The effect on GDP is multiplied. In other words, a $10,000 investment by a business does not simply increase the "I" in C + I + G, and thus GDP, by $10,000. It increases GDP by a multiple of that amount. That's why this effect is called the *multiplier effect*.

For such a technical concept, the multiplier effect is quite easy to grasp. When a company invests $10,000 to expand its building, it hires workers, buys materials, pays for building permits, and so on. And I mean "and so on." When the building is complete, the business will equip it, furnish it, and hire workers to staff it, clean it, and repair it as needed.

EconoTalk

The **multiplier effect** refers to the fact that an increase in investment eventually raises or lowers national income by an amount greater than itself. The **multiplier** is the number that expresses the magnitude of that effect. For example, if a $100 investment eventually increases national income by $300, then the multiplier is three.

Unfortunately, the multiplier works both ways. When a business decides to slash its inventories and reduce its production, it will buy fewer materials and less fuel, and lay off workers. Say the business saves $10,000 through these measures. The sellers of the materials and the fuel, and the laid off workers receive less money to pump back into the economy. As a result, the economy contracts by more than the $10,000 that the business chose not to spend.

The multiplier stands as another case of everything relating to everything else in economics. The economy is one system in which, one way or another, sooner or later, all players are linked.

The Least You Need to Know

♦ Households must either spend or save their disposable income, that is, their after-tax income. The average propensity to consume is the percentage of disposable income that a household spends. The marginal propensity to consume is the percentage of additional income that goes to consumption.

♦ The average propensity to save is the percentage of total disposable income that a household, population segment, or nation puts into savings. The marginal propensity to save is the percentage of additional income that goes into savings.

♦ As income increases, the marginal propensity to save increases and the marginal propensity to consume decreases.

♦ Saving and investing are done by two very different sets of players in the economy and for unrelated reasons. Consequently, the levels of savings and investment in the economy often do not match one another. Therefore, forces relating to production, employment, and income are usually pushing the economy toward an equilibrium point, which tends to remain elusive.

♦ The multiplier amplifies the effect of business investment on the economy.

Chapter 8

The Business of Business

In This Chapter

- ◆ Production decisions and how they are made
- ◆ How to analyze a business's cost structure
- ◆ All about economies of scale
- ◆ How monopolies and cartels operate

Having examined the consumer in some depth, let's take a look at his counterpart, the producer. Everything that makes its way into the market, every good or service that's up for sale, must somehow be produced. In Adam Smith's world, the butcher, the baker, and the candlestick maker are guided in their production decisions by the famous "invisible hand." Modern economists, however, have worked hard to make that hand at least partly visible.

In this chapter, we learn how production decisions are made, how fixed and variable costs add up, and how some businesses become so large. We'll also examine some of the ways that businesses intervene in the market, with the aim of increasing their profits.

Business Realities

A business takes inputs, which it pays for, and transforms them into outputs, which it gets paid for, and must make a profit in the process. As anyone who as ever run a lemonade stand knows, to make a profit you must sell the output for more than you paid for the inputs. Profit is what remains after the cost of the inputs—land, labor, plant, equipment, raw materials, transportation, and so on—is subtracted from the revenue received for the output. (Actually, taxes must also be subtracted.)

The Real World

Politics in the United States, like politics elsewhere, has often been characterized by hostility toward profits. As you learned in Chapter 1, Karl Marx blazed a trail in this area, believing that businesses made profits only by exploiting labor.

Although some political viewpoints (Karl Marx's for instance) are hostile to profits, from the economic standpoint, profits are necessary. First, entrepreneurs provide a valuable service in organizing the factors of production. If they weren't compensated for providing that service, why would they do it? Second, profits reward the entrepreneur for taking the risks associated with failure. Rents, wages, and interest are guaranteed by contracts, but profits are not guaranteed. Entrepreneurs must be rewarded for risking their time and talent to produce goods and services that may or may not sell. Third, profits encourage investment and are often used to buy more productive capital for the business.

Many people are misinformed not only about the purpose of profits, but about the level of profits most companies earn. Several years ago, a survey revealed that many Americans believe that 20 to 25 percent or more of a company's revenue goes to profits. The actual figure averages about 5 percent.

How does a business manage its costs? How does a business find the right mix among the factors of production?

Let's find out.

Decisions, Decisions

Every business owner or management team must combine the factors of production, particularly labor and capital, in a way that generates profits. Let's take a very simple business—landscaping. Landscaping is fairly *labor-intensive*, as opposed to *capital-intensive*. It requires a good amount of human labor, but the productivity of that labor can be boosted with machinery. Giving the workers power mowers rather than hand mowers and leaf blowers rather than rakes will increase their productivity.

However, power mowers and leaf blowers are more expensive to purchase, operate, and maintain than hand tools. They increase insurance expense by increasing the risk of injury. Transporting equipment to the work site requires larger trucks, which require fuel, drivers, and insurance. The purchase price of the equipment and trucks and the insurance premiums are all fixed costs. Labor and the fuel to operate the equipment are the major variable costs.

EconoTalk

A **labor-intensive** business is one that relies more heavily on labor than capital as a primary input. Restaurants and most personal service businesses are labor intensive. A **capital-intensive** business relies more heavily on equipment than labor. Mining is a highly capital-intensive industry.

Suppose that, over the first few years in operation, the owner of the landscaping outfit developed the figures shown in Table 8.1.

Table 8.1 Fixed, Variable, Total, Marginal, and Average Costs

(1) Quantity (Acres)	(2) Fixed Costs	(3) Variable Costs	(4) Total Cost	(5) Marginal Cost Per Acre	(6) Average Fixed Cost	(7) Average Variable Cost	(8) Average Total Cost
0	5,000	0	5,000	—	—	—	—
50	5,000	300	5,300	6.00	100.00	6.00	106.00
100	5,000	550	5,550	5.00	50.00	5.50	55.50
150	5,000	750	5,750	4.00	33.33	5.00	38.33
200	5,000	1,050	6,050	6.00	25.00	5.25	30.25
250	5,000	1,550	6,550	10.00	20.00	6.20	26.20
300	5,000	2,250	7,250	14.00	16.67	7.50	24.17
350	5,000	3,150	8,150	18.00	14.29	9.00	23.29
400	5,000	4,250	9,250	22.00	12.50	10.63	23.13
450	5,000	5,550	10,550	26.00	11.11	12.33	23.44
500	5,000	7,050	12,050	30.00	10.00	14.10	24.10

Please follow along as I walk you through this important table. Column 1 shows the number of acres the company can landscape in, say, a week. Column 2 shows fixed costs of $5,000—fixed because they remain the same regardless of the number of acres. Column 3 shows the variable costs—labor, fuel, repairs, and so on—which increase as the number of acres landscaped increases. Column 4, total cost, is simply the sum of the fixed costs (Column 2) and the variable costs (Column 3) for a given number of acres.

Now here's where it gets interesting, because a businessperson is always interested in costs per unit. In this case, the "unit" of production is an acre. Marginal cost per acre, shown in Column 5, is the *increase* in total cost divided by the *increase* in acreage. So at 150 acres, total costs are $5,750. That's an increase of $200 over the previous level of cost, which is $5,550. If it costs another $200 to landscape 150 acres rather than 100 acres, then the marginal cost per acre is $4.00, which equals the additional $200 divided by the additional 50 acres.

As volume increases, marginal cost per unit decreases *up to a point*. Notice that, in this example, marginal cost per unit is lowest at that 150-acre volume. After that point, marginal cost rises. At 200 acres, it is back up to $6.00. We'll examine the reason for this in a moment.

Average fixed cost, shown in Column 6, is just the fixed cost in Column 2 divided by the number of acres in Column 1. Average fixed cost decreases as volume increases. The reason for this is simple: Average fixed costs are the fixed cost *per unit*. As the number of units increases and fixed costs remain constant, the fixed cost per unit must decrease. The more units that a piece of equipment produces, the more cheaply it is producing each unit.

Average variable costs, shown in Column 7, are the variable costs in Column 3 divided by the total acres in Column 1. Average variable cost, which is variable cost per unit, also decreases *up to a point* and then increases. Again, we will see why in a moment.

Finally, average total cost, shown in Column 8, is the total cost in Column 4, divided by the number of acres. Average total cost, which is total cost per unit, also decreases and then increases.

Figure 8.1 shows the behavior of various per-unit costs at various levels of output.

Let's start with average fixed costs, represented by the curve AFC. Average fixed costs decrease as volume increases, so the curve slopes downward as the number of acres landscaped increases.

Average variable costs, represented by the curve AVC, first decrease and then increase as volume rises. This is due to the *law of diminishing returns*, which states that, if fixed inputs are held constant, additional units of a variable input will yield higher returns up to a point. After that point, each additional input will produce less output. In other words, at some point the extra worker will produce less than the worker who was added before him.

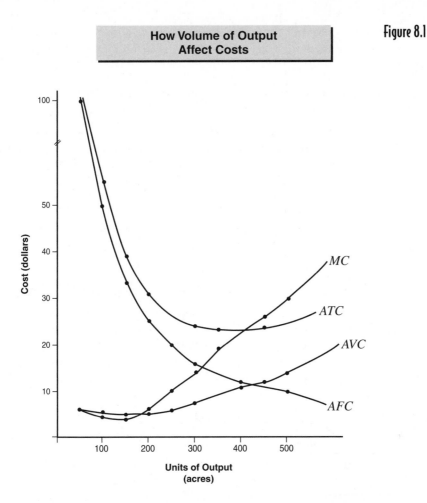

How Volume of Output Affect Costs

Figure 8.1

In our example, adding more laborers will at first enable the business to landscape more acreage. More workers can get more work done *until* they start running into limiting factors. For example, if they don't have enough equipment, their contribution to output will be less than that of workers with equipment. (They will only be able to pick up leaves by hand, for instance.) If the business kept adding workers, they would ultimately undermine the productive process by trampling the grass and bushes. There simply wouldn't be enough land for them to work on.

EconoTalk

The **law of diminishing returns** states that after a certain point, each additional unit of a variable input will yield less output than the previous unit of input. This concept also underlies diminishing marginal utility, which consumers experience.

The diminishing returns to labor are reflected in the variable cost curve AVC. Variable costs first decrease, but then increase as the productivity of each added worker decreases.

Average total costs are the sum of average fixed costs and average variable costs. That is, Column 8 in Table 8.1 is the sum of Columns 6 and 7. Similarly, the distance of the total average cost curve (ATC) from the horizontal axis equals the distance between curve AFC and the horizontal axis plus the distance between curve AVC and curve ATC.

One final point: The marginal cost curve MC intersects the average total cost curve ATC where the cost of the marginal unit equals the cost of the average unit. After that point, marginal cost—the cost of producing each added unit (each additional landscaped acre)—increases, which in turn *raises* the average total cost.

The Real World

Managers of small businesses usually combine fixed and variable inputs intuitively and figure their costs using accounting rather than economics. But managers in heavy manufacturing operations analyze their costs more scientifically.

For instance, microchip manufacturers such as Intel and AMD work very hard to drive their costs down. Fixed costs in the business run into the billions for factories and equipment before chips can be produced. A chip manufacturer must produce as many chips as possible to spread these fixed costs over as many units as possible. To control variable costs, each company produces as many chips as it can from each silicon wafer it processes.

Intel claims that its costs are the lowest because it has more advanced factories that can process larger silicon wafers. This enables Intel to produce more chips per wafer. AMD claims that its costs are lowest because its chips are smaller. This enables AMD to produce more chips per wafer, even from the smaller wafer.

External analysts believe that the companies' costs per chip are about equal. Whichever company is the lower cost producer, each of them uses very sophisticated economic analyses to determine the type of factories to build and the size of the wafers to be processed and chips to be produced.

What's a Business Person to Do?

What does all this mean for the business owner?

First, a business owner must understand the cost structure of her business—the costs of the fixed and variable inputs needed to produce various levels of output.

Second, she must find the right mix of fixed and variable inputs. Sometimes the decision to replace people with capital is a "no-brainer." For example, one worker with a leaf blower will be more productive than two workers with rakes.

Third, the owner must minimize total costs by using the right mix of inputs to produce the right quantity. The mix of inputs that will minimize costs will be the combination where the *marginal product per dollar* of the variable inputs is equal to the *marginal product per dollar* of the fixed inputs.

EconoTalk

Marginal product per dollar is the amount of additional output produced by the last dollar spent on input. This can be calculated for variable inputs, for fixed inputs, or for total inputs.

Here, marginal analysis does for the producer something like what it does for the consumer. You'll recall that the consumer maximizes his total satisfaction when the marginal utility produced by the last dollar he spends on an item equals the marginal utility of the last dollar spent on any other item he buys. Otherwise, he could get more satisfaction by changing the mix of items he buys—and, presumably, he would change to that mix.

The same is true, in its way, for the producer. The marginal product of the last dollar spent on variable inputs should equal the marginal product of the last dollar spent on fixed inputs. Otherwise, he would get more output for the money spent by changing the mix of variable and fixed inputs, just as the consumer could get more satisfaction by changing the mix of items he buys.

"Output" is the utility that the producer wants to maximize for the money he spends on variable and fixed inputs. This happens at the volume of output where the marginal cost curve MC intersects the total average cost curve ATC. In Figure 8.1, this output level is about 400 acres. Finally, the owner will maximize profits by producing the right level of output at the right price. In a competitive market, a business trying to maximize its total profit should produce the quantity of output where the marginal cost per unit equals the price.

Think about it. If the marginal cost—the total fixed and variable cost—of the last unit produced is greater than its price, then the company loses money on the last unit. If the marginal cost is below the price, the company is not maximizing its profits because it is producing fewer units than it could profitability produce. The company makes additional profit as long as the marginal revenue (from selling one more unit) is higher than the marginal cost (of producing one more unit).

So total profit is maximized when the company produces the level of output where marginal cost per unit equals the price of the unit. But in reality, prices—even prices of the same brand of product in the same size—fluctuate with changes in demand, competitive conditions, and so on. Therefore, a business must use pricing strategies that take the external market—as well as internal costs—into consideration.

Let's take a look at these pricing strategies.

Three Pricing Strategies

There are three basic pricing strategies: cost-plus pricing, competitive pricing, and value pricing.

In *cost-plus pricing*, you look at the cost of what you sell—that is, the total marginal cost—then add on the profit you need to make. That's your price. Cost-plus means "cost plus profit." So if it costs the landscaper $25 to landscape an acre, and he has targeted a pre-tax profit of $5 per acre, he should charge $30 per acre. (There are other ways to set the price using cost-plus pricing, but all are based on clearing a certain profit above the costs.)

This method of pricing is straightforward and ensures that you will make money on what you sell. Unfortunately, it does not ensure that you will sell it. The success of this pricing strategy depends on targeting a "reasonable" profit and controlling your costs. It also depends on not being under-priced by a competitor.

A *competitive pricing* strategy aims to price the product at the lowest price among all recognized competitors. Low prices are one way to compete effectively, and sometimes competitive pricing is essential. For instance, in an industry selling a *commodity*, the outfit with the lowest price will usually succeed. That's because when the products themselves are not differentiated, price becomes the differentiating factor.

EconoTalk

A **commodity** is a product that is the same in characteristics and performance regardless of who is selling it. Iron ore, coal, lumber, rice, and many other products drawn from the earth are commodities.

Competitive pricing is not just for commodities. In retail, for example, portable CD players are not a commodity, but once a customer has decided she wants to buy one, price will play a big role in which type she buys. So competitive pricing is common in retailing. In fact, some retailers offer to beat any other advertised price.

In general, the success of a competitive pricing strategy depends on achieving high volume and low costs—preferably the lowest in the industry—so you can maintain the lowest price and still make a profit. Success also depends on avoiding a destructive *price war*.

EconoTalk

In a **price war,** two or more competitors repeatedly undercut each other's prices. This usually occurs in a commodity business, and so two gas stations on opposite corners are the classic example. In a price war, each competitor can wind up selling the product at a loss. When that occurs, they are trying to drive one another out of business. The "winner" will be the one that can afford to lose money the longest and still stay in business.

A *value pricing* strategy is the alternative to basing your prices on your costs or your competitors' prices. Instead, you base your prices on the value you deliver to customers. In this strategy, you deliver as much value as possible to your customers—and charge them for it. With this strategy, you charge a high price and justify it by delivering high value.

Value pricing is common in high technology and luxury items, such as clothing, restaurants, and automobiles.

In practice, a business considers all three pricing strategies. You have to consider your costs, or your profits will suffer. You have to consider your competitor's prices, even if you're not competing on price. You must consider the value you deliver because no matter what you sell, customers want value for their money.

Why the Big Get Bigger: Returns to Scale

Why are so many industries in the United States dominated by a handful of very large companies? For decades, the Big Three automakers—General Motors, Ford, and Chrysler—dominated the U.S. market. Now they share it with several other foreign car companies that are the large automakers in their nations: Toyota and Honda of Japan, Mercedes Benz and Volkswagen of Germany, Volvo of Sweden, and several others.

Three major companies—General Mills, Kelloggs, and Post—dominate the cereal business. Proctor & Gamble and Colgate Palmolive dominate personal care products, such as soap and toothpaste. Independent booksellers have been supplanted by chains such as Barnes and Noble and Borders. Other chain operations, such as CVS, Kinko's, and McDonald's have superceded the local drugstore, copy shop, and hamburger joint.

These companies all became large partly due to *economies of scale*. In many businesses, there are very real advantages to large size, but not in every business. It all depends on how much the level of output increases when the size of the business increases. Scale here means the size of the business. As the business becomes larger (or "scales up"), it can experience constant, decreasing, or increasing economies of scale.

Constant economies of scale mean that a certain percentage increase in scale brings about an equal increase in output. If you double the size of the operation, you double the amount of output. There are no true economies of scale in such a business. Many personal service outfits face this situation. If a hair salon doubles the number of chairs and hair stylists, it will roughly double its output. This doesn't mean that a chain of hair salons couldn't compete more effectively by establishing a first-rate training program and a strong brand. Nor does it mean that a chain of salons couldn't cut costs by buying supplies in volume. It means that the output of 10 stylists is about double that of 5 equally skilled stylists.

Decreasing economies of scale mean that a certain percentage increase in the size of the business brings about a less than equal increase in output. If you double the size of the operation, output will increase by less than 100 percent. This amounts to diseconomies of scale in which "too many cooks make less broth." Many companies find that inefficiencies arise with large size and people become less productive (probably because they spend so much time in meetings!).

EconoTalk

Increasing economies of scale means that when the size of an operation increases by a certain percentage, output increases by a greater percentage. **Decreasing economies of scale** means that as the size of an operation increases, output increases by a smaller percentage—or decreases. **Constant economies of scale** means that increases in the size of an operation yield the same percentage increase in output.

Increasing returns to scale mean that a certain percentage increase in scale brings about a greater increase in output. If you double the size of the operation, output more than doubles. Business people typically refer to increasing economies of scale as "economies of scale."

Increasing economies of scale are why the large companies get larger. They are also why a few large companies dominate many industries. And they are why Karl Marx predicted that most industries would become dominated by a few large companies, or one large company.

The returns to scale can be enormous. Here are several factors that both contribute to, and result from, increasing economies of scale:

◆ **Capital intensiveness:** In a highly capital-intensive business, large size is essential for survival, let alone success. The extractive industries (oil, gas, coal, and metals) are so capital intensive that a small outfit is not economically feasible. The fixed costs of drilling rigs, refineries, and pipelines demand a high volume of production. High volume drives down the average fixed costs, which increases cost-effectiveness.

◆ **Volume buying:** Average variable costs also decrease for many large operations thanks to volume buying. A high volume producer usually passes some of the cost savings on to high volume buyers in the form of lower prices. A high-volume buyer of raw materials can in turn lower its prices and compete more effectively against lower volume producers. In this way high-volume operations often push low-volume outfits out of business—and then sometimes raise their prices when the competition is gone.

◆ **Administrative efficiencies:** Administrative costs include the finance and per-sonnel departments, the cost of employee benefit plans, and so on. There are both fixed and variable costs involved. For instance, every company needs a computerized billing system and someone to run it. That's a fixed cost. The variable costs occur when the number of customers grows and accountants must be hired. These costs, however, typically do not grow as fast as the output. Therefore large size brings increasing economies of scale in administration.

◆ **Distribution:** Some transportation costs, such as the cost of a truck, are fixed. Others, such as the cost of gasoline, are variable. But in general, the more prod-uct that can be delivered for the fixed costs, the more efficient the operation will be. Great Bear Spring Water, an East Coast company that delivers bottled water to offices, prospects for new customers along its established delivery routes. New customers along the route drive down the costs of the delivery operation, which is among the company's largest costs.

◆ **Market and marketing power:** A large operation can allocate its marketing costs over a larger number of customers. Plus, large advertisers get volume dis-counts from the media. Perhaps even more important, international brands ben-efit from "brand power" because of their size. It is easier for most people to trust (and notice) an internationally known brand.

Economies of scale have driven much of business history over the past century. Many U.S. industries—oil, automobiles, food processing, financial services, consumer pack-aged goods, advertising, and software—started out with many competitors and are now dominated by a few large companies.

Large companies and the economics of mass production have provided a tremendous range of goods and services to consumers at reasonable prices. But the concentration of power and profits among the largest players in an industry can be quite significant.

The Real World

The merciless economics of economies of scale are most evident in farming. In 1935, there were over 6.5 million family farms in the United States; today there are fewer than 2.0 million. The major reason for this is consolidation in the farming industry, driven mainly by economies of scale. By some measures, which omit social costs, large farms are more efficient than small ones. Large agribusiness companies, such as ConAgra, Cargill, Tyson, and Dole, drive down the costs of food production and thus prices and force smaller farms out of business.

Political storms surround farming. First, all developed nations have government programs to temper the financial difficulties of farming that arise from weather, crop damage, and market forces. These programs cost taxpayers money, which some taxpayers resent. Second, many—but not all—Americans, Europeans, and Asians believe that family farms should be preserved as a way of life and as strong threads in the social fabric.

Finally, the definition of "efficiency" can change once items beyond the cost of inputs are considered. The costs and impact of pesticides, hormones, ecological damage, lower food quality, food-borne illnesses, and inhumane treatment of animals are often thought to be higher in large-scale farming. Thus, while large scale may yield efficiencies in farming, it may also yield serious inefficiencies.

Let's examine ways in which concentrated power can be, and has been, used and abused in business.

Monopoly and Oligopoly

As you learned in Chapter 4, in a free market, the dynamics of supply and demand are resolved through the price mechanism. Yet this occurs only when numerous suppliers must compete for customers, and customers "bid up" or "bid down" the price.

What happens when there is one supplier, or only a few?

If there is one supplier, the result is a monopoly. If there are several suppliers, the result is oligopoly. First, we'll examine monopoly and then oligopoly, and then look at how a cartel works.

Monopoly: The Power of One

A monopoly occurs when a single producer controls the supply of a good or service that has no real substitute and where the *barriers to entry* are high.

Many people think of a monopoly as a company that set out to dominate its industry illegally. In fact, many monopolies develop for more benign reasons. A "natural monopoly" occurs because a single supplier owns the entire supply or most of it, or a single provider can supply the market at a lower cost than several competitors could.

EconoTalk

Barriers to entry are conditions that make it hard for new suppliers to enter a business. Any business presents some barriers to entry, but in many industries they are quite low, as they are, for example, in the employment agency business. You need a desk, a phone, a few open jobs, and money for classified ads. Generally, however, barriers to entry refer to significant impediments to new entrants in an industry. These include historical position, technology advantages, patent protection, and the like.

Single suppliers often own the supply for historical reasons. De Beers diamond company has dominated the diamond market since 1889 by controlling most of the world's diamond mines and the supply of rough diamonds. For many decades, Dun & Bradstreet had about 90 percent of the commercial credit reporting business to itself because they started the industry in the mid-1800s and kept building it.

The economies of scale in some industries result in a lower cost to the consumer if a single and often regulated supplier serves the market. Until the late 1980s, power generation was thought to be such an industry. Competition among electric utilities was deemed inherently inefficient compared with having a single utility serve a designated area, subject to regulation of its prices. Power generation was deregulated and opened to competitive market forces in certain areas in the 1990s, with decidedly mixed results. California consumers were overcharged billions of dollars by producers who created artificial shortages to drive up electricity prices.

Another type of natural monopoly centers on a single standard of technology for an industry. A single standard ensures compatibility and helps users get the most from the technology. Microsoft is the best example of this. Microsoft developed DOS (Disk Operating System), which enabled personal computers to run applications software. DOS served as a single platform that enabled software developers to write software for a large market. The common platform provided by DOS created a large installed base that would allow a successful software developer to spread its costs over a huge number of users. This introduced real efficiency into the PC market. The Windows operating system had the same effect.

Many people believe that the worst aspect of a monopoly is the excess profit it receives by charging a price above the free-market price. That's bad. But worse yet, consumers also receive a lower quantity of the product than they would in a competitive market. A monopoly usually limits the supply and moves the supply curve to the left. This raises the "forced equilibrium" price upward on the demand curve. So consumers pay an above-market price for a below-market total quantity of the product.

The Real World

In the late 1800s, John D. Rockefeller founded Standard Oil (now ExxonMobil) to standardize the oil business, which had been composed of small drilling and refining operations battered by wild price fluctuations. With sometimes ruthless but legal tactics, Rockefeller bought up refineries and consolidated them into larger operations.

As Standard Oil became larger, increasing economies of scale kicked in, making it impossible for smaller outfits to compete. In the process, Rockefeller created the template for the modern corporation and executive team. Although he was vilified as a "robber baron," Rockefeller also established a model of corporate and personal philanthropy that endures to this day.

Over the past 10 years or so, the United States has broken up several monopolies and introduced market forces into some formerly regulated industries, such as telephone service, power generation, and air travel. Results have been mixed. In the telephone business, greater innovation and lower prices for services have resulted. Lower prices have also resulted in air travel, but extremely high costs may render the industry ill equipped to function in a truly competitive environment. The jury is still out on power generation, but early signs in from California are not promising.

Oligopoly: The Chosen Few

Oligopoly occurs when a few producers share a market, but no single one among them controls the supply or the price of the product. Oligopoly tends to occur in industries with high barriers to entry, high fixed costs, and the need for large size (relative to total demand) to reach the optimal size for efficient production.

EconoTalk

Price-fixing refers to agreements between producers to maintain a certain level of prices for certain goods or services. This enables the producers to maintain their profits above the level they would earn if they did compete on price. This and other forms of collusion are generally illegal.

Oligopoly occurs in situations where marginal costs persistently decrease as larger quantities are produced. The key feature of an oligopoly is tacit agreement (as opposed to actual *price-fixing*) to not undercut one another's prices. The oligopolists maximize their long-run profits by maintaining a level of prices designed to do exactly that.

Oligopolists try to avoid competing on price. In oligopoly—like industries such as breakfast cereal and consumer packaged goods—prices are pretty much in line with one another. However, the players pour huge sums into advertising to differentiate products that are actually quite similar, such as raisin bran and shampoo. Competing on price would be potentially destructive and almost certainly result in lower total profits for all the major companies.

Cartels Mean Control

Members of a cartel agree to limit the supply of a good in order to raise its price and their profit. Cartels arise in industries with few producers, because too many producers would present a cartel with too much competition. Competition is exactly what the members of a cartel don't want—especially among themselves.

OPEC, which pumps about one-third of the world's crude oil, is the best example of a cartel now in operation. Representatives from the 11 member nations meet periodically and agree to a target price per barrel of crude oil—say, $25 per barrel—and agree to limit the amount of oil they produce to a level that will achieve that target price.

The share of the total output that each nation gets to produce is decided through quotas, which have a mixed history of success. In any cartel, there is an incentive for a member to produce more than its quota in order to sell more and profit at the expense of the members who stick to their quotas. One thing that has made OPEC successful is the willingness of Saudi Arabia to cut its production when another nation does exceed its quota and to absorb the revenue loss. With the world's largest proven oil reserves, Saudi Arabia may well be able to afford this gesture.

OPEC must play its game carefully. If it targets too low a price, it may not maximize its profits (while encouraging usage of the finite resource it depends on). On the other hand, if OPEC targets too high a price, it encourages oil production among non-OPEC nations. A higher price increases the amount supplied by other producers, gives OPEC more competition, and puts downward pressure on prices.

OPEC clearly benefits its member nations and does bring some price stability to the oil market. On its website (www.opec.org), the cartel admits to controlling the price of oil in the 1970s and 1980s, but states that since then larger forces have more effect on price. However, if those larger forces become more political than they already are, OPEC's prices could rise substantially or the world oil market could become unstable, or both.

Meanwhile, Out in the Marketplace

Regardless of how a business structures its costs, it must make a tradeoff between fixed and variable inputs. Also, every business must decide how large or small it wants to be. Of course, market realities and management skills have as much to do with the growth of a business as its underlying economics. However, as the dot-com boom demonstrated, business people and investors ignore the microeconomic fundamentals of a business at their peril.

The Least You Need to Know

- The costs of every business can be broken down into variable costs and fixed costs. Variable costs are expenses that change with the volume of production. Fixed costs do not change with the level of production.

- Total costs are minimized at the point where the marginal product of an additional dollar spent on variable inputs equals the marginal product of an additional dollar spent on fixed inputs.

- Total profits are maximized at the level of output where, for the last unit produced, marginal cost equals marginal revenue.

- Increasing economies of scale occur when a percentage increase in the size of an operation brings about a higher percentage increase in production.

- A monopoly is a single supplier that can control the price of a product. A monopoly raises the price and lowers the supply of a good beyond the market levels.

- An oligopoly is a group of a few suppliers who price their products in a way that limits price competition among them and maximizes their long-term profit.

Wages, Workers, and the Workplace

In This Chapter

- ◆ Labor and management relations
- ◆ The effect of unions on supply, demand, and wages
- ◆ Wages for skilled versus unskilled workers
- ◆ The economic effect of discrimination

Steve Martin once said, "All I've ever wanted was an honest week's pay for an honest day's work." It is an aspiration that has taken him pretty far. Those of us less fortunate, meaning most of us in the workforce, face the harsher economics of the labor market. This market is unique among all markets because the "commodity" being bought and sold is a human being's time, talent, and energy. That may indeed be the case when any product is sold. After all, everything we buy in stores and showrooms is the product of human labor. However, in the labor market the exchange is extremely direct and personal.

Employees rent *themselves*, not their land or machinery, out to the employer. Employees are then largely under the control of the employer.

While it's true that workers are usually free to leave their jobs, the loss of any single employee does not threaten the income of most employers. But if the employer abandons the employees, for example, by laying them off or moving the business out of the region, the employees lose their livelihoods. Without the protection of union contracts or other legal agreements, most employers in the United States are free to lay off employees or move the business at will.

Although the exchange is direct and personal, impersonal economic forces prevail in the workplace, just as they do whenever money changes hands. In this chapter, we examine some of those forces and the behavior of people in the workplace. We'll start with an overview of the economic relationship between employers and employees.

Fighting Over the Pie?

Many business people—particularly entrepreneurs, capitalists, and business owners— picture wages coming out of the pockets of landlords, capitalists, and entrepreneurs. It's especially easy for entrepreneurs, managers, or business owners to conjure this image. They often feel that every dollar paid in wages is a dollar less going to profits. Similarly, workers often feel that the profits of the business are coming out of their wages. In every picket line, you will see a striking worker or protester holding a sign that says, "People before profits."

The traditional battle—wages versus profits, employees versus employers—still goes on. But the terms of engagement, and even the scene of the battle, have shifted a bit. The old terms of engagement called for collective bargaining, in which union officials confronted tightfisted employers with demands for higher wages and better working conditions. The battlefield was the sidewalk, the shop floor, the union hall, and the smoke-filled rooms where union chiefs and factory bosses argued far into the night.

All of that still exists (although the rooms may be less smoky). Yet for many workers, the terms of engagement have shifted because they are no longer represented by unions. Many traditionally unionized jobs have been moved to foreign production facilities by companies eager to avoid the relatively high costs of U.S. workers. As manufacturing jobs have been moved out of the country, they have been replaced by nonunion service jobs. Most service industries, such as retail, restaurants, and personal services (for example, beauticians and masseurs) have been slow to unionize.

Moreover, expanded access to education over the past 50 years has created a huge class of "knowledge workers," such as financial analysts, computer programmers, and engineers, and swelled the ranks of the professions, which traditionally have included law, medicine, accounting, and architecture. Knowledge workers and professionals— and, of course, managers—are rarely, if ever, unionized in the United States.

Much of the battle has shifted from the plant floor and the union hall to the Senate floor and the halls of Congress. Today, regulations, mandated employee benefits and work rules (for instance, the Employees with Disabilities Act), and international trade policies can affect both employers and employees as much as any union contract. Unions and employers now have lobbyists do much of their fighting for them.

The Real World

In reality, the conflict between management and workers goes beyond the issue of profits versus wages. It also centers on salaries (of management) verses wages (of hourly employees).

Given the finite sum available to pay managers and workers, managers may feel that they are taking money out of their own pockets when they give workers a raise. They often act that way.

The clearest case of managers pocketing salaries at the expense of workers (and profits) has been the skyrocketing compensation of senior executives at major corporations. According to *Business Week*, from 1980 to 1990, the ratio of CEO compensation to the average factory worker's pay rose from 42 to 85 times. By 1997, the ratio had climbed to 419. In virtually all other industrial nations, the ratio of CEO to average-worker pay is less than 75, and often significantly less.

Many books on economics, particularly textbooks, delve deeply into the history and effect of unions. We will examine their effect, but unions are on their way to becoming history, at least in the United States. According to the Bureau of Labor Statistics (BLS), from 1984 to 2001, union membership declined from 20.1 percent to 13.5 percent of the workforce. Before 1984 (the first year for which the BLS data are comparable over the years), union membership was even higher, with almost 30 percent of U.S. workers carrying a union card.

For many workers, the demise of unions has probably not been a good thing.

The State of the Unions

Unions exist to address the imbalance of power between employer and employee. In a union, workers band together to bargain collectively with management regarding their pay, hours, and working conditions. Under collective bargaining, the union leaders negotiate a contract that governs these and other aspects of work at the company or in the industry. A union shop is a plant or other location, such as a construction site, where the workers are covered by the union contract. In many instances, workers are obligated to join the union in order to work at the location.

During contract negotiations or protests of management decisions, a union may hold a strike or slowdown. A strike usually shuts down an operation, costing the business large amounts of money, hurting its customers and the public, and putting pressure on management to meet the union's demands. Striking workers form a picket line to protest management's reluctance to meet their demands. Anyone attempting to cross a picket line to work in the place of a striking worker is subject to intimidation (sometimes even physical violence). When they can, managers will often take the place of striking workers to keep the business functioning on some level. Nonunion workers who work in the place of striking workers are known as "scabs."

For their part, managers work fairly hard to avoid unionization of their businesses in the first place. The history of the labor movement in America offers as many tales of violent union-busting and strike-breaking as there are of union intimidation and violence. In some cases, where the economic well-being of the nation or a region or industry is at stake, the president of the United States will order the workers back to work.

The Real World

When the air traffic controllers' union went on strike in 1981, President Ronald Reagan declared the strike illegal, which it was according to established regulations, and ordered them back to work. When they refused to return to work, he authorized the Federal Aviation Administration to hire and train new workers, which it did.

In 2002, President George W. Bush ordered the dock workers on the west coast back to work after deciding that their strike against the shipping industry was causing too much damage to the economy and the shipping and farming industries. In this case, the workers complied.

According to the BLS, in 2001 about 16.3 million workers were union members. Most of these, however, were government workers and "protective service workers," such as police officers and fire fighters. Less than one in ten private-sector workers belonged to a union. Unionization rates for government workers has held steady at about 37 percent since 1983, while those of private sector employees have fallen to 9 percent. The highest unionization rate occurs in the protective services at 38 percent. (Note, however, that this means that, even in this line of work, over 60 percent of the employees are *not* in unions.)

The most heavily unionized private-sector industries are construction and manufacturing, at about 18 percent and 15 percent respectively. The least unionized are sales at 3 percent and finance, insurance, and real estate at 2 percent.

Despite the decline of their influence in the private sector, unions remain a powerful force in America. They make the news in stories ranging from baseball and basketball players' strikes, to controversies over how to improve public schools in which unions make it hard to fire teachers. The major point of contention in the legislative battle over the Department of Homeland Security in 2002 was whether the government workers being moved into the department would still be covered by union rules. Democrats favored continued coverage, while Republicans did not.

The Real World

Traditionally, the Democratic Party has been viewed as the "labor party" in America while Republicans are viewed as the "party of big business." In reality, elected officials at all levels cheerfully accept campaign contributions from all sources. Major labor unions, corporations, and industrial groups contribute to both parties. Yet in general, unions still tend to favor the Democrats and vice versa, and big business still tends to favor the Republicans and vice versa.

Speaking of politics, union membership and political influence tends to be much stronger in Europe than in the United States.

What Good Are Unions?

Labor unions, like most aspects of labor, are mostly about money. They generally perform the function of getting more money for their members fairly effectively. Table 9.1 shows the median full-time wages, and the wage differentials, between union and nonunion workers for the U.S. workforce and by gender and race.

Table 9.1   Union versus Nonunion Wages Median Full-Time Weekly Wage for 2000 (current dollars and percentage differential)

	Union Members	Nonunion Members	Differential*
All workers, 16–years and older	$696	$542	28.4%
Men	739	620	19.1
Women	616	472	30.5
White Workers	716	565	26.7
White Men	757	641	18.1
White Women	631	482	30.9

continues

Table 9.1   Union versus Nonunion Wages Median Full-Time Weekly Wage for 2000 (current dollars and percentage differential) (continued)

	Union Members	Nonunion Members	Differential*
Black Workers	596	436	36.7
Black Men	619	479	29.2
Black Women	564	408	38.2
Hispanic Workers	584	377	54.9
Hispanic Men	631	394	60.2
Hispanic Women	489	346	41.3

* Calculated by subtracting nonunion wage from union wage and dividing the difference by the nonunion wage.
Source: Bureau of Labor Statistics

The difference between union and nonunion wages is significant in all cases. White men who are members of unions earn about 19 percent more than their nonunion counterparts. Hispanic men who are union members earn about 60 percent more than Hispanic men who are not union members. The differential between the median union and nonunion wage is greater for women than for men in all categories of workers excluding Hispanic women.

Please view these wage statistics with caution. While the differences between union and nonunion wages are significant for all groups, union membership is only one factor in that difference. First, to some extent unions choose their members. Perhaps they choose better-educated workers, leaving those less educated in the nonunion workforce. Second, unions typically try to unionize established, profitable industries that are able to pay a decent wage. Third, the Hispanic population in particular includes many recent immigrants, who may have a harder time getting into a union. Fourth, the same gender and racial differences in pay occur for both union and nonunion workers. White men are paid more than white women in both union and nonunion settings. White workers are paid more than black and Hispanic workers, and so on, in both settings. However, the differential between the median wage for men and women is smaller in the union wage than in the nonunion wage for all categories of worker, except Hispanic.

EconoTip

When is a difference "significant" in economics? The rule of thumb that I use is 10 percent or more. If an indicator moves at a rate that's at least 10 percent more than the previous period's rate or if the difference between two values is at least 10 percent, it *could* be significant. In many cases, however, a smaller difference could also be significant.

Finally, the jobs of unionized government workers, police officers, firefighters, and teachers tend to be very secure. As workers gain seniority in these jobs, their wages steadily increase. In the private sector, workers deemed "too expensive" can be laid off, and they often find it difficult to find new jobs at their previous pay.

Yet, these qualifiers notwithstanding, workers in unions are, on average, doing significantly better than their nonunion counterparts.

How Unions Skew Labor Economics

We saw the effect of a minimum wage on the supply and demand of labor in Chapter 4. Now let's turn to the effect of unions on the labor market, which is like that of a minimum wage. A union aims to enforce a "minimum wage" either by demanding one or by restricting the supply of workers, by limiting the number of workers in the union.

Figure 9.1 shows the general effect of unions on the supply of labor. Note that this effect does not apply to the overall labor market, but to the specific supply of and demand for the type of workers covered by the union.

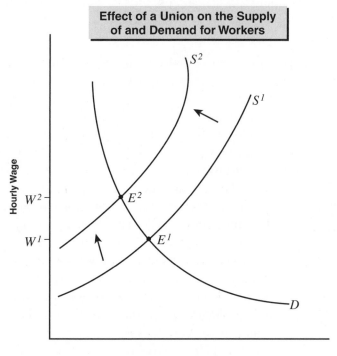

Effect of a Union on the Supply of and Demand for Workers

Figure 9.1

The goal of the union is to raise the wage from W^1 to W^2 by making wage demands in the union contract, or to reduce the supply of workers from S^1 to S^2 by limiting union membership. In practice, a union often does both. In any case, the effect is essentially the same. If the wage is increased to W^2, the supply curve shifts from S^1 to S^2. If the supply curve shifts to S^2, then the wage increases to W^2.

In both cases, the supply of workers is artificially limited. (By "artificially" I mean by means other than free-market dynamics.) If the union demands a high—that is, above-market—wage, then the business hires fewer workers, just as it would if the minimum wage were well above the market wage. If the union limits the number of workers, then the labor supply falls and management must pay the higher wage that prevails at that lower level of supply.

Unions also try to shift the demand curve upward. Union work rules are a common way of doing this. For example, a railroad union contract might stipulate that there must be a conductor for every two cars on a passenger train when one for every three or four cars would be enough. A bricklayers' contract might state that a mason may lay only so many bricks per seven-hour shift, leaving the contractor no choice but to hire more masons or pay overtime to get more done.

Although a union affects the supply and demand only for its members, the effects extend to the general labor market, and to the overall economy. These effects are both positive and negative.

Among the negatives, unions raise the cost of doing business and of products because they move the cost of labor above its market equilibrium level. This *can* make U.S. products less competitive in the global market. (I stress "can" because if skilled union workers produce higher quality products, the higher prices may indeed be fair and competitive.) Also, businesses try to avoid or escape unions by moving to *right to work* states or moving jobs out of the country. This takes jobs away from an area that was used to having them. To avoid unions, companies have moved jobs in the textile industry from the north to the south, jobs in the garment industry from the United States to Asia, and jobs in the auto industry from the United States to Mexico. Unions protest these management decisions, but are also at least partly responsible for them.

EconoTalk

In a **right to work** state, a worker cannot be required to join a union or pay union dues or fees in order to get or keep a job. There are some exceptions. For example, in certain states, airline or railroad employees may have to pay union fees, but are not required to join a union. Twenty-two states have right to work laws.

Among the unions' positives, they have helped neutralize the power of employers over individual employees. In doing so, they have probably required managers to manage more professionally, and to maximize the productivity of capital equipment. Unions have also raised the standard of living of millions of workers, and have boosted their purchasing power and thus the nation's economic growth.

By and large, unions are both a negative and positive force, just like the management teams that they often oppose. Unions are a blunt instrument for accomplishing economic goals, but one that has often worked.

Peace over the Pie?

Whatever your personal and political views on unions, management, and the positions of each side—both of which have validity—another fact has altered the dynamics between labor and management. Unions in America enjoyed their most rapid growth between 1930 and 1960. During those years, Marx's view of the worker as an exploited pawn of capitalism became familiar to much of public even in fervently non-socialist nations, such as the United States, as well as in those more open to socialism, such as Russia.

But since the middle of the last century, capitalism has proven itself to be quite effective at bringing prosperity to workers as well as to landlords, capitalists, and entrepreneurs. By some measures, it has brought more prosperity to workers than to the other players in production. Since 1950, the entire pie—measured by national income or GDP—has grown larger *and* workers (including salaried managers) have shared in that growth. Table 9.2 shows this to be the case.

Table 9.2 Amounts and Shares of National Income (billions of current dollars [percent of total])

	1950	1960	1970	1980	1990	2000
Wages & Salaries	155 [64]	296 [69]	617 [73]	1,651 [74]	3,351 [72]	5,723 [72]
Rent	47 [20]	68 [16]	100 [12]	209 [9]	430 [9]	861 [9]
Interest	3 [1]	11 [3]	38 [5]	184 [8]	452 [10]	612 [10]
Profits	36 [15]	52 [12]	82 [10]	199 [9]	409 [9]	788 [9]
Total	241 [100]	427 [100]	837 [100]	2,243 [100]	4,642 [100]	7,984 [100]

Source: Bureau of Economic Analysis, National Income and Product Accounts

Since 1970, the share of national income going to wages and salaries has been about 73 percent, and the share going to profits has been about 9 percent. Money is *not* being steered away from wages and toward profits. Instead, both workers and entrepreneurs—and, since 1980, landlords and capitalists—are maintaining steady shares in the growth of the U.S. economy.

The Real World

Profits supposedly exploded in the 1990s, with "record earnings" driving stock prices to record heights. While stock prices reached record heights, profits most certainly did not. As we learned in the corporate scandals of 2001 and 2002, the heralded profits were sometimes achieved by accounting gimmicks. (See *The Complete Idiot's Guide to MBA Basics* by Tom Gorman for a discussion of those gimmicks. Or simply forgive my naked attempt at cross selling.)

Here's the interesting part: A number of economists examining the National Income and Product Account (NIPA) data—where the profits reported have to be real—were puzzled by the companies' continual claims of record profits and therefore by the dizzying stock prices. The NIPA income data have to be real because they are based on tax-accounting rules, which deal in actual receipts and actual expenses. In contrast, the income figures reported on financial statements released to the investing public are based on financial accounting rules, which are more, ah, liberal in their treatment of revenue and expenses.

In other words, Karl Marx's vision of workers exploited by employers hogging profits has not come to pass. As we will see in Chapter 11, the *distribution* of income among wage earners has become uneven. That has to do with higher wages for skilled workers and lower wages for unskilled, as well as with the shift to a "service economy" in the United States. But the shares of national income going to wages and to profits clearly indicate that workers and business owners are sharing equitably in the growth of the economy.

But, if workers' slice of the national income pie has remained the same, why did I say that the demise of unions may be a bad thing for many workers? Because, as we will see in Chapter 11, a much larger slice of the wage and salary pie is going to people in upper income brackets. If you are an educated, skilled, flexible knowledge worker, manager, or professional, you don't need a union to represent you. As it so happens, there are more such people in the workforce than ever. Yet less educated wage earners are having a tougher time making a good living. Lack of union jobs is one—but only one—of the reasons.

Yet unions are having a hard time maintaining, let alone increasing, their membership. They have failed to unionize even poorly paid white-collar workers, such as clerks and other office workers, and workers in the retail and restaurant industries. So unions are not going to "save" most American workers from the realities of the domestic and international labor markets. Two things that can help American workers would be increasing their skills and ending racial and gender discrimination on the job.

Got Skills?

Skilled workers earn more than unskilled workers, for several reasons. First, if the law of supply and demand is operating (and it usually is), the supply of workers with a specific skill is far smaller than the supply of people without that skill. If the demand is high relative to the supply, people with that skill can command a wage well above the wage of unskilled workers.

Second, it takes time to acquire a skill. Time is money, so people who learn a skill forgo some or all of their earnings during the education or training period. Few people will forgo earnings unless they can make more money later by doing so. Therefore, people must be compensated for their training. This is one reason that doctors are paid more than nurses, and why nurses are paid more than orderlies.

Third, relative to unskilled workers, skilled workers add more value to the goods and services they produce. That means that they also generate more revenue. This is also true of people with a higher level of skills than other people with the same skill set. For instance, a senior partner in a law firm who litigates cases adds more value for her firm's clients than an associate two years out of law school. She therefore bills out at a much higher rate—and is paid a lot more—than the associate.

As we saw in Chapter 8, economists analyze the factors of production at the margin— they examine the effect of adding one more unit of the factor being analyzed, including labor. Recall that the marginal product of a factor is the extra output added by one extra unit of that factor, holding all other factors constant. Remember also that the worker will be paid an amount equal to his or her marginal revenue product. That fact clearly works to the advantage of skilled workers.

In general—and this will be quite apparent when we look at the U.S. distribution of income in Chapter 11—education, training, and skills are the key determinants of higher wages.

Discrimination Doesn't Pay

To an economist, the issue of job discrimination is one of optimizing the value of *human capital* and, on a more political note, economic justice.

From the truly dismal economics of slavery to recent efforts to exclude immigrants, the United States has a long history of discrimination in the workplace.

What, exactly, is the economic effect of job discrimination?

Let's take racial discrimination against African-Americans as a case in point, although the effects also apply to gender and to other racial and ethnic discrimination.

EconoTalk

Broadly, **human capital** is the total of all that people bring to an economy. It is also the base of knowledge and skills that the population or a subset of a population has acquired through training, education, experience, and similar endeavors (including reading!). People invest in human capital through education, research, job training, scholarships, coaching, and mentoring.

You can probably guess that the overall effect of discrimination would be to artificially increase the wages of white workers and decrease those of black workers. White wages increase because whites are given greater access to higher paying jobs, while blacks are relegated to lower paying jobs. This reduces the supply of labor for higher paying jobs and, as a result, the white wage rises.

However, society pays a price in lost productivity from African American workers. If a black person who qualifies for a position as loan officer is kept in the position of bank teller or a black customer service representative is refused a promotion to salesperson, their productivity—their contribution to GDP in that higher, better paying position—is forgone.

Therefore, when discrimination ends, the wages that white workers lose is small relative to the gain that black workers—and the economy—achieve. White workers do lose a portion of their wages, because the total supply of workers, black and white, for higher paying jobs increases. When the supply of labor increases, the wage decreases. Yet most of the gains that black workers achieve come from their increased productivity in their new jobs. Those new jobs enable them to contribute higher marginal revenue product. In addition, the (often white) business owners obtain that increased productivity at a slightly *lower* total wage.

While white workers do lose a bit, the overall gain to those discriminated against and to society as a whole warrants the end to discrimination on economic grounds. Of course, there are no moral grounds for discrimination either. In Chapter 11, we will see some of the long-term effects of discrimination and similar economic inefficiencies in the U.S. economy.

What Works?

On an economic level, human labor is just one more factor of production. However, unlike land, materials, and machinery, people think and talk back. They form unions, engage in collective bargaining, move jobs to other nations, differentiate themselves by their skills, practice discrimination, and generally behave in ways that skew the forces of the free market.

Labor economics is among the most fascinating areas of economics. In no other part of the economy have buyers and sellers come to such deep, lasting, and violent conflict. There are few areas where the stakes are as high. The best path forward for workers and employers lies in understanding the role of human capital and how to enhance it and put it to the best use for the greatest number of people. When all factors of production—including human labor—reach their highest degree of functionality, an economy will realize the greatest good for the greatest number of people.

The Least You Need to Know

- In a union, workers band together to engage in collective bargaining with management regarding their pay, hours, and working conditions. Union membership and influence has waned in the United States, yet over 16 million workers still belong to a union.

- Union membership is heaviest among government workers, police officers, firefighters, and teachers. About 37 percent of government workers are union members compared with about 9 percent of private-sector workers.

- Since 1970, the share of national income going to wages and salaries has been about 73 percent, and the share going to profits has been 9 percent. Money is *not* being steered away from wages and toward profits.

- Skilled workers are paid more because of supply and demand, the need to compensate them for the time and money spent in school and training, and their higher marginal revenue product compared with less skilled workers.

- Discrimination relegates the minority to lower paying jobs, leaving more highly paid jobs to the majority. However, society loses a portion of the productivity of the minority. When discrimination ends, the majority loses some pay, but less than the wage gain to the minority and the productivity gain to the business owner.

Chapter 10

The Ups and Downs of the Business Cycle

In This Chapter

- ◆ The nature of the business cycle

- ◆ Causes of expansions and recessions

- ◆ Unemployment, inflation, and the economy

The forces of supply and demand play themselves out in the economy in ways that tend toward equilibrium, but never quite get there. Over the very short term or in very specific areas of the economy, supply, demand, employment, unemployment, wages, and prices may remain somewhat steady. That can create the impression that a kind of equilibrium has been reached. But the short term, by definition, never lasts long, and here we are focusing on the economy as a whole.

The economy as a whole is always either growing or contracting at a rate that usually changes from one quarter—or even one month—to the next. In this chapter, we examine the dynamics of growth and contraction. As I mentioned earlier, every business wants to grow, every household wants higher income, and every government wants a growing economy. Over the long term, the U.S. economy does grow, at the average of about 3 percent that I mentioned earlier, but that's the average. In this chapter, we look at the swings around that average.

What Is the Business Cycle?

The economy, as measured by gross domestic product (GDP), goes through alternating phases of growth and contraction. Phases of growth are called *expansions*, upswings, or recoveries. Phases of contraction are called *recessions*, downturns, or periods of "negative growth" (yes, it's an oxymoron, but one that economists insist on using).

During an expansion, consumer, business, and government demand all usually rise, but not at the same pace or at the same time. Expansions are often led by the consumer. In a consumer-led expansion, households demand more goods and services. In response, businesses increase production of goods and services, hire new workers, and put existing employees on overtime. This sets off a virtuous cycle of rising consumer demand, rising sales for business, and rising employment. Rising employment generates rising incomes for consumers, which fuels rising consumer demand, rising sales for business, and so on. Businesses increase their purchases of raw materials and expand their productive capacity by investing in new plant and equipment and offices. This kicks the sales of other businesses—contractors, builders, and producers of materials and capital equipment—into high gear.

Meanwhile, the federal government enjoys rising tax receipts. Elected officials can spread the wealth among their constituents by funding programs and increasing pay for government workers and the military (and themselves). They also usually increase government purchases and employment in health and human services, defense, public works, space exploration, and scientific research. If the federal budget runs a surplus, in which tax receipts exceed the federal budget, officials may even pay down some of the nation's debt, but don't count on it. We'll discuss the national debt in Chapter 12.

EconoTip

When GDP rises, the government collects more in taxes without increasing tax rates. When people's incomes rise, they automatically pay more in federal and state income taxes. Revenue from sales taxes also increases, which benefits almost all states and some cities. Property values usually rise during expansions, and that increases the property-tax receipts of local governments. All this extra revenue enables the government at all levels to buy more goods and services, provide more services to citizens, and pay down their debt—or to reduce tax rates.

Even poor people fare relatively well in an expansion—that is, relative to their situation during a recession. As unemployment approaches the full-employment level of 4 percent, almost every worker can find employment. Unfortunately, those without skills are destined to remain relatively poor and vulnerable to job loss when the next downturn arrives.

In a recession, demand falls—we'll examine why in a minute—and when demand falls, production contracts. In a typical recession, a decrease in consumer demand sets off a vicious cycle. When consumer demand decreases, businesses cut back production. They buy fewer raw materials, stop hiring workers, and even lay off some workers. They put expansion plans on hold, and may even shut down plants and offices.

> **EconoTalk**
>
> Officially, a **recession** is defined as two consecutive quarters of contraction in GDP (or "negative growth"). An **expansion** is growth in GDP, but unless it lasts, the result is a double dip recession—a recession in which the economy recovers for one, two, or three quarters and then contracts again. A **flat economy** is one registering zero growth—neither growth nor contraction.

These moves by businesses decrease consumers' incomes, which prompts consumers to reduce their consumption. When consumption falls further, businesses cut back production even more, laying off workers, further reducing income, and so on.

So in a typical recession consumption—the "C" in C + I + G—and investment—the "I" in the GDP formula—both fall.

What happens to government spending? You would expect it to fall, particularly when tax receipts decrease as incomes decrease. However, the federal government usually continues to spend during a recession. That provides a cushion—a baseline level of demand—so demand doesn't fall too far too fast. How much to spend is a fiscal policy decision for the government. We will deal with fiscal policy in Part 3.

When does a recession end?

A recession ends when demand is rekindled and starts rising, setting off a new virtuous cycle. Demand usually increases again because consumers reach a point where they simply have to increase their spending. Cars have to be replaced. Clothing wears out. Appliances break down for the fifth time. Even during a recession, some consumers continue to buy. However, they merely keep the economy from sinking into *depression*, which we discuss

> **EconoTalk**
>
> A **depression** is a prolonged period of extremely low consumer demand and investment, reduced business activity, high unemployment, and pessimism about the future of the economy.

later in this chapter. Their demand does not cause demand to rise and cannot make the economy grow. It is the rekindling of demand from the consumers who cut back because they lost their jobs, overtime pay, or sense of security that kicks off the next expansion.

The Inflation-Unemployment Tradeoff

For much of the past century, economists and business people believed that there was a tradeoff between inflation and unemployment. Many still do. Here's the theory, which has often been borne out in the real world.

An economy enjoying high demand and high employment experiences inflationary pressure—that is, upward pressure on prices. That's because when demand for goods and services is high, consumers bid up the prices of goods and services. Sellers, of course, are happy to accommodate them. This is called *demand-pull inflation*, because buyers' increasing demand pulls up prices.

There's another type of inflation, too. When the unemployment rate is low (say, below the full-employment rate of 4 percent), we have a tight labor market. In a tight market, employers increase wages in order to keep good workers and hire new ones. This upward pressure on wages raises the cost of doing business. But to maintain their profits, businesses have to raise their prices. This is called *cost-push inflation*, because the increased costs push prices upward. (It is also, more properly but less commonly, called *wage-push inflation*.)

EconoTalk

Demand-pull inflation occurs when consumers bid up prices, usually because employment is strong and incomes are increasing. **Wage-push inflation** occurs when businesses must raise wages to keep and attract workers in an environment of low unemployment, and then raise their prices. **Cost-push inflation** can include wage-push inflation, but also refers to price increases by business due to increased costs of one or more inputs other than labor.

Regardless of which comes first—the chicken of increased prices or the egg of increased wages (or is it the other way around?)—the result can be a price-wage inflation spiral. Demand for goods pushes up prices and keeps production high and unemployment low. Low unemployment pushes wages up. With higher incomes, consumers can afford the higher prices. Production is stepped up even further, and that pushes unemployment even lower and wages even higher, and so on.

Where does the spiral end? It ends when the government reins in the money supply or when the level of demand and the level of real wages reach the equilibrium, full-employment level and stays there. We will see how the government reduces the money supply in Part 4. The demand and supply for goods and services, which determine prices, and the demand and supply of labor, which dictate wages, reach equilibrium levels when demand cools down, but does not fall too sharply.

If demand falls too sharply, the economy is pushed into a recession. A recession wrings inflation out of an economy by reducing income. When businesses cut back, people lose their jobs and overtime pay. That stops the wage inflation and dampens consumer spending. When consumers cut back their spending, businesses lower their prices—or at least stop increasing them—to get people to buy. That stops the price inflation.

The inflation-unemployment tradeoff is the "classic" view of the two phenomena and of the business cycle. However, two relatively recent and very different developments have complicated things: the stagflation of the 1970s, and the low-inflation boom of 1990s.

Stagflation

Stagflation, a combination of stagnation and inflation, means rising prices in the face of fairly high unemployment.

Why would such a thing occur? If unemployment is relatively high, how can people have the income to bid up prices of goods and services?

They don't. Stagflation results from an increase in the price of inputs other than labor. It's not wage-push inflation. In fact, the price of even one input can generate inflation, even in a slack economy, if that input is important and widely used—like oil, for instance.

EconoTalk

Stagflation refers to rising prices in an environment of relatively slack demand and high unemployment. It usually arises from cost-push inflation, when the cost of one or more inputs—other than labor—increases.

Indeed, the term stagflation arose to describe the economy of the 1970s after the Organization of Petroleum Exporting Countries (OPEC) sharply increased the price of oil in 1973. Oil, gasoline, and other petroleum products are key inputs in virtually every aspect of the U.S. economy, as either raw material or fuel. There are few short-term substitutes for oil and gasoline, so the economy had to absorb the "oil price shock." Businesses raised their prices, but incomes didn't rise and consumer demand stayed sluggish.

Stagflation can be quite persistent. In the short term there is little to be done about it. Over the longer term people can use less of the input or develop substitutes. They also absorb the shock and ride it out until overall wage and price levels adjust and stabilize. This eventually occurred after the oil shock of the early 1970s and after the milder, but also jarring, oil shock of the early 1980s.

EconoTalk

Economists and business people watch two widely reported measures of inflation: the consumer price index (CPI) and the producer price index (PPI). The CPI measures the increase (or decrease), over a month, quarter, or year in the prices that consumers pay for a "market basket" of popular goods and services. The PPI measures the increase (or decrease) in the general price that producers pay for raw materials, labor, and other inputs.

In the late 1990s, some economists concluded that increased productivity in the U.S. economy had done away with the traditional trade-off between inflation and unemployment. Indeed, during the 1990s recovery, inflation remained quite low—about 2 percent or less per year—even as unemployment approached the rock-bottom rate of 4 percent. Other economists argue that the inflation-unemployment trade-off may still exist because the 1990s were an unusual period of unsustainable productivity growth. They see that growth as being driven largely by advances in technology, particularly information technology, which will not soon occur again.

Changes in the Cycle

The business cycle and the relationship between inflation and unemployment that I've described are those that prevailed in theory and reality until the 1970s. There have been some changes since then. Most important among these are the following:

♦ **Lower inflation:** Inflation erodes the value of the currency, and therefore the government, through monetary policy administered by the Federal Reserve, tries to prevent or at least control it. We will examine monetary policy in Part 4. In recent years, the Fed has been quite successful in keeping inflation low, especially under Fed Chairman Alan Greenspan (appointed in 1987 by President Ronald Reagan and reappointed every four years by each succeeding president).

♦ **Higher productivity:** Some economists believe that increased productivity in the U.S. economy has moderated the trade-off between inflation and unemployment. If productivity rises, businesses can produce more with roughly the same resources. That means that prices don't get pushed up. During the 1990s expansion, the Fed's aggressive management of the money supply helped, but an increase in productivity due to improved technology and management methods may have also helped. (I say "may" because economists are still divided on this.)

- **Faster response by businesses:** Thanks to better information systems and inventory management, businesses now respond more quickly to changes in the business cycle than they did before the 1980s. They reduce production more quickly, lay people off faster, and do not rehire workers as quickly as they did in past decades. When businesses respond faster to changing demand, they shift a bit more of the burden of recession to consumers, who are laid off faster. Yet many employees have learned to cope with this. I'm not saying they enjoy coping with it—for instance, by taking second jobs or whatever work they can find—but most are coping.

- **Investment-led recession:** In the recession that occurred in the last three quarters of 2001, consumer demand kept growing. However, business investment decreased enough to put the economy into recession. In the 1990s, businesses invested very heavily, particularly in telecommunications and information technology. It takes time for companies to digest that amount of investment and integrate it into their operations. Also, many companies invested heavily in Web-based e-business initiatives that didn't pay off. That, plus the post-9/11 atmosphere of uncertainty, further dampened investment.

How permanent these changes will be remains unclear. The fundamental dynamics of the business cycle remain largely unchanged, except for the lack of significant inflation over the past 10 years. But the mechanism of increased demand leading to increased production and rising incomes, followed by a decrease in demand, decreased production, and falling incomes still operates in the economy.

But we've yet to answer one question: What causes demand to decrease in the first place?

Seasons of Wither

Demand falls because consumers reduce consumption, businesses reduce investment, or the government reduces spending. But *why* do they reduce these activities?

Let's start with the government. The government may curtail its spending because it sees less need to spend in certain areas. This has not been a determining factor in a recession since the early 1960s. But up to then, periodic cutbacks in military spending without increases in other spending or reductions in taxes occasionally caused a contraction in demand that flowed through to the broader economy.

Since the late 1960s, government has occasionally tried to produce *mild* recessions to reduce inflationary pressure in the economy. This is done through monetary policy. To solve the problem of "too many dollars chasing too few goods," the Federal Reserve increases interest rates, which makes borrowing more difficult, and curtails the growth of the money supply, which takes some of those excess dollars out of the economy. (Don't worry, Part 4 will cover this in detail.) If the Fed miscalculates and raises interest rates too fast or too high, the result is a not-so-mild recession.

So, believe it or not, the government sometimes initiates a recession.

Businesses generally want to invest, but they need to see opportunities. If they go on an investment binge, as they did in the 1990s, they need time to integrate the plant and equipment into their operations.

They also need money to invest. As we saw in Chapter 7, a mismatch between the amount households want to save and the amount businesses want to invest can cause trouble. If consumers want to save more than business wants to invest—if consumers "sit on their wallets"—production may decrease. If it decreases enough to raise unemployment and lower incomes, recession may follow. (Over-saving by consumers has not been a problem in the U.S. economy lately.)

Consumers (bless 'em) are predisposed to demand goods and services. They want to buy, but they need two things: income, which we've discussed, and *confidence* in the economy.

The Conference Board's Index is available to the public at www.conference-board. org. Each month, a different sample of 5,000 households is mailed a questionnaire, and about 70 percent respond to the survey's five questions. The questions concern current business conditions, expectations of business conditions six months from now, current employment conditions, expectations of employment conditions six months from now, and expectations of total family income six months from now. Each question calls for a "positive," "negative," or "neutral" response.

EconoTalk

Consumer confidence, also known as consumer sentiment, is a measure of the "mood" of consumers regarding the current economy and their optimism or pessimism about their economic prospects.

There are two widely followed measures of the consumer's mood: the Conference Board's Consumer Confidence Index and University of Michigan Consumer Confidence Index.

The responses are compiled and used to calculate the Index. The Index is pegged to the year 1985. This means that the value of the Index is relative to the base year 1985, for which the Index is pegged at 100.

The real value of the Index is in its trend and in relative high and low points. For example, knowing that the index stood at 79.4 in October 2002 tells you very little. But knowing that October was the fourth straight month of decline, and that the September level was 93.7, tells you more. Knowing that in October 2002 the Index was at its lowest level since 1993, when it was 71.9, tells you still more.

If you are a retailer who, like many retailers, does 30 to 40 percent of her business during the Christmas season, it tells you to advertise aggressively, avoid overstocking, and discount slow-moving merchandise quickly.

The University of Michigan Index is based on a monthly survey of 500 consumers and the base year is 1966, meaning that the value of the Index in 1966 equals 100. The survey questions are similar to those in the Conference Board Survey, but focus on a one-year horizon and gauge the respondents' purchasing plans. From September to October 2002, the University of Michigan Index fell from 86.1 to 80.4.

These indexes are fairly well related to consumer spending in the near future. The overall trend is much more important than month-to-month values or changes. Economists follow these indexes and use them in their analyses and forecasts of the economy.

Serious Depression

Economists call a deep, prolonged contraction a depression. A depression is not as clearly defined as a recession, but is characterized by rising unemployment, falling incomes, falling prices, excess inventories and productive capacity, lack of confidence, and a generally low level of business activity. Fortunately, depressions are very rare. The Great Depression of the 1930s was the only true depression to occur in the United States and Europe in the past century.

The Great Depression lasted from 1929, when the stock market crashed on October 25 ("Black Thursday"), to 1941, when the United States entered World War II. During the Depression, unemployment reached 25 percent, families lost their savings and homes and survived on charity and odd jobs, farms and banks failed by the thousands, and two generations formed lifelong memories of tough economic times. Real GDP contracted by 8.6 percent in 1930, 6.4 percent in 1931, 13.0 percent in 1932 and 1.4 percent in 1933.

Economists disagree about the exact causes of the Great Depression, but a stock market bubble driven by the wild buying of the Roaring Twenties is a candidate. Much of that buying was on margin, meaning with borrowed money, so when stock prices peaked and a sell-off began, it quickly snowballed into a crash. While the Crash of 1929 did not actually *cause* the Great Depression, it certainly reduced people's wealth and, perhaps more important, induced pessimism and fear regarding their economic prospects. That lack of confidence prevailed for much of the 1930s.

In the view of many economists, the Federal Reserve's decision to reduce the money supply in the very early 1930s reduced demand too sharply. (You'll see how this works in Part 4.) Some economists "blame" the Fed for pushing the nation into depression, but a lot of money was actually taken out of the economy by bank failures. When people put a "run" on a bank, that is, when all or most depositors want to withdraw their money at once, the bank typically fails. The bank will close its doors, because the depositors' money is not in the bank—it has been loaned out as mortgages, auto loans, and personal loans. Bank failures reduced the money supply and that, apart from the Fed's actions, reduced demand.

Moreover, business investment collapsed. Why? The market crash hobbled companies' efforts to raise capital by selling stock. Consumer pessimism and falling demand left businesses with fewer reasons to invest. A reduced money supply and high interest rates made money harder to come by and expensive to borrow.

Actually, economists agree that all of these factors—the stock market crash, collapse in confidence, reduction of the money supply, bank failures, high interest rates, and reduced business investment—all played a role in initiating, prolonging, or worsening the Great Depression. The disagreement concerns their exact roles and relative importance in the debacle.

Fortunately, economists agree that the United States now has safeguards in place that make a repeat of the Great Depression unlikely. These safeguards include a social safety net in the form of unemployment insurance, welfare, and Medicare. They also include a more active government role in economic policy, better regulation of the securities markets, and insurance of bank deposits up to $100,000 thanks to the Federal Deposit Insurance Corporation (FDIC), which was created in 1933 to insure bank deposits and put an end to runs on banks.

The Real World

In March 1933, Franklin D. Roosevelt succeeded Herbert Hoover as president of the United States. Roosevelt immediately began efforts to reform the banking and securities industries, provide relief for farmers and the unemployed, and stimulate the economy. By June 30, the Emergency Banking Relief Act (providing for federal bank inspections), Agricultural Adjustment Act and Farm Credit Act (subsidizing farmers), Reforestation Relief Act (putting people to work on conservation projects), and the Federal Securities Act and Glass-Steagall Act (reforming the securities industry) were all passed. The FDIC and the Tennessee Valley Authority were both created in that period as well.

These measures initiated the New Deal, which expanded the role of the government in the economy as both regulator and participant. This made Roosevelt a hero to many and a demon to others, depending on their politics and economic situation.

Booms and Bubbles

When consumers and businesses increase or decrease demand gradually, the cycle of recession and recovery will be relatively smooth, although hardly painless. But exaggerated responses by consumers or businesses can create a boom or a bust. (A bust is a colloquial term for a sharp, severe downturn.)

A boom occurs when demand increases sharply over a sustained period. The increase in demand can be broad-based and affect the entire economy, or a boom can be more specific. For example, a nationwide housing boom may be driven by a dramatic increase of adults in the population who are ready to become homeowners. More specifically still, a housing boom can occur in a rapidly growing city, as occurred in Las Vegas from the late 1980s through most of the 1990s.

In general, an economic boom means good times for most people. However, if a boom continues long enough and strong enough, it can generate over-expansion by business or inflation. If businesses over-expand, they wind up with too much productive capacity and too many employees for the existing level of demand. When that happens, they must cut their costs by cutting back on purchases of materials and equipment and decreasing the number of employees through layoffs. When employees are laid off, they cut back their spending, too. If businesses and employees cut back their spending sharply enough for long enough, a recession begins. If economic conditions become bad enough, the result can be bust.

Look Out Below: Falling Prices

Until recently, very few economists worried about *deflation*, but in the early 2000s many have started re-examining the phenomenon. Deflation is defined as a sustained period of falling prices for most goods and services. It is a situation of "too few dollars chasing too many goods," and is therefore the opposite of inflation.

For this reason, deflation might strike you as a wonderful development. Indeed, it helps households, at least initially. Consumers can buy more for their money because, if prices are falling *and* wages remain stable, the purchasing power of the currency is rising. But that is about the only benefit to consumers, and it can be short lived.

EconoTalk

Deflation is a period of falling prices across a broad range of products and services. It is the opposite of inflation, in that "too few dollars are chasing too many goods." In such a situation producers have no choice but to reduce their prices.

During deflation, a business that's able to increase its sales volume enough to offset the effect of lower prices may continue to do business more or less as usual. But many businesses find that lower prices mean lower sales or lower profits, or both. (Recall our discussion of elasticity of demand in Chapter 5?) Businesses facing declining profits will have to reduce their payrolls and other costs. This reduces employment and income, which can set off the vicious cycle of lower demand, lower production, and recession.

In addition, deflation hurts debtors because they must pay back their debts with "more expensive" dollars. This is in contrast to the benefits debtors derive from inflation, when they repay their debts with "cheaper" dollars. Also, returns on savings and investments may decrease during deflation because interest rates tend to fall, along with profits and, by extension, stock prices and dividends.

Remember, the goal of sound economic policy is a stable currency, not one that is gaining or losing purchasing power. For this reason, economists take a dim view of deflation.

The cause of deflation is too much capacity—the ability to produce too many goods and services given the level of demand. In the United States, the huge investment in technology made during the 1990s expanded capacity while reducing production costs.

One cure for deflation is to reduce capacity, which is painful for the businesses that must close factories or stores—and for their employees. The other is to increase demand, which isn't always easy to do. Lower interest rates can help spur borrowing and spending, but sometimes the only "cure" is time. Sooner or later the car, clothes, and appliances need replacing, demand rises, and the virtuous cycle begins again.

Recent Events

The most recent prolonged expansion officially started in March 1991 and ended in March 2001, lasting exactly 10 years. The recession that preceded that expansion officially lasted a mere eight months. In fact, since the end of World War II, the longest recession, the "oil shock" induced downturn of 1973 and 1974, lasted 16 months.

In the 1990s, consumers and businesses went on a spending spree. Consumers bought goods and services on a level that outdid the "glitzy" 1980s. Business investment also went into high gear. But much of the consumption and investment focused on something new: the personal computer and the Internet. Consumers made household names out of companies such as Compaq, Dell, AOL, and CompUSA. Businesses put a personal computer on every desk, and then networked them, and then became so enamored of the Internet and "the promise of e-business" that they invested heavily in projects that often promised little more than a website.

In the background, or perhaps the foreground, was a bull market in all stocks and a bubble in Internet-related stocks—the dot-coms—in which even some companies without any earnings (or even a rational business plan) were able to go public and raise millions of dollars. Ultimately, the bubble burst, the stock market lost about one-third of its value, and businesses curtailed investment.

EconoTip

The example of a bubble that you'll encounter in every economics book concerns the incredible run-up in the price of tulip bulbs in Amsterdam in the 1630s. Although tulips were all the rage as flowers, as investments they got to the point were a single tulip bulb could command a price equal to 25, 50, or even 100 percent of a well-to-do merchant's annual earnings. "Tulipmania" ended, as all bubbles do, when people started realizing that they were paying huge sums for something that did not have anything remotely like that level of intrinsic value.

Starting in March 2001, the U.S. economy experienced three quarters of slightly negative growth. A contraction of -1.6 percent (at an annualized rate) in the second quarter of 2001 was the worst of it, although March alone was bad enough to turn growth for the entire first quarter of 2001 negative. However, the recovery that began in the fourth quarter of 2001 was uneven. Growth was 2.8 percent in the fourth quarter of 2001, shot up to 5.0 percent in the first quarter of 2002, drifted down to 1.3 percent in the second quarter, hit 4.0 percent in the third quarter, and sank to 0.7 percent in the fourth quarter. However, growth for 2002 was positive at 2.4 percent, despite the unevenness and uncertainty surrounding the expansion.

Rather than a good, steady expansion, the U.S. economy has been progressing unevenly, posing the risk of a "double dip" recession. At this point, the relative mildness of the recession has been attributed to the consumer's continued willingness to spend. In fact, some economists marvel at the strength of consumer demand, and wonder whether it can continue in the face of a shaky stock market, the threat of terrorist attacks, and sluggish business investment.

Also the threat of deflation has risen in the United States. Inflation stands at 30-to 50-year lows, depending upon which indicator of prices you examine. Retailers and some manufacturers, have had to reduce prices and have seen their profits take a hit. In the early 2000s, deflation was already a serious problem in most Asian economies. A number of economists believe that the United States and Europe are not immune from falling prices and their ill effects on economic growth.

Stay tuned. Also, Chapter 21 discusses a broad range of economic indicators and shows you how to interpret them and the economic news, especially with regard to the business cycle.

The Least You Need to Know

- The business cycle is the alternating pattern of expansion and recession caused by fluctuating demand by consumers, businesses, and (to a lesser extent) government, and by mismatches between supply and demand and between savings and investment.

- Demand-pull inflation occurs when consumers bid up the prices of goods and services. Wage-push inflation occurs when businesses must raise wages to keep and attract workers in an environment of low unemployment. Cost-push inflation refers to price increases by business due to increased costs of inputs other than labor.

- A recession is defined as at least two consecutive quarters of contraction in GDP. A depression is a prolonged period of rising unemployment, falling incomes, falling prices, excess inventories and productive capacity, and lack of confidence.

- The long-accepted relationship between inflation and unemployment is that low unemployment eventually generates inflation, and a mild recession is the cure for that inflation. However, the phenomenon of stagflation shows that inflation can occur even in the presence of relatively high unemployment.

- The business cycle and the relationship between inflation and unemployment may have changed in the past 20 or 30 years due to faster responses by businesses, better inventory management, the Federal Reserve's success at controlling inflation, and higher productivity.

Part 3

The Government and the Economy

Although the government plays a smaller role in the U.S. economy than the governments of most other nations play in theirs, that role is important, and multifaceted. First, it is through the government that society produces goods and services that everyone needs but that markets can't really deliver. Defense is a good example. Second, total government spending accounts for about 28 percent of GDP, and that spending has a huge effect on the economy. Third, the government has the power to levy taxes, and the way in which it uses that power generates strong responses in people as well as in the economy. Finally, the government issues currency and controls the supply of money in the economy.

In this part, we examine all of these government roles except for the last one, having to do with money, which we cover in Part 4.

Chapter 11

To Have and Have Not: Wealth and Poverty

In This Chapter

◆ How economists define wealth and poverty

◆ Income patterns in the United States

◆ Public policy and income redistribution

People tend to be quite judgmental when it comes to wealth and poverty. On the one hand, the so-called Protestant work ethic—the idea that wealth comes to those who work—leads many people to blame the poor for their poverty. On the other hand, compassion for the poor (and perhaps envy of the wealthy) leads others to blame the wealthy for poverty, judging them too selfish and unfeeling to assist the poor.

Here is where the science of economics comes in handy. As a social scientist, an economist examines wealth and poverty from a more objective viewpoint than the noneconomist. In this chapter, we examine poverty and wealth from the economist's viewpoint. The goal is, first, to develop a clear picture of the extent of wealth and poverty and, second, to examine trends in the distribution of income in America. Finally, we will examine the government's current role in addressing poverty.

What Is Poverty?

Economists measure wealth and poverty in several ways. The three most common measures are income, assets (meaning accumulated wealth in the form of money, securities, and real estate), and socioeconomic metrics. Measures in the last category go beyond financial data to account for health, nutrition, infant mortality, sanitation, and other aspects of human well being.

In this chapter, I will usually examine wealth and poverty in terms of income. Data on income is readily available, reliable, and relevant, especially in discussing poverty in the United States, where inherited wealth is a minor factor and most people live on wages and salaries.

It's useful to think of wealth and poverty in relation to one another. That's because *income inequality* is really the underlying issue in poverty, especially in developed nations.

EconoTalk

Income inequality refers to the differences in income between and among various groups of individuals and households in an economy.

Human social systems being what they are, it is often the differences in wealth that make people feel rich or poor. In a Third World nation, a family with indoor plumbing, running water, decent food and clothing, and access to health care and education is quite well off. In the United States, however, millions of people who have those things are considered poor, because they have little else and those things constitute the bare essentials in America. In this most developed of economies, dwellings without plumbing are not legally fit for habitation; public assistance programs, such as Food Stamps, Medicare, and Medicaid, assure at least adequate levels of nutrition and health care; and public education is compulsory for children.

Perhaps Webster's Dictionary provides the most accurate definition of poverty, at least in America: the state of one who lacks a *usual or socially acceptable amount* of money or material possessions (italics mine). This is not to minimize the plight of the poor in America. It's easily arguable that poverty of any kind is unacceptable in a society with the riches and opportunities of the United States. Also, many poor Americans do live without adequate nutrition, shelter, and health care. This is especially true of the rural poor, for instance in Appalachia, and for the physically, emotionally, and mentally disabled poor. I am only pointing out that poverty can be a relative condition.

For instance, the World Bank identifies areas of the world where significant portions of the population live on less than $1 a day. These are the poorest people in the world's poorest regions, where food, shelter, health care, and other necessities are in dangerously short supply. Table 11.1 reveals the sad statistics.

Table 11.1   People Living on less than $1 a Day in 2000

Region	Total Population (millions)	People Living on Less than $1 a Day (millions)	Percent of Region's Population
Latin American and Caribbean	432	49	12
West Asia and North Africa	204	5	3
Sub-Saharan Africa	388	169	44
South Asia	1,266	515	41
East and Southeast Asia	1,726	320	19

Source: World Bank

Poverty is most widespread in Sub-Saharan Africa and South Asia, where over 40 percent of the population lives on less than $365 a year. All told, over 1 billion people in the world are in this situation, which is considered absolute, rather than relative, poverty.

We will look at the economic issues of the developing world in Part 5. But one of the worst of its problems is the human suffering caused by persistent poverty.

Who's Got How Much?

To measure income inequality—a measure of wealth and poverty that can be applied to any geographical area—economists use quintile rankings. These rankings divide households into five groups according to income. Each group accounts for one-fifth of the number of households. Table 11.2 shows the income breakpoints for each quintile of U.S. households for 2000, 1990, 1980, and 1970, according to the U.S. Census Bureau.

Table 11.2   U.S. Household Income Limits by Quintile (upper limit of each quintile—with the exception of the fifth quintile, in current dollars, rounded to nearest 100)

Year	Lowest	Second	Third	Fourth	Lower Limit of Top 5%
2000	18,000	33,000	52,300	82,000	145,500
1990	12,500	23,700	36,200	55,200	94,700
1980	7,600	14,100	21,600	31,700	51,500
1970	3,700	7,100	10,300	14,700	23,200

Source: U.S. Census Bureau

Just to clarify, this table is saying that in the year 2000:

- 20 percent of U.S. households had incomes of $18,000 and under

- 20 percent had incomes between $18,001 and $33,000

- 20 percent had incomes between $33,001 and $52,300

- 20 percent had incomes between $52,301 and $82,000

- 20 percent had incomes above $82,000

It is also saying that in 2000, 5 percent of households had incomes of $145,500 and higher. (This 5 percent is also counted in the top 20 percent.)

To analyze the data in this table accurately, however, we should use real, rather than nominal, dollars to correct for the effects of inflation. Table 11.3 shows the same data in real dollars (adjusted for inflation by the Census Bureau using the Consumer Price Index).

Table 11.3   U.S. Household Income Limits by Quintile (upper limit of each quintile, in real dollars, rounded to the nearest 100)

Year	Lowest	Second	Third	Fourth	Lower Limit of Top 5%
2000	18,500	33,900	53,700	84,200	149,600
1990	16,400	31,100	47,500	72,500	124,400
1980	15,400	28,700	44,000	64,500	104,800
1970	14,600	27,900	40,600	57,900	91,500

continued

Year	Lowest	Second	Third	Fourth	Lower Limit of Top 5%
Increase in Breakpoint, 1970–2000	26.7%	21.5%	33.3%	45.4%	63.5%

Observers who point out that the wealthiest Americans have been doing better than the rest of the population are clearly correct. In real dollars, from 1970 to 2000, the upper limit of the fourth quintile (that is, the lower limit of the fifth quintile) rose by 45.4 percent while the upper limit of the lowest quintile rose by 26.7 percent. Meanwhile, the lower limit that defines the top 5 percent—the very wealthiest households—rose by 63.5 percent.

That's interesting, but changes in the *share* of total income going to the various quintiles tell an even more interesting story. Table 11.4 shows the percentage share of total income going to each quintile and to the top 5 percent of households.

Table 11.4 Share of Income Received by Each Quintile and the Top 5 Percent

Year	Lowest	Second	Third	Fourth	Fifth	Top 5%
2000	3.6	8.9	14.9	23.0	49.6	21.9
1990	3.9	9.6	15.9	24.0	46.6	18.6
1980	4.3	10.3	16.9	24.9	43.7	15.8
1970	4.1	10.8	17.4	24.5	43.3	16.6

Source: U.S. Census Bureau

It doesn't take a raving socialist to see that the shares of total income going to U.S. households in the top 20 percent—and in the top 5 percent—increased from 1970 to 2000, while the shares going to those in the lower four quintiles—the lower 80 percent—decreased. What you think should be done about this trend, if anything, is another matter. Yet clearly, over the past 30 years, a larger share of income has gone to those who were already earning the highest incomes.

That is a major point of contention in the political, social, and economic argument over income distribution in the United States. Very few Americans seriously argue that income *equality* is a reasonable, or even desirable, goal. Americans recognize that the incentive to earn a higher income drives people to get an education and work hard, fuels economic growth, and informs our national character. If incomes were "equalized" through taxation or other means, the labor market would fall into disarray and people would lack economic incentives to better themselves.

EconoTip _____

Don't confuse income distribution with income redistribution. Income distribution refers to the amounts and shares of income that go to various segments of a population. It's actually a frequency distribution, which you learned about in Chapter 3.

Income redistribution refers to government programs to even out income disparities to some degree. This involves taking money from relatively wealthy segments of society and transferring it to relatively poor segments, through public assistance and other government programs.

However, despite very real disparities in income, Americans pride themselves on being a "classless society," or at least on being a nation with such a large middle class that it may as well be composed of one class. This may be wishful thinking, given the actual distribution of income.

Through work, education, innovation, and financial savvy, people in America can move to a higher socioeconomic class more easily than in most other societies. This is another source of national pride and economic incentive in the United States. Might that change if people with the largest slice of the economic pie keep getting an even larger slice? If we became a nation in which the economic deck were stacked against average people—those with average education and skills—both social mobility and incentives to work could diminish. Moreover, with much of the fruits of economic growth going to a relatively small segment of the population, the once tight social fabric of the country could fray.

There is some evidence that that fabric has frayed since the "glory days" of World War II and the 1950s. The urban riots of the 1960s arose in part from economic issues. The character of many U.S. cities changed during and after that period, in many instances leaving a much smaller middle class to fill jobs, attend schools, spend money, and pay taxes. Suburban sprawl, "white flight," and the need for more housing transformed large portions of cities like Detroit, Baltimore, Los Angeles, and New York into urban societies with two-classes: wealthy and poor.

Some people point out that even if the lower four quintiles each have a lower share of the economic pie than they did 30 years ago, their incomes are still larger than they were back then. That may be true, but relative to the top quintile, they are poorer, and the distribution of the shares of national wealth is the key measure of wealth and poverty in a nation as rich as the United States.

Why Incomes Are Becoming More Unequal

Incomes have become more unequal in the United States for three primary reasons:

- Changes in employment patterns
- Increased returns to education
- Changes in households

Let's take a look at each of these reasons.

Changes in Employment Patterns

As we discussed in Chapter 9, the percentage of workers who belong to a labor union decreased dramatically in the past 30 years. That in itself results in a lower wage for millions of workers, because unions exist to push wages upward, and they usually succeed.

As a result, however, management often moves jobs to lower-wage locations. Many high paying U.S. manufacturing jobs have been replaced by lower paying jobs in service industries, such as retail and restaurants. This trend is expected to continue. The Bureau of Labor Statistics states that, of the ten occupations with the largest projected job growth from 1998 to 2008, five pay less than $10 an hour (retail salespersons, cashiers, office clerks, home health aides, and teachers' assistants).

Growth in service-sector employment is also being driven by changes in consumers' spending patterns. Spending on services has been growing faster than spending on nondurables, such as food, beverages, and clothing, and that trend is also expected to continue. Spending on durables, such as motor vehicles, furniture, appliances, and consumer electronics is growing. But those industries have been moved to lower wage nations, such as Mexico, Malaysia, and China.

Increased Returns to Education

More educated and highly skilled workers have always earned higher incomes than less educated and less skilled workers. That tendency has become more pronounced in the United States due to increased demand for "knowledge workers" and managers in an economy where industries such as high technology, financial services, media, communications, and academe have been growing.

Table 11.5 relates education with income levels for men and women.

Table 11.5   Higher Education Means Higher Income (average annual income in dollars, rounded to nearest 100)

	Men	Women
Some High School	21,600	12,300
High School Graduate	32,100	17,700
Some College	40,200	23,500
Associate Degree	42,400	25,200
Bachelor's Degree	61,200	32,800
Master's Degree	71,800	42,700
Doctorate	98,800	61,300
Professional Degree (M.D., etc.)	119,000	59,500

Source: U.S. Census, 1999

For both men and women—admittedly with a significant gender gap—income increases with education. (Professional degrees do not increase income for women the way they do for men.) A man with a bachelor's degree earns 90 percent more than one with a high school diploma. A woman with a bachelor's degree earns 85 percent more than one with a high school diploma.

Higher education also means lower unemployment. In 2000—a low-unemployment year—unemployment was 3.5 for high school graduates and, at 1.7 percent, about half that for college graduates.

A bright, motivated individual worker stands a good chance of earning a higher income by obtaining more education. But increased education and skills training will not be enough to shift the current trend in income distribution significantly. Even if it were possible to give *all* U.S. workers a college education, millions of the jobs being created in the future—in retail, restaurants, home health services, and so on—simply don't require high levels of education. Getting a college degree only to wind up selling hardware or frying potatoes makes no economic sense. Nor does paying a hardware salesperson or a fry cook $25 an hour.

These structural changes in the labor force represent a high obstacle to improving the incomes of the bottom 40 percent of households.

Changes in Households

Households themselves have changed, and these changes have affected household income. The tendency toward more single-adult households, due to people marrying later and divorcing more frequently has, over the past 30 years, created more households for a given level of population. When people marry later and couples divorce, the number of households increases in proportion to the population. Indeed, this is exactly what has occurred in the United States since 1970.

Table 11.6 summarizes key population statistics for 1970 and 2000.

Table 11.6   Population, Households, and Married Couples (1970 and 2000, nearest million)

	1970	2000	Change
Total Population	203,000,000	282,000,000	39%
Households	63,000,000	105,000,000	67%
Average Household Size	3.2 people	2.7 people	–15.6
Married Couples	45,000,000	55,000,000	22%
Married Couples as Percent of Pop.	22.2%	19.5%	—

From 1970 to 2000, the U.S. population increased 39 percent while the number of married couples increased by only 22 percent, due to later marriage, increased divorce, and, perhaps, increased acceptance of gay lifestyles. The rise in the number of households relative to the population (67 percent versus 39 percent) increases the number of households that total income is divided by, resulting in lower income per household.

Consider this: If a married couple heading a household—even a two-earner household—divorces, their income is divided between two households rather than one. That halves the household income figure generated by that couple. (And that's assuming that their incomes remain the same, which is not always the case: Women's incomes often decrease after divorce.)

On the surface, this may seem to be a "mathematical" issue rather than a true problem of income inequality. After all, if people want to remain or become single, why shouldn't they? They probably should. But being divorced or an unmarried head of a household (or both) falls harder on the poor. As difficult as divorce and single-parenthood can be, it's tougher for people in the lower income quintiles, because they lack the income and other resources that help a person cope with child-rearing and other challenges of daily living. Society also bears the social cost of a continuing cycle of poverty and the ills that poverty generates.

What's the Government's Role?

The U.S. government is already working to address income inequality and poverty. Some people believe that the government should be doing more, some believe it should be doing less, and some feel that the current role is about right.

EconoTalk

A **progressive income tax** levies higher taxes on higher incomes. Typically, marginal income is taxed at marginally higher rates. For example, income up to $20,000 may be taxed at 15 percent, income between $20,000 and $35,000 at 20 percent, and so on. (If only the tax code were that simple.) In other words, the higher rate does not apply to all income, but rather to the marginal income.

Here are some of the policies that the government has in place to address income inequality and assist poor households:

♦ **Progressive income tax:** A progressive income tax taxes people with higher incomes at higher rates. In 2001, U.S. federal tax rates started at 15 percent and climbed to 39 percent, with three intermediate brackets. Except for transfer payments and public assistance programs, all U.S. citizens receive the same basic federal services in terms of defense, law enforcement, food and drug regulation, and so on. Yet wealthier citizens pay more for these services. This smacks of the Marxist principle, "from each according to his means," yet most Americans (but not all) feel that progressive taxation is ultimately fair. So, while the wealthiest Americans have a larger share of the income pie, they also pay more in taxes.

♦ **Public assistance programs:** Federal unemployment insurance, Medicare, and federal welfare programs, such as Food Stamps, all help poor and temporarily hard-pressed households make ends meet. While Social Security is not a welfare program (because workers pay a specific Social Security tax for these benefits), it does provide financial assistance to millions of retirees and people unable to work.

♦ **Economic development programs:** Federal programs that help finance minority- and women-owned business, such as those of the Small Business Administration, help redress the imbalances created by job discrimination in the past, and so do efforts that encourage these businesses to apply for government contracts. Federal money also finds its way into state and municipal programs to train unskilled workers and encourage business formation, for instance in "enterprise zones" designed to foster redevelopment in the inner city.

♦ **Managing the economy:** The federal government implements economic policies aimed at generating full employment as well as low inflation. While this benefits wealthy Americans as well as the less well off, the emphasis on controlling unemployment arguably helps wage earners more than it does "the moneyed class."

All of that said, the United States generally provides its citizens with a lower level of government support for health and human services than most developed European nations. This is true for services that benefit the middle class as well as those for the poor. Most European nations provide, insure, or mandate higher levels of health care, childcare, employee benefits, and job security. They also generally levy higher taxes on their citizens, particularly on the wealthiest, to finance these programs.

In Chapters 12 and 13 and in Part 4, we will examine the role of the federal government in managing the economy. The government's role in addressing income inequality falls into the political realm, and this is not a book about political economics. Very few people, regardless of their political persuasion, want to see their fellow human beings in poverty. However, there is no political consensus on further addressing the effects of poverty in the United States.

Other Aspects of Wealth and Poverty

Before completing our examination of wealth and poverty, there are a few related topics to cover: general spending patterns, consumer debt, and inflation.

Where It Goes

As I mentioned earlier, there are three broad classes of personal consumption expenditure: durables, nondurables, and services. Table 11.7 shows the dollar amounts of spending and the growth rates in these categories for 1977 and 1993, and the projected amounts for 2005.

Table 11.7   Personal Spending Patterns Are Changing (billions of 1987 dollars)

	1977	1993	Average Annual Percent Growth, 1977–1993	Projected 2005	Average Annual Projected Growth, 1993-2005
Durables	280	490	4.7	746	4.4
Nondurables	820	1,079	2.0	1,299	1.7
Services	1,197	1,890	3.6	2,510	2.7
Total	2,297	3,459	3.2	4,555	2.6

Sources: Bureau of Economic Analysis (1977 and 1993); Bureau of Labor Statistics (2005)

As the table shows, consumers spend most of their money on services. The five largest service expenditures are housing, health care, financial services, utilities, and transportation. Spending on nondurables—food, beverages, clothing, toys, and so on—is the next largest category. Although spending on durables—motor vehicles, furniture, appliances, home computers, and so on—is the smallest, it is the fastest growing category of spending.

As household income falls, the percentage of income spent on necessities such as food, housing, utilities, and transportation becomes larger. This leaves little or nothing to save, and little to spend on durables such as new cars, furniture, and appliances. Therefore, much of the growth in spending on durables has been fueled by educated, higher income baby boomers purchasing vehicles, as well as homes and condominiums that require furniture and appliances as they have moved through adulthood.

New Highs in Deep Debt

As I mentioned in Chapter 6, American consumers use large amounts of credit. Consumer credit takes two basic forms: mortgages, which are used to buy real estate and are *secured* by the homes, condominiums, or other property being purchased; and consumer loans. Home-equity loans, which are personal loans secured by the equity in houses and condominiums, may be lumped in with mortgages. Consumer loans include both secured loans, such as auto loans, and *unsecured* loans, such as purchases made with credit cards.

Over the past 10 years, consumer debt in all forms has hovered around record levels, both in absolute terms and as a percentage of income. Mortgages to finance America's widespread homeownership are one reason, but so is the proliferation of credit cards and other installment debt. Growth in these borrowings has not been fueled only by people trying to make ends meet. Debt for the top 20 percent of U.S. households reached 120 percent of disposable income in 2002, compared with 100 percent in 1995. In the lower 80 percent of households, consumer debt stood at about 80 percent of disposable income in 2002, up from 70 percent in 1995. In each case, the 1995 levels were already high by historical standards.

EconoTalk

A **secured** loan is one in which the borrower provides a tangible or financial asset—such as a home, car, boat, stocks, or bonds—to the lender as collateral. In the event the borrower cannot repay the loan, the lender takes possession of the collateral and sells it to recoup the borrowed money. An **unsecured** loan is one on which the borrower provides no collateral.

The consequences of high consumer debt are twofold. First, it usually indicates a low rate of savings, and, as we saw in Chapter 7, that is indeed the case in the United States. Second, when a recession results in fewer working hours and lower incomes, consumers can find repaying their debt difficult or even impossible. Indeed, according to the October 9, 2002 *Wall Street Journal*, auto repossessions, personal bankruptcies, and mortgage foreclosures were all at or near their highest levels in decades.

Moreover, consumers may also find it difficult to maintain, let alone increase, spending while carrying this debt burden. That can prolong lackluster economic growth or even contribute to a recession. Also, if interest rates rise, many consumers who had difficulty making debt payments at lower rates, may find themselves unable to do so at higher rates.

Nonetheless, many economists feel that American consumers can handle their debt, even at these levels. They point out that many people have come to accept debt and interest payments as part of their household expenditures. They also point out that incomes generally keep growing and that interest rates (except on credit cards) have been quite low for the past five years.

Inflation Hurts—and Helps

We discussed the types of inflation and their causes in Chapter 10. Except in times of stagflation, incomes generally rise during periods of inflation. But if incomes are not rising as fast as prices, then inflation is eroding the currency's purchasing power. This hurts everyone, wealthy, middle class, and poor, but can make life especially hard for the poor.

That's because of a second effect of inflation. During inflation, the value of assets, particularly real estate but also financial assets such as stocks, generally rises. This rise in asset values helps the wealthy and the middle class because they own real estate and stocks. The poor do not. The rise in asset values in the 1990s produced what is know as a "wealth effect," which occurs when even people who don't sell their homes or portfolios feel wealthier because they are wealthier on paper. As a result of the wealth effect in the 1990s, consumers probably spent (and borrowed) more freely than they otherwise would have.

Price stability, along with high employment, are the goals of government economic policy. A stable currency enables everyone, wealthy or poor, consumer or businessperson, debtor or creditor, to make better, more confident financial plans and decisions.

The Ultimate Issue: Quality of Life

Ultimately, wealth and poverty are quality of life issues. Wealth obviously improves it, but poverty undermines the quality of life for everyone in an economy, not just the poor. Poverty generates crime, broken families, drug addiction, illness, illiteracy—and more poverty. Many people decry the cost of government programs to deal with poverty and its side effects. However, the "hidden costs" of poverty, which go beyond the suffering of the poor, are staggering. These costs include property loss, deteriorating real estate values, bodily injury, and increased public and private expenditures for insurance, law enforcement, court cases, prisons, and health care, plus the lost productivity of people who could be employed or more gainfully employed.

These costs are borne by everyone. The wealthy arguably bear the largest share of the cost because they pay the largest share of income taxes. They also insulate themselves from the effects of poverty by inhabiting exclusive suburbs, using private schools, and so on, yet the social repercussions of poverty are difficult to escape.

Ensuring minimum levels of nutrition, shelter, safety, health care, and education for everyone may well be within the capabilities of the most productive economy in human history. Again, however, that is a political issue. Moreover, as we will see in the next two chapters, the federal government has its hands full simply managing its budget and keeping the economy stable and growing.

The Least You Need to Know

- Often, it is income inequality rather than actual destitution that creates poverty in an economy.

- A little over 10 percent of U.S. households are defined as living in poverty, which translates to a family of three living on about $14,000 a year.

- Income inequality is a fact of life in the United States, and it is becoming more pronounced.

- The reasons for growing income inequality include changing employment patterns, increased returns to education, and changes in the composition of households.

- The U.S. government helps the poor through progressive income taxes, public assistance programs, economic development programs, and management of the economy for low inflation and unemployment. Yet the United States provides a lower level of government support for health and human services than most developed European nations.

Chapter 12

Hey, Big Spender! The Federal Budget

In This Chapter

◆ What the government does in the economy

◆ The federal budget and where it goes

◆ Government agencies that affect the economy

The main title of this chapter—Hey, Big Spender!—is meant to be somewhat ironic. Americans tend to distrust government in general and big government in particular. But, as I've noted, the U.S. government plays a smaller role in the U.S. economy than the governments of most developed nations play in theirs. U.S. taxes are lower, and public programs are smaller.

Still the government's role in the economy is one area where politics can be expected to intrude on economics, and it does. In this chapter, I will try to keep politics at bay and *describe* the role of the government, the money involved, where it comes from, where it goes, and the government agencies that most affect the economy. In other words, in this chapter our goal is to understand the government as the "G" in the C + I + G formula for GDP. The next chapter and Part 4 deal with economic policy.

Role of Government in a Capitalist Economy

In a way, the political arguments that rage on in America are relatively trivial. While there are serious situations to address—poverty, crime, drugs, and terrorism—the vast majority of Americans largely agree on the basic principles that rule the economy.

Most Americans agree on the individual's right to private property; the government's right to issue currency, levy taxes, and borrow money; and the rights of businesses and consumers to enter agreements and to resolve their differences through legal channels. (Immigrants marvel at how easy it is to start a business in America.) Few people believe that laws regarding child labor, toxic waste, food and drug purity, and the financial markets should be repealed.

For some 90 percent of the adult population, the political and economic arguments really amount to whether the federal government should account for 20, 22, or 18 percent of the economy. Legislators of both parties in both houses of Congress grab as much federal money as they can carry back to their constituents, and the constituents don't send it back to Washington in protest.

By and large there is general agreement on the role of government in the U.S. economy, which is to …

- ◆ Provide the public goods that society requires

- ◆ Issue currency, levy taxes, and borrow money

- ◆ Maintain economic order, stability, and growth

Let's examine each of these roles.

EconoTalk

A **public good** is a good that society requires and that benefits everyone but that the private sector holds no economic incentive to provide. Public goods cannot be divided up and distributed through a market to consumers, who may or may not choose to buy them. Rather, they are made available to everyone, and everyone benefits from them.

The Government Provides Public Goods

Public goods are those that society requires and that benefit everyone, but that the private sector has no economic incentive to provide. Public goods benefit everyone, whether they pay for them or want them or not. The most basic public good is defense of the populace from attack and invasion. This begins at our borders and extends inward to the formation of police forces at the federal (the Federal Bureau of Investigation), state, and local levels. Other public goods include the highway system and traffic lights, clean air and water, and public education.

There is a tradeoff—as always in economics—between public goods and private goods. Societies allocate their resources to both, in a mix that works for them. Some societies employ a mix weighted toward private goods, while others prefer a mix weighted toward public goods. In general, the more developed an economy becomes, the more resources it devotes to public goods.

> **EconoTip**
>
> In economics, the term government often means government at all levels: federal, state, and local. For instance, the "G" in C + I + G includes all three levels of government. In this book, I have generally indicated which levels of government are under discussion.
>
> It's wise to understand what people mean when they say "government." For instance, many people oppose "big government," meaning the federal government, because they want more governmental decisions made at the state and local levels, where they have more control. They simply prefer local government to federal government.

The government provides public goods by administering the budget and overseeing the delivery of the goods. However, in most cases the goods are actually provided by the private sector. The personnel for the armed services are an exception, but even for defense, most of the equipment and weapons are manufactured by the private sector.

Currency, Taxes, and Borrowing

The federal government issues the nation's currency, levies taxes, and, when taxes don't cover federal spending, borrows money by issuing government securities. We will discuss the federal agencies responsible for these functions later in this chapter.

Each of these three functions are subject to debate, especially taxes and deficit spending, which we cover in Chapter 13. Currency arouses little debate, although many people first hated the redesign of U.S. money a few years ago.

Order in the Economy!

The federal government in any society tries to maintain order and growth in the economy. Disorder in the economy leads to social unrest and political upheaval. Lack of economic growth leads to unemployment, which also generates unrest. If poor economic growth persists, a nation may even wind up unable to defend itself from attack or invasion. For instance, the economy of the USSR under socialism could not sustain itself, which led to the breakup of the Soviet Union.

Most modern governments take an active role in managing their economies through economic policies. These policies aim to maintain a stable currency and economic growth at a rate that balances inflation and unemployment.

In socialist and communist economies, such as China and North Korea, the government uses central planning to gauge demand and make production decisions. This stands in sharp contrast to the role of government in a market economy. In a market economy, the government usually acts as a referee, ensuring that the market works properly and achieves the goal of delivering the greatest good to the greatest number of people.

EconoTalk

Antitrust suits are legal actions initiated by the Justice Department to stop companies from engaging in anti-competitive practices or from becoming so large that they constitute a monopoly. Anti-competitive practices include any agreements or actions designed to limit competition, such as agreements among competitors to fix prices at a certain level.

Toward that end, the U.S. government regulates certain activities in the market. For example, the Justice Department occasionally launches *antitrust suits* to limit monopolistic business practices, as it did against Microsoft in the late 1990s. The federal government will occasionally levy tariffs and erect other barriers to trade to protect a domestic market from foreign competition, as it did with certain steel imports in 2002. The Securities and Exchange Commission initiates suits against companies that violate securities law, as it did in 2001 and 2002.

In other words, society uses the government to limit behaviors that could distort the workings of the market for the benefit of a few unscrupulous or powerful competitors at the expense of everyone else.

The Government Share of the Economy

In the U.S. economy, total government spending at all levels represents about 28 percent of GDP. Private spending makes up the other 72 percent. That 28 percent figure breaks down as shown in Figure 12.1.

As the figure shows, of the 28 percent of GDP that government spending represents, direct federal programs (programs administered by the federal government) represents 16 percent while state and local spending represents the other 12 percent. Of that 12 percent, about 9 percent is raised by the states and local jurisdictions, and about 2 percent comes from federal government grants. The two numbers—9 and 2 don't add up to 12 because of rounding differences in the government data. That reminds me of a quote attributed to Senator Everett Dirksen: "A billion here, a billion there, and pretty soon you're talking about real money."

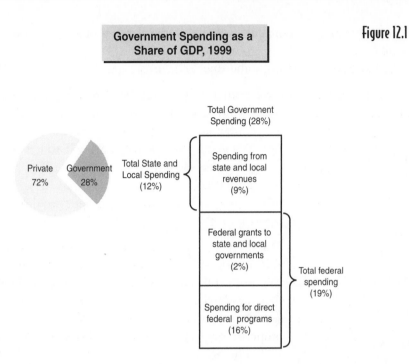

Government Spending as a Share of GDP, 1999

Figure 12.1

The government share of GDP is substantially larger in other industrialized economies. In the 1990s in Italy, France, and Germany, government expenditures accounted for 45 to 55 percent of GDP, and in the United Kingdom, 40 to 45 percent.

Budgeting Billions

As is the case in most financial situations, understanding the budget is the key to understanding the government's finances. Each year the federal government undergoes a budgeting process in which the White House Office of Management and Budget (OMB) develops a budget that the president proposes to Congress.

Congress reviews this proposed budget and goes through its own budget process. In that process, Congress passes a budget resolution with targets, expressed in dollars, for total spending and revenues and for the surplus or deficit. Congress also allocates total spending between *discretionary spending* and *mandatory spending*. Finally, Congress approves its spending and revenue bills, which then are turned over to the president to be signed.

The distinction between discretionary and mandatory spending is key. Discretionary spending accounts for only one-third of all federal spending. This amount is what the president and Congress must decide to spend in the next year, which they do by means of 13 annual appropriations bills, which Congress passes and the president signs. These bills allocate money to activities such as the FBI, Coast Guard, housing, education, space programs, highways, defense, and foreign aid.

Mandatory spending accounts for two-thirds of federal spending and is authorized by permanent laws, not by the 13 annual appropriations bills. These include entitlements, such as Social Security, Medicare, veterans' benefits, and Food Stamps. They are called entitlements because citizens are entitled to the benefits, based upon their age, income, military service, or other criteria. Mandatory spending also includes interest on the *national debt*.

EconoTalk

Discretionary spending accounts for one-third of the federal budget and pays for activities that require annual approval and appropriation of the amount to be spent. **Mandatory spending** accounts for the rest of the budget and pays for entitlements—payments that citizens are entitled to because of their age, income, disability, or military service—and interest on the federal debt.

EconoTalk

The **national debt**, also called the federal debt, is the sum of all outstanding borrowings of the federal government. This debt is owed to the holders of U.S. government securities, such as savings bonds, treasury bonds, and treasury bills. Essentially, it is all the money borrowed to finance past budget deficits that has not been paid back.

Mandatory spending could be changed by changing the laws that govern the entitlements. But otherwise, that money has to be spent according to the law. Discretionary spending requires the Congress and president to appropriate the money to fund it. As a practical matter, changing the laws regarding entitlements is politically quite difficult, and annual appropriations, especially for activities such as defense and education, are not exactly optional in the true sense of the term. The allocation of discretionary spending may be at issue—foreign aid, for example, is usually controversial—but huge sums for discretionary spending always wind up in the budget.

The federal government's fiscal year begins on October 1. Fiscal year 2004, for instance, begins on October 1, 2003 and ends on September 30, 2004. During the fiscal year, the relevant government agencies spend and disburse the budgeted money. As they do, the agencies, OMB, congressional committees, and General Accounting Office (GAO), all monitor the amounts spent and the effectiveness of the programs being funded. (The GAO is the main auditing department of Congress.)

Where It Comes From

The federal budget is managed like most household and business budgets: money comes in from various sources of revenue, and money goes out to pay various expenses. If revenue does not cover the expenses in a given period, the household or business borrows the money to meet the expenses.

Increasing levels of debt usually indicate a need for a course of action other than continued borrowing. One is raising revenues. The householder can take a second job or find a higher paying one. The business can raise its prices or push into new markets. The government can raise revenues in various ways, such as raising tariffs on imports. But the only meaningful way for the federal government to increase revenue is to increase taxes.

Economically, increasing taxes can make sense, as we'll see in Chapter 13. Politically, it can mean professional suicide for the president and legislators. It's the old story: Everyone wants to go to heaven, but nobody wants to die. People want government services, but they don't want to pay for them.

Income taxes on individuals account for about 48 percent of total federal revenue. That percentage may sound low to you, but payroll taxes, which are paid by individuals and businesses, account for another 33 percent. Payroll taxes include taxes for Social Security, Medicare, and unemployment insurance. That brings total revenue from income and payroll taxes to about 80 percent.

Corporate income taxes contribute about 10 percent of total revenue. The other 10 percent comes from excise taxes, estate and gift taxes, customs duties, and miscellaneous revenues, such as fines.

EconoTip

User fees and service fees charged by the federal government are not included in revenue. The government subtracts collections from business-like activities, such as entrance fees at national parks, from spending instead of adding them to revenues. In 2001, these collections came to about $215 billion, or about 12 percent of the $1.8 trillion budget that year.

Figure 12.2 shows the breakdown of federal revenues by source.

As of this writing, the federal government must raise over $2 trillion a year, every year. That's tough to do when you're cutting taxes. So, can the government cut spending?

In theory, yes. Since 1980, the beginning of President Ronald Reagan's first term, presidents and legislators have been promising to reduce taxes *and* make the federal government smaller. Attempts to reduce taxes have occasionally succeeded: President Reagan reduced taxes in the early 1980s—and a decade of higher deficits ensued because no one remembered to reduce federal expenditures. George W. Bush may succeed in locking in long-term tax cuts, but don't bet the ranch on a reduction in federal expenditures.

Figure 12.2

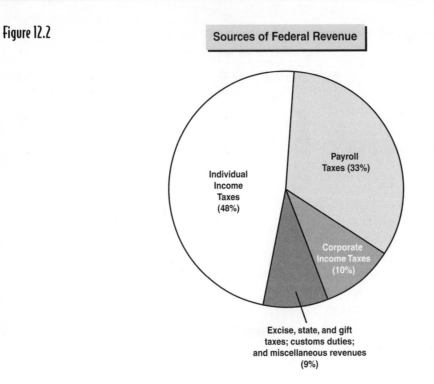

Sources of Federal Revenue

Individual
Income
Taxes
(48%)

Payroll
Taxes (33%)

Corporate
Income Taxes
(10%)

Excise, state, and gift
taxes; customs duties;
and miscellaneous revenues
(9%)

A closer look at where the money goes will reveal why.

Where It Goes

Recall that two-thirds of the federal budget is spent on entitlements. Of these mandatory expenditures, the largest one is for Social Security, which accounts for about 23

EconoTalk

Means-tested entitlements are those that people are eligible for only if they meet certain criteria. The criteria usually have to do with income, age, assets, and other measures of a person's financial and living condition.

percent of total federal expenditures. The next largest mandatory expenditure is for Medicare (12 percent) and Medicaid (7 percent), which add up to 19 percent of total federal expenditures. So about 42 percent of the federal budget is going to Social Security and subsidized health care. Other *means-tested entitlements* and mandatory payments and *net interest* on the federal debt add up to 23 percent. So, the 42 percent for Social Security and subsidized health care and the 23 percent for other entitlements and net interest equal 65 percent, or about two-thirds of total expenditures.

Figure 12.3 shows the breakdown of federal expenditures.

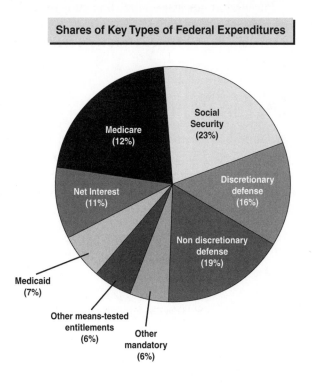

Shares of Key Types of Federal Expenditures

Figure 12.3

(Source: Office of Management and Budget)

Here's why it's so difficult to reduce federal expenditures. The so-called entitlements are mainly either agreements between the government and certain citizens, or forms of assistance for people who need health care, in the case of Medicare and Medicaid, or food, in the case of Food Stamps. These are difficult areas in which to reduce spending. That's especially true of Social Security.

How discretionary is discretionary spending? The United States cannot decide to spend nothing on defense for a year or two, or even cut it by $10 or $20 billion (especially now that the nation faces the threat of terrorism). As for nondefense spending, programs such as government financed research in science and technology require ongoing support or they will fall apart. If they are already in place and achieving progress, they stand a good chance of receiving continued funding. The same goes for programs that support education, transportation, and law enforcement.

EconoTalk

Net interest is the interest paid out on government securities, minus interest earned. The federal government earns interest on loans it extends domestically (such as student loans) and to foreign governments, and on its holdings of foreign government bonds. (The U.S. government does not buy corporate stocks and bonds.)

Is there really much spending that can be cut? The average citizen thinks so, and the average politician says so, but with an annual budget that runs to thousands of pages and a constituency for every program, elected officials seem unable to find much to cut. A look at the largest program, Social Security, provides some insight regarding the reasons.

Social Security: A Case in Point

Let's try to clear the air around Social Security, which has become quite cloudy. First, many people seem to think that Social Security is a "welfare" program. It may be one in the sense that it aims to ensure people's welfare. But the term "welfare" typically refers to programs for poor people. There are some extremely well off—even wealthy—people cheerfully cashing their Social Security benefit checks every month.

Why? Because people who receive Social Security typically spent years paying Social Security taxes believing that they were accruing those benefits for themselves by paying those taxes. That is, in fact, the agreement between the government and those who pay Social Security taxes.

Social Security was enacted by Congress in 1935 as a social insurance program in which workers pay into the system during their working lives and earn entitlement to family benefits upon retirement, disability, or death. About 44 million Americans currently receive benefits, including 30 million elderly retirees and their dependents, 6 million disabled workers and their dependents, and more than 7 million survivors of deceased workers. These figures include more than 3 million children.

About 96 percent of U.S. workers contribute to Social Security, currently paying 6.2 percent of their wage income up to $68,400. That amount is matched by the employer, while the self-employed pay the entire 12.4 percent themselves. These payroll taxes are by far the largest source of funding for the program.

Unfortunately, the system operates on a pay-as-you-go basis, which means that the money being paid into the fund by current contributors is going to the people who currently receive Social Security benefits. The system collects more in payroll taxes than it pays out to beneficiaries. Where, you might be wondering, does the rest of the money go?

It goes into the Social Security Trust Fund, which now has about $600 million in it. But that's not entirely accurate. The *money* is not going into the Trust Fund. The money is being spent on other government expenditures. Government bonds are going into the Trust Fund, in the amount of the excess Social Security taxes collected for the benefits paid each year. In other words, the government is borrowing the money from the Trust Fund.

Problems Ahead

Regardless of political viewpoint, everyone agrees that if no changes to the system are made, at around 2012 or 2014, the Social Security system will be collecting less in revenues that it will be paying out in benefits. That's because the famous baby boomers, the 77 million people born from 1945 to 1964, will be retiring in numbers that will suck up more money than the contributors will be paying in.

One solution to this financial dilemma is to raise the payroll taxes or to lower the benefits at that time, now, or between now and that time. Another is to reduce government spending in other areas. Each of these measures is unpopular and politically difficult. Other proposals abound, but mostly they just reduce benefits, either by raising the retirement age or paying people only the benefits that they need (in other words, means-testing). Another proposal is to partially or completely privatize the system, which would radically alter its character. Besides, doesn't the marketplace already provide thousands of ways to invest privately? Yet another proposal is to invest the money in stocks, but that brings market vagaries into the picture. (What happens, for example, in a multiyear bear market?)

Some people look to the Social Security Trust Fund to make up the shortfall. They say that the fund, which will continue to grow until 2014, will be sufficient to make up the shortfall until 2034. The question those people must answer is this: If the government will not have the money to pay full benefits from taxes being collected at the time, where will it get the money to repay the bonds in the Trust Fund?

In 1983, Congress started taxing the Social Security benefits of high-income retirees, raised the retirement age, and raised the payroll taxes. In raising the payroll taxes, the government promised that the accumulated balances in the Trust Fund would guarantee future benefits. But the government put bonds in the Trust Fund and spent the money on other things. To "take money" out of the Trust Fund to pay benefits, the government must first "put money" into the fund by repaying the bonds (with interest, I might add). There really is no way for the government to do that without raising taxes, cutting spending, or cutting Social Security benefits.

What's the Solution?

Economics can indeed be a dismal science, because ultimately it is about addition and subtraction. No household, business, or society can borrow money to pay for something in the future, spend the money now, and expect the money to be there in the future. That is exactly what the Social Security Trust Fund enables people to expect. The Trust Fund does represent the Social Security system's claim on future government funds. But those funds will have to come from somewhere, and the only source is the taxpayer, who must pay more in taxes or make do with fewer government services.

The "solution" in any situation ruled by economics is for people to face the facts. But, as in many households and businesses, people avoid unpleasant facts. These people eventually go bankrupt. The U.S. government will not go bankrupt, and in all likelihood neither will the Social Security system. But the system will not pay benefits at the current rate to retiring baby boomers without a tax hike or reduced spending on other programs at some point.

The Real World

The United States experiences intense conflict over the mix of public and private goods that society should have. In the past 20 years, it has become fashionable to discuss public goods in pejorative terms. But nobody wants to do without the public goods that benefit them personally, whether it's Social Security benefits, public education, low prices for farm products, or the presence of the FBI. The conflict over the mix can be healthy, and Americans are suited to resolving arguments through adversarial means (as our legal system demonstrates).

What disturbs the economists I know is the lack of honesty that pervades arguments over the mix of public and private goods. Democrats lean toward government solutions to societal problems, but they refuse to tell people about the price in higher taxes or lower government services in other areas. Republicans lean toward lower taxes and private solutions to societal problems, but they refuse to tell people about the reduced services that go along with lower taxes, or about the lack of private solutions to certain problems.

In the absence of honest discussion about these kinds of decisions, the process is reduced to a "battle of the bumper stickers" that serves people badly and drives economists crazy.

Government Agencies That Affect the Economy

Virtually every government agency affects the economy by its very existence, by doing its work, and by keeping people gainfully employed. But some government entities exist mainly to deal with the nation's business, economic, and financial matters. Here we briefly examine the most important ones aside from the president and the Congress, which we've already discussed.

The Treasury (www.ustreas.gov)

The Department of the Treasury was established by an act of the first Congress and has been overseeing the nation's money ever since. Key areas of the department include the following:

- **Internal Revenue Service:** assesses and collects taxes within the country and is the largest of the Treasury's bureaus

- **Office of the Comptroller of the Currency:** regulates and supervises national banks

- **Bureau of Printing and Engraving:** designs and manufactures U.S. currency

- **U.S. Mint:** designs and manufactures coins

- **Bureau of the Public Debt:** borrows money to finance the deficit and administers the public debt

- **Financial Management Service:** receives and distributes public funds, maintains government accounts, and prepares reports on the government's finances

Along with a few other bureaus, the U.S. Customs Service, the Secret Service, and (of all things) the Bureau of Alcohol, Tobacco, and Firearms also come under the Treasury Department. (Alcohol and tobacco are heavily taxed, but how do guns figure in this?)

Department of Commerce (www.commerce.gov)

Established by an Act of Congress in 1903, the Department of Commerce deals with commercial and industrial matters within the nation's borders. Significant areas include:

- **Bureau of Economic Analysis:** compiles and analyzes economic data for the government and the public, with assistance from the Economic and Statistics Administration

- **Census Bureau:** compiles and analyzes demographic data on the population

- **Patent and Trademark Office:** ensures that inventors can register and benefit from ownership of their inventions

- **Economic Development Administration:** stimulates job, commercial, and industrial growth in economically distressed areas

- ◆ **Small Business Administration:** promotes the formation and sound management of small business

- ◆ **Minority Business Development Agency:** promotes formation of minority businesses

- ◆ **International Trade Administration:** encourages and monitors export and import activity

Federal Reserve (www.federalreserve.gov)

The Federal Reserve (the Fed) regulates the banking system, implements monetary policy, maintains the stability of the financial system, and provides certain services to financial institutions. The Fed is so important to the U.S. economy that it is discussed in depth in Part 4.

Council of Economic Advisors (www.whitehouse.gov/cea/about.html)

The President's Council of Economic Advisors is a team of three professionals from the worlds of business, finance, and economics, appointed by the president, and served by a staff of about 20 additional economists and four statisticians. (The chairman of the council is almost always a professional economist.) The Council monitors and interprets economic developments in the nation, appraises the effects of various programs, and advises the president on economic policy.

Regulatory Agencies

Federal regulatory agencies, such as the Federal Aeronautics Administration, the Food and Drug Administration, the Federal Communications Commission, among many others, affect segments of the economy by virtue of the roles they play in important industries. Essentially, these agencies oversee their respective industries and try to balance the industry's interests against those of the public and the economy.

State and Local Governments

Finally, state and local governments work hard to ensure that their economies grow and remain robust. Through the power to tax, spend, regulate, and support programs that benefit education and the industrial infrastructure, these governments strongly affect the environment for business and household formation, employment, construction, and other key economic activities.

In 2002, most state and many local governments, including those of some of the largest U.S. cities, were facing serious financial challenges. Most of these revolve around budget deficits generated during the recession in 2001 and slow growth in 2002. The situation regarding increasing taxes and decreasing services at the state and local levels resembles that at the national level. Nobody wants to do either.

However, unlike the federal government, states and cities cannot print money and do not have virtually unlimited access to the debt markets. They must be more realistic about raising taxes, cutting services, and avoiding debt, and manage their budgets far more aggressively. When they do raise or reduce taxes the effect is similar to that at the national level, but on a far smaller scale. We learn about the effect of changes in taxes in Chapter 13.

Government the Enemy?

Although it's fashionable to knock the government, the fact is that the U.S. economy wouldn't be the powerhouse that it is without it. Aside from the federal government's 19 percent share of GDP, its economic policies have clearly contributed to the stability and growth of the U.S. economy.

Moreover, in a democracy, people get the government they vote for. Thus, if the government appears to be at odds with itself over the mix of public and private goods that society wants, it may well be because society is at odds with itself over the matter. If elected officials won't discuss economic realities honestly, then perhaps the citizens have given them no incentive to do so. Fortunately, the U.S. economy appears to be sound enough to absorb these imperfections and still provide one of the highest standards of living in the world.

The Least You Need to Know

- ◆ All government spending amounts to about 28 percent of gross domestic product (GDP). Of that 28 percent, about 16 percent goes to federal programs, and 12 percent goes to state and local programs.

- ◆ Discretionary spending accounts for one-third of the federal budget and requires annual appropriation of the amount to be spent. Mandatory spending accounts for the remaining two-thirds of the budget and pays for entitlements and interest on the federal debt.

- ◆ Although elected officials talk about cutting taxes and reducing spending, either is extremely difficult to do because the taxes and spending pay for programs that people want—even if they don't want to pay for them.

◆ The Social Security system will face a crisis around 2014, when the baby boomers begin to retire and payroll taxes will no longer cover the payments to beneficiaries.

◆ The real issue between the government and citizens is the mix of public and private goods society wants.

13

Fiscal Policy and Economic Growth

In This Chapter

◆ Goals of fiscal policy

◆ How fiscal policy works

◆ The record of tax, spend, and borrow

Although two-thirds of the federal government's expenditures are manda-tory and many of the discretionary expenditures are not all that discre-tionary, even a small portion of the federal budget represents billions of dollars. Those billions can make a big difference to an industry, region, or segment of the population, and to the economy.

Moreover there are decisions about taxes, which may be even more impor-tant. Cutting taxes is popular, so elected officials are always happy to talk about it and sometimes actually do it (as President Kennedy did in 1963 and President Reagan did in 1981). Officials also occasionally raise taxes, which can profoundly affect the economy—and their careers.

This chapter examines fiscal policy—the budget decisions of the federal government—and its consequences. It also covers deficit spending and the national debt, both of which have been major topics in the public discussion about the economy.

Government's Unique Situation

As you know, if any element of the C + I + G + (Ex − Im) formula increases, then GDP—total demand—increases. If the "G" portion—government spending at all levels—increases, then GDP increases. Similarly, if government spending decreases, then GDP decreases.

EconoTip

The interest rate on U.S. bonds is considered the risk-free interest rate because there is no credit risk associated with them. There is, however, the risk of inflation. Therefore, the rate on a government security represents the price to "rent" that money for that period of time with the certainty that it will be paid back, plus any inflation premium.

EconoTalk

The **tax base** in a nation, region, state, or city is the number of workers and businesses who can be taxed. The term usually refers to income taxes, but in the case of states and cities, it also refers to sales and property taxes.

When it comes to financial management, four characteristics of the government set it apart from households and businesses (the "C" and "I" in the formula):

♦ **Government has the power to tax, which gives it greater control over its revenue.** Federal, state, and local governments can mandate higher taxes and increase their revenues. Households and businesses have the more difficult task of selling their labor, goods, and services in order to raise revenue.

♦ **By increasing or decreasing taxes, the government affects households' level of disposable income (after-tax income).** A tax increase will decrease disposable income, because it takes money out of households. A tax decrease will increase disposable income, because it leaves households with more money. Disposable income is the main factor driving consumer demand, which accounts for two-thirds of total demand.

♦ **The federal government can finance budget deficits by borrowing in the financial markets.** Investors consider U.S. government bonds to be risk free, because they are backed by the taxing power of the government. States and cities also issue bonds to finance deficits. These bonds, however, are considered riskier because the *tax base* of the state or city could erode.

♦ **The federal government—and only the federal government—can print more money.** Like raising taxes, this has potential economic consequences (in the form of higher inflation) as well as political consequences. Nevertheless, the federal government does have that option, which is certainly not open to households and businesses.

These unique characteristics set the government apart from the other players in the economy. They also position the federal government to formulate and implement economic policy.

Fiscal Fundamentals

Fiscal policy is the general name for the federal government's taxation and expenditure decisions and activities, particularly as they affect the economy. (Monetary policy refers to policies that affect interest rates and the money supply.)

Figure 13.1 shows how C + I + G add up to determine the equilibrium level of GDP. (For convenience, we're assuming that net exports (Ex – Im) are zero.) Line "C" represents consumption by consumers. Line "C+I" represents consumption by consumers plus investment by businesses. Line "C+I+G" represents consumption plus investment plus government spending.

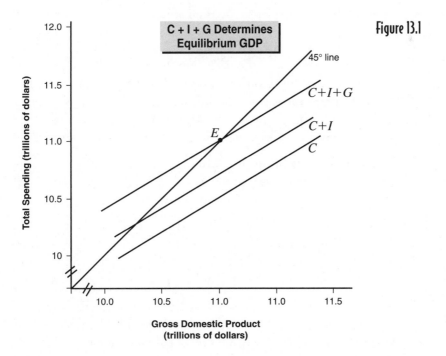

Figure 13.1

The 45 degree line shows all the points at which total spending equals gross domestic product. At any point on that line, the quantity demanded by the households, businesses, and government in the economy (total spending) equals the amount being produced (GDP). Whenever total demand equals total spending, the economy is in equilibrium.

Where is the actual equilibrium point for the economy? Where the total demand of households, businesses, and government—C + I + G—equals their production. That equilibrium point occurs where the line C + I + G intersects the 45 degree line. At that point, which is point "E" on the chart, total spending (total demand) and total production (GDP) are equal.

What About Taxes?

Figure 13.1 ignores taxes, but they are a crucial element in fiscal policy.

Taxes lower households' disposable income. The amount collected in taxes doesn't find its way into consumption ("C"). But if the government spends every dollar that it collects in taxes, then that amount does find its way into total demand through government expenditures. When that occurs, the GDP remains unaffected by taxes. The size of the economy is the same whether people choose to produce and consume private goods (angora sweaters) or public goods (army uniforms). The mix of goods doesn't affect the level of GDP, as long as the total amount spent on them doesn't change.

What happens when the government collects more in taxes than it spends?

Total spending—and therefore the equilibrium level of GDP—decreases. Suppose that the money for army uniforms is collected but not spent. In that case, there's no need to manufacture the uniforms, no need to staff the uniform factory, and no need to pay the workers, who now have less income to devote to consumption.

In general, when the government brings in more in taxes than it spends, it reduces disposable income and slows the growth of the economy. So, the fiscal policy prescription to stabilize an overheated economy is higher taxes.

In times of inflation—when too much demand is bidding up prices—a tax increase, coupled with no increase in government spending, will dampen the upward pressure on prices. The tax increase lowers demand by lowering disposable income. As long as that reduction in consumer demand is not offset by an increase in government demand, total demand decreases.

A decrease in taxes has the opposite effect on income, demand, and GDP. It will boost all three, which is why people cry out for a tax cut when the economy is sluggish. When the government decreases taxes, disposable income increases. That translates to higher demand (spending) and increased production (GDP). So, the fiscal policy prescription for a sluggish economy and high unemployment is lower taxes.

Spending policy is the mirror image of tax policy. If the government were to keep taxes the same, but decrease its spending, it would have the same effect as a tax increase, but through a slightly different channel. Instead of decreasing disposable income and decreasing consumption ("C"), a decrease in government spending decreases the "G" in C + I + G directly. The lower demand flows through to the larger economy, slows growth in income and employment, and dampens inflationary pressure.

Likewise, an increase in government spending will increase "G" and boost demand and production and reduce unemployment.

Those are the fundamentals of fiscal policy, and they are summed up in Figure 13.2.

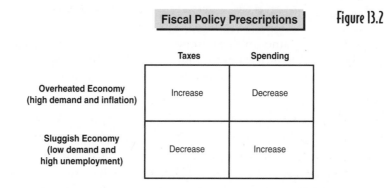

Fiscal Policy Prescriptions   **Figure 13.2**

	Taxes	Spending
Overheated Economy (high demand and inflation)	Increase	Decrease
Sluggish Economy (low demand and high unemployment)	Decrease	Increase

To dampen economic growth and inflationary pressure, the government can increase taxes and keep spending constant, or decrease spending and keep taxes constant. To stimulate growth and reduce unemployment, the government can decrease taxes and keep spending constant, or increase spending and keep taxes constant.

Finally, the government can pursue its fiscal policy objectives more aggressively by simultaneously adjusting both taxes and spending. For instance, in a sluggish economy, the government could decrease taxes *and* increase spending at the same time. Each could be adjusted either by small amounts, so that neither taxes nor spending are changed too radically, or by large amounts to deliver a stronger dose of fiscal stimulus. Similarly, in an overheated economy, the government could increase taxes *and* decrease spending, if it wanted to dampen growth (and enrage voters).

The Real World

I am discussing fiscal policy and monetary policy separately, but in practice they are often used together. Moreover, in recent years, monetary policy has become the more useful tool in economic policy. It can be implemented more quickly than fiscal policy because the Fed stands largely apart from politics. It also works more quickly because the financial markets and the public respond more quickly to changes in interest rates and the money supply than they do to changes in taxes and spending.

Fiscal policy is now primarily more of a tool for stabilizing the economy—for softening the negative effects of a downturn on employment and income and for dampening inflationary pressures. Fiscal policy has also become politicized to the point where useful projections are hard to find in the debate over taxes and spending.

Other Issues in Fiscal Policy

To keep things simple, the previous section omitted three other aspects of fiscal policy: the automatic stabilizing influence of fiscal policy, the multiplier effect, and the propensity to spend or save.

First, fiscal policy exerts an automatic stabilizing effect on the economy, even when the government makes no explicit changes in its tax or spending plans.

When the economy contracts, tax receipts automatically decrease (because incomes decrease). This effect is magnified by progressive taxation, our system applying higher tax rates to higher incomes. Workers who are laid off or lose their overtime pay automatically fall into a lower tax bracket. Their lower taxes bills will partially offset the effect of their lost income. Similarly, when incomes rise, particularly during inflation, *bracket creep* pushes people into higher tax brackets. The higher taxes they pay takes money out of their pockets—money they can no longer use to bid prices up even higher.

Government spending also acts as an automatic stabilizer, especially during downturns. The federal government tends to maintain its general level of spending during recessions, which ensures a solid baseline level of demand from the "G" in C + I + G. Also, programs of unemployment insurance and public assistance help to ease the burden of tough times on households.

Second, the multiplier will boost the effect of an increase or reduction in taxes or spending. For instance, an extra dollar of government spending will

EconoTalk

Bracket creep occurs when inflationary pressure increases wages and pushes a worker into a higher tax bracket. This puts a "double whammy" on the worker, who loses purchasing power—wage-push inflation often increases prices faster than wages—and pays more in taxes. But it helps keep inflationary pressures under control.

flow through the economy and, by being repeatedly respent, will magnify the stimulus provided by that incremental dollar. Likewise, a dollar of reduced spending will take a dollar out of the economy, and the multiplier applies to that as well.

Finally, like the multiplier, the propensities to spend and to save are at work. If the government reduces taxes to stimulate consumption, but households save the money rather than spend it, consumption will not rise, nor will investment. If people save the money, they are "sitting on their wallets" and consumption remains low. If consumption is low, businesses won't invest. This has been a problem in the application of fiscal stimulus in Japan, where people tend to save increases in income.

The Real World

The propensity to spend or to save can alter the effect of fiscal policy. President George W. Bush's proposed long-term reduction in income taxes, which is to be phased in over 10 years, generated controversy. Critics cite the fact that, by the end of the decade, over 50 percent of the reduction in taxes will go to the wealthiest 1 percent of taxpayers. That happens to be true, but if the goal is to stimulate savings—rather than consumption—that may not be a bad thing.

Wealthy households have a higher propensity to save, so giving a disproportionately large share of the tax reduction to them may stimulate savings and, by extension, investment. If, however, the goal is to stimulate consumption, more of the tax reduction should be going to lower income households. Actually, however, the only clearly articulated goal has been to reduce taxes.

Of Deficits and Debt

Aside from taxes, few topics in economics excite more emotion than *deficit spending* and the national debt. Citizens decry the fact that the government spends money more than it takes in, but they blanch at the idea of decreased services or increased taxes. Each of the two major political parties accuses the other of fiscal irresponsibility, and in a way, they are both correct.

As of autumn 2002, the national debt totaled $6.2 trillion—a lot of money. Of that amount, $3.6 trillion was held by the private sector and $2.7 was held in government accounts. I'll discuss the growth of the deficit later in this chapter. First, however, let's look at the two

EconoTalk

Deficits occur when government expenditures exceed revenues. The practice of maintaining or increasing expenditures when revenues will not cover them is called **deficit spending**. Surpluses occur when government revenues exceed expenditures.

prevailing views of deficits and the national debt. One is that deficits and debt harm the economy, the other is that they don't matter.

EconoTip

I am lumping the two issues—deficits and the national debt—together in this discussion. This is proper given the reality of the federal budget, which ran a deficit for all but five years from 1960 to 2001 (1969 and 1998–2001). Continual deficit spending has created the $6.2 trillion U.S. national debt.

However, it would also be proper to treat the deficit and national debt separately. That's because a person could believe in the value of deficit spending, but not believe in accumulating a large national debt. In theory, the government could run deficits in years that required economic stimulus and pay that debt down with surplus revenues in years of expansion. But, as I said, that's in theory. It has certainly not been tried.

Stay Out of Debt!

People who believe that deficits and the national debt do matter point out that …

◆ Continual deficit spending displays lack of fiscal discipline on the part of the government and on the part of the citizens, who want government goodies without having to pay for them.

◆ This lack of fiscal discipline spills over into the private sector, where households and businesses have become "addicted to debt."

◆ Interest payments on the national debt represent a substantial claim on tax revenues that could be better spent on other things.

◆ Future generations will bear the burden of today's debt and either have to pay the interest on it or pay down the principal, or both.

◆ Deficit spending and high debt limit the government's fiscal policy options: If deficit spending is the norm, how much more (deficit) spending will be needed to stimulate a sluggish economy?

◆ Foreign entities now hold about $1 trillion of U.S. government securities. If their willingness to buy or hold that debt diminishes, we would have to absorb it.

These points are hard to contradict, except perhaps for the last one: Foreign entities seem to enjoy the safety, liquidity, and interest rates provided by U.S. government securities.

No, Debt's Okay!

The arguments in favor of continued deficit spending and high national debt are:

♦ The size of the national debt or budget deficit is not an indicator of the condition of the economy. Other factors, such as growth, productivity, employment, and price stability, are all more important. The entire issue is one of politics, not economics.

♦ We owe the debt to ourselves (mostly) and therefore should not be overly concerned about paying it back. Also, we pay the interest on the debt mainly to ourselves, and that money remains in the economy.

♦ While the burden of the deficit is passed on to future generations, so are the Treasury securities and, more important, the assets financed with the debt.

♦ The deficits and the national debt have not grown substantially relative to other measures of the economy's magnitude, including GDP, total income, and total assets in the economy.

♦ Paying down the national debt is not something the nation has to do because the debt can be rolled over indefinitely—that is, continually refinanced by issuing new government securities.

♦ Deficit spending has helped the nation to establish a solid baseline level of demand and has contributed to the outstanding U.S. record of economic growth.

Economists' Two Cents' Worth

Elected officials, candidates for office, and the public tend to move between the two poles. Economists themselves view the issue as quite complex, but on balance generally believe that …

♦ Future generations bear an unfair burden if the debt being passed on to them is not accompanied by a corresponding level of productive capital.

♦ Debt in foreign hands sends money out of the country, but this may be offset if the debt is used to finance capital that produces additional income.

♦ We make the interest and principal payments (mostly) to ourselves. However, these amount to transfer payments when the people paying the taxes are not the same as the people holding the securities and receiving the interest and principal payments.

◆ Indefinite and unbridled deficit spending can lead to inflation and, potentially, economic instability. It can undermine credibility in the government's ability to manage the economy.

The Nobel Prize-winning economist Milton Friedman (who you will meet in Part 5) said it best: "There is no such thing as a free lunch." Is it conceivable that each generation of citizens could consistently demand more public goods and services than they are willing to pay for and generate no economic consequences? Doesn't the situation looming ahead for Social Security (described in Chapter 12) indicate that even the government can run out of rope? Might an aging population find itself unable to handle the level of debt the nation continues to incur? Also, how much of that debt has actually gone into productive plant and equipment? Our review of the budget in Chapter 12 showed that most of the budget, if not the deficit, is in fact not going into productive plant and equipment.

Also if interest rates increase, won't the interest payments on the national debt—which now consume 11 percent of the budget—rise? In the late 1970s, they accounted for 14 percent of the federal budget.

The Real World

Virtually no economist believes that balancing the federal budget every year is possible or even desirable. And they are, after all, the people helping elected officials develop fiscal policy.

However, there are also conservative economists and liberal economists. Republicans bring conservative economists on board, while Democrats bring liberal economists on board. But the definition of "conservative" and "liberal" is in flux when applied to economics.

For instance, from the economics standpoint, a "conservative" has historically been a "deficit hawk"—an official out to minimize deficit spending. Yet since the 1980s, conservatives have become comfortable with deficit spending. Similarly, an economic "liberal" would favor deficit spending in order to stimulate job growth. Yet in the 1990s, Democrats sounded like the deficit hawks. As for government spending, both parties appear to favor it—although often on different programs.

A Look at the Recent Record

Figure 13.3 provides some historical perspective on how the U.S. national debt reached $6.2 trillion.

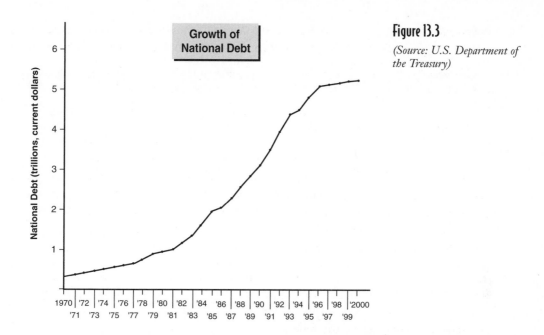

Figure 13.3

(Source: U.S. Department of the Treasury)

From 1970 to 2000, the national debt rose from $389 million to $5.7 trillion, a more than thirteen-fold increase in 30 years. In the preceding 30 years, which included World War II and the mobilization for the war in Vietnam, the national debt rose from $43 million to $389 million, an eight-fold increase.

The largest sustained increase in the national debt occurred from 1980 to 1992, when it rose from $930 million to $4 trillion. Ironically, this is the period of the administrations of Ronald Reagan (1980–1988) and George H. W. Bush (1988–1992)—ironic because Republicans had long been associated in the public mind with fiscal responsibility. Indeed, President Reagan regularly spoke of "those tax-and-spend Democrats." The program of his administration was to "spend and borrow" after cutting taxes. As a result, the national debt tripled during his two terms. Yet President Reagan's strategy for igniting strong growth worked.

As I mentioned earlier, the 1970s had been a period of stagflation: slow growth along with high unemployment, high interest rates, and high inflation. The economic stimulus provided by President Reagan's tax cut in August, 1981—which scaled back marginal tax rates by 25 percent over three years—clearly set the economy on a growth trajectory.

But it also set the national debt on a growth trajectory. The debt rose from $930 million in 1980 to $2.6 trillion in 1988. Some observers point out that this doesn't matter because after the tax cut, government tax receipts doubled from about $500 billion to $1 trillion from 1980 to 1990, due to the higher income in a growing economy. But whatever the increase in tax receipts, it clearly did not come near to covering the increase in government spending—for which each party blames the other.

The Real World

Around 1980, the notion of supply-side economics became popular in some circles. Its central idea is that tax cuts cause economic growth (without deficits) by stimulating investment. Entrepreneurs and executives invest the tax savings in capital equipment, which increases the supply side of the economy—hence the name supply-side economics. The economy grows and tax receipts rise, which eliminates the deficit.

Supply-side economics was promoted by conservative journalists rather than mainstream economists. Many partisans still argue that supply-side economics worked—despite the huge deficits it created and its being disavowed by David Stockman, who was President Reagan's budget director and a main promoter of the program.

Essentially supply-side economics places too much faith in the ability of tax cuts to increase investment. In practice, tax cuts have failed to boost economic growth to the point that the higher tax receipts close the budget deficits. Also, if consumers aren't buying, an increase in investment isn't going to get them to start. They have to be hired first, which they won't be until consumption starts growing. So rather than directly boost investment, the 1981 "supply side" tax cut probably boosted consumption.

Democrats enjoy taking credit for the slower growth of the national debt from 1992 to 2000, President Clinton's administration. During that period, the debt increased from $4.1 trillion to $5.7 trillion, or by 39 percent, well under the almost 300 percent of the Reagan administration. However, the Clinton administration had two things going for it: First, from 1992 onward, the economy grew even more rapidly than it did in the 1980s. Tax receipts rose dramatically, generating budget surpluses from 1998 through 2001. Second, inflation and interest rates remained at historical lows, and the monetary policy that partly engineered that phenomenon clearly contributed to the length and growth rate of expansion. (President Clinton wisely reappointed Fed Chairman Alan Greenspan, twice.)

The Clinton administration also benefited from a new focus on fiscal discipline in both parties, prompted by the deficits of the 1980s. Groups like the Concord Coalition and individuals like Ross Perot—who based his quixotic presidential campaign on deficit reduction—were emblematic of this concern. In 1990, President George H.W. Bush even agreed to a tax increase. It was politically difficult given his famous campaign promise: "Read my lips: No new taxes." Recession followed in 1991, and given the reaction of the public, candidate Clinton won the presidency in 1992.

Some observers trace the expansion of the 1990s to President Clinton's tax *increase* in 1993, which boosted rates on the wealthiest households. The credit may be misplaced, yet the tax increase certainly didn't hurt the economy, and may well have helped.

Wait! How could a tax *increase* help a recovery? Isn't a tax increase supposed to cool a recovery by lowering disposable income?

Ordinarily, yes. However, with the deficits and debt at high levels, some economists believe that "crowding out" and high interest rates hampered the growth of investment at the time. Crowding out occurs when government borrowing makes it harder for the private sector to obtain funds. The resulting competition for the nation's savings also increases interest rates.

The logic of the 1993 tax increase bolstering the expansion is that the financial markets saw it as a harbinger of declining deficits and lower interest rates. Indeed, deficits and interest rates both did decline in the mid-to late-1990s, and investment soared to record levels. It's quite possible that the financial markets and the business community responded positively to the tax increase. Again, it certainly did not hamper the recovery.

So, Who's Right About Fiscal Policy?

Did the tax cut of 1981 lead to the deficits of the 1980s and the need to raise taxes in 1990 and 1993? Did the 1981 tax cut also lead to the expansion of the 1980s? Did the tax increases of 1990 and 1993 help bring about the 1990s expansion?

For what it's worth, I believe the answer to all three questions is yes. But a) I have no political ax to grind, and b) I believe that other factors helped both recoveries, which together actually amount to one, long, nearly 20-year expansion. The period from 1982 to 2000 was a long boom interrupted by a recession in 1991.

By "other factors" I mean the natural business cycle and long-term population trends. These may be the most important factors of all. After the depressed demand of the 1970s, the economy was poised for expansion due to "pent-up demand." The early 1970's tripling of gasoline prices had to be absorbed into the economy. That happened in the 1970s, a time of lackluster growth. In the 1980s, that pent-up demand was released.

In addition, baby boomers had to find employment, get married, buy condos and houses and furniture and appliances, start purchasing new cars, have children, go to Disney World, get divorced and remarried, buy computers and software, join health clubs, get hair transplants, and generally make their contribution to production and consumption. That they did, and it may well be the single largest factor driving the 20-year boom.

However, a business cycle and population-driven boom gives neither political party credit for economic genius. In truth, each major party has its share of good and bad economic policy prescriptions. (I say "major parties" because the flat tax, the Libertarian Party's idea of the federal government paying only for defense, and most economic notions of the Green Party are all too far-fetched for the United States.) Also, as I've noted, the hurly-burly of politics is a better place than most to thrash out the economic questions facing U.S. society.

Fortunately for all of us, there is a less politically charged and equally useful tool for keeping the economy on a long-term, low-inflation, low-unemployment growth trajectory. That would be monetary policy, which we take up in Part 4.

The Least You Need to Know

- ◆ Fiscal policy refers to changes in the federal government's taxation and expenditure decisions and activities aimed at achieving certain economic goals. (Monetary policy refers to the pursuit of those goals by changing interest rates and the money supply.)

- ◆ To dampen inflationary pressure and economic growth, the government can increase taxes and keep spending constant, or decrease spending and keep taxes constant. To stimulate growth and reduce unemployment, the government can decrease taxes and keep spending constant, or increase spending and keep taxes constant.

- ◆ People who oppose high deficits and federal debt believe that they indicate lack of fiscal discipline, that money paid in interest could be better spent on other things, and that future generations will unfairly bear the burden of interest and debt payments.

- ◆ People who believe that high deficits and debt don't matter believe that they are not indicators of the condition of the economy. They hold that we're paying the interest and principal to ourselves, that future generations will inherit the assets financed with the debt, and that deficit spending helps to keep the economy growing.

- ◆ Economists believe that future generations bear an unfair burden if the debt being passed on to them is not accompanied by a corresponding level of productive capital.

- ◆ Each political party has good and bad economic policy ideas, but neither party wants to deliver bad news to voters, who'd rather not hear it anyway.

Part 4

Money, the Banking System, and Monetary Policy

Another realm of government economic activity exists apart from taxes and spending and deficits and debt. This involves the nation's money supply and its banking system. Compared with fiscal policy and its decisions about taxes and spending, the level of interest rates and the supply of money are remote and somewhat mysterious subjects.

They are not, however, remote in their effect on the economy. In fact, monetary policy is in some ways a more useful and powerful tool for achieving the goal of high employment and low inflation. Certain monetary policy measures can change the growth rate, and even the direction, of economy.

This part of the book covers monetary policy and the Federal Reserve System, the institution primarily responsible for formulating and implementing that policy. Here the reasons for the movement of interest rates, the relationship between the banking system and the economy, and the workings of monetary policy itself will all become clear.

14

The Colors of Money

In This Chapter

◆ Definitions of money

◆ How money fuels the economy

◆ Interest rates and credit

It's been said that the most confusing thing in the world to an economist is a $10 bill lying on the sidewalk. He doesn't know whether to pick it up, leave it to be found by someone with a higher propensity to spend, or convert it into pesos.

Indeed the topic of money is far more complex to an economist than it is to a businessperson, consumer, or taxpayer. That's good, because in a modern economy, money takes many forms and behaves in ways that profoundly affect growth, employment, and prices. The better an economist understands the forms that money takes and the ways in which it behaves, the better she will understand our economy. The same goes for us.

This chapter puts money in all its forms under a microscope. It defines money and the money supply and shows how money serves as the lifeblood of the economy. It also explains the basic beliefs of monetarism.

What Is Money?

In Chapter 1, you learned that virtually all economic activity occurs in the form of transactions in which goods or services are exchanged for money. No money, no transactions. Wages, prices, taxes, spending, deficits, surpluses, and debt are all expressed in money.

That's what we mean when we say that money is a medium of exchange. It facilitates exchanges. The alternative is a barter economy, in which people exchange goods and services for goods and services. In a barter economy, people spend a lot of time facilitating exchanges, because an exchange can occur only when each party has what the other one wants.

Barter is so inconvenient that early societies soon came up with mediums of exchange. Gold, silver, furs, and many other substances have been used as money. Money might have intrinsic value, as in the case of furs, which can be used to keep you warm, but it doesn't have to have any intrinsic value whatsoever. Money might also *represent* something that has intrinsic value, such as gold, which can be used to make tableware or to fill dental cavities. In that case money, in the form of paper currency, is said to be "backed by gold" and the economy is said to be on the *gold standard*.

EconoTalk

In a nation with currency on the **gold standard**, the currency represents a certain amount of gold deposited in the nation's treasury. Typically, the currency can be converted into a defined amount of gold, and gold can be converted into the currency. For decades, the U.S. dollar was worth $\frac{1}{35}$ of an ounce of gold, and gold was priced at $35 an ounce.

The United States was on the gold standard for much of the last century, but abandoned it in August 1971, when President Nixon formally ended the convertibility of U.S. currency into gold.

Doing away with the link between the dollar and gold gave both the U.S. economy and the international monetary system, which you'll learn about in Part 5, much greater flexibility.

Today, dollars are backed by "the full faith and credit" of the U.S. government, as the saying goes. With the power to tax individuals, businesses, and imports—among other things—in the world's largest economy, there's a lot of faith and credit backing the dollar. However, the currency can no longer be exchanged for gold. Which brings us to money's true nature: It has value because people will accept it in exchange for goods and services, and they accept it because they know they will also be able to exchange it for goods and services.

Aside from functioning as a medium of exchange, money also serves as a unit of value—a single measure for assessing the value of all the various goods and services produced and sold in an economy. Money is also a store of value—a way of accumulating wealth so it can be used at a later date. Stocks and bonds serve a similar function because they can be quickly converted to money. But money already is money, the most readily available form of wealth.

The Money Supply

Economists have many definitions of money, or, more accurately, the money supply. The money supply includes money as we usually think of it, plus various bank deposits and financial instruments. These deposits and instruments have one thing in common: They are *liquid assets*. A liquid asset is one that can readily be converted into currency.

EconoTalk

Liquid assets are assets that can be quickly converted to money. These include short-term government securities and a variety of other financial assets. Liquid assets are also referred to as **near money**.

The terms liquid assets and *near money* invariably mean short-term assets. For instance, a demand deposit can be accessed almost instantly. It is therefore more liquid than a six-month certificate of deposit.

Economists break the money supply into four groups based on how accessible they are, as follows:.

M-1   currency in circulation

commercial bank demand deposits (checking accounts)

NOW accounts and ATS accounts (Negotiable Order of Withdrawal and Automatic Transfer from Savings)

credit union share drafts

mutual savings bank demand deposits

traveler's checks

M-2   all M-1 assets

overnight repurchase agreements of commercial banks

overnight Eurodollars

savings accounts

time deposits (certificates of deposit) under $100,000

money market mutual fund shares

M-3	all M-2 assets
	time deposits over $100,000
	term repurchase agreements
L	all M-3 and other liquid assets such as:
	Treasury bills
	Savings bonds
	Commercial paper
	Bankers' acceptances
	Eurodollar holdings of U.S. residents

A few of these terms are probably unfamiliar, so I'll define them here:

◆ **Overnight repurchase agreements** (or "repos") are overnight loans between corporations and banks. In this type of transaction, a company with excess cash buys a security from a bank, with the agreement that the bank will buy it back the next day. The security is usually a government security. Both the bank and the company benefit. The bank has the use of the money, and the company gets a higher yield on its money than it would in a checking account.

◆ A **term repurchase agreement** is similar to a repo, but with a longer term. For instance, the bank may agree to buy the security back in 14 days.

◆ **Eurodollars** are dollars in demand deposits in banks outside the United States (not just in Europe).

◆ **Money market mutual fund shares** represent money invested by mutual funds in short-term securities, usually short-term government securities. A mutual fund pools money from various investors and invests it in a designated type of security. For instance, a bond fund invests in bonds.

◆ **Treasury bills** are U.S. government securities with terms of one year or less.

◆ **Commercial paper** consists of short-term—2 to 270 days—obligations (basically IOUs) of large, extremely creditworthy corporations and banks. These are traded in the financial markets and give large institutions easy access to short-term borrowings.

◆ **Bankers' acceptances** are time drafts—checks payable at a specific time in the future—that have been accepted, that is, formally approved for payment, by a bank. Bankers' acceptances are used to finance import and export transactions.

Before 1980, the money supply was mainly thought of as currency and demand deposits. Since then, the definitions of money have expanded to cover new types of liquid assets and the increased amount of funds in these assets. There is still debate about the composition of the money supply, and economists have developed at least 10 different definitions of the money supply. The proliferation of consumer credit gives them even more to worry about. Consider, for example, the "liquidity" that a credit card with an open $10,000 line of credit gives a person.

The Demand for Money

Money is both a medium of exchange and a store of value, which points to the two major types of demand for money: transaction demand and asset demand.

Transaction demand is the amount of money people need to conduct their exchanges in the economy. This includes demand for "walking around money" for lunch and tickets to the movies, as well as demand for money in checking accounts to pay the bills.

Asset demand is the amount of money that people in an economy want to hold as money, usually in bank accounts or in the form of near money, such as shares in money market funds.

Asset demand is motivated by people who save for unexpected contingencies and who would rather hold money than stocks or bonds. For example, when an investor says he has 40 percent of his portfolio in stocks, 40 percent in bonds, and 20 percent in "cash," he is saying that 20 percent is in money market funds, Treasury bills, or similar assets. People increase their holdings of cash when the stock market is shaky. During a bull market, most people who buy stocks are "fully invested," meaning they are holding no cash in their portfolios.

Three forces mainly drive the demand for money: prices, incomes, and interest rates, as follows:

♦ When price levels rise, goods and services cost more, and people need more money to purchase them. Therefore demand for money increases. When prices fall, people need less money and demand for it decreases.

♦ When incomes rise, consumption rises and people spend more money. This, too, increases the demand for money. However, when incomes fall so does consumption, and the demand for money decreases.

♦ When interest rates rise, demand for money *decreases*. That's because high interest rates increase the opportunity cost of holding (that is, not investing) money—the interest forgone. So people don't what to hold money. However, when interest rates fall, people are willing to hold money because the opportunity cost of doing so is low. Therefore, when interest rates fall, demand for money increases.

Of course, we all know that people's demand for money is literally unlimited. The supply, however, is not. That's one reason that money keeps changing hands.

In Circulation: The Velocity of Money

In 2001, M-1—the money used to purchase goods and services—amounted to about $1.1 trillion. That represents the stock of money, the amount of money in the economy. But we know that money exists to facilitate transactions. We also know that the transactions in the economy add up to GDP. If that's so, then what is the relationship between the stock of money—M-1—and GDP?

The stock of money constantly flows through the economy, circulating and repeatedly changing hands in transactions until the end of the year when all those transactions add up to GDP. If GDP in 2001 was about $10 trillion and the stock of money was about $1.1 trillion, then how many times did the stock of money change hands in transactions? Put another way, how many times did the inventory of money turn over?

The answer is nine times, because $10 trillion divided by $1.1 trillion equals nine. In this case, nine is what economists call the *velocity* of money in 2001.

Stated mathematically:

$$\text{Velocity} = \text{GDP} \div \text{M1}$$

EconoTalk

The **velocity** of money is the average number of times that a dollar changed hands in the economy in a period of time. It is calculated by dividing gross domestic product (GDP) by the money supply as measured by M-1.

The velocity of money changes gradually over time with changes in interest rates and other factors. For instance, if interest rates rise, the velocity of money also rises because money flows into investments. That leaves a smaller M-1 to circulate through the economy, and a smaller amount of money must turn over more frequently to produce the same GDP. If incomes rise, the velocity of money also rises, because demand for money increases. When demand for money increases, the stock of money must turn over more frequently.

From the formula for velocity, it is also clear that if velocity increases and the money supply remains the same, then GDP will rise. Why? Because if we rearrange the velocity formula to solve for GDP we get:

$$GDP = M \times V$$

which means that GDP equals the money supply (using M instead of M-1, for simplicity) multiplied by velocity (represented by V).

GDP *has* to equal the money supply times velocity because, by definition, GDP is the sum of all transactions, and transactions are facilitated by money changing hands. Indeed if we plug the real figures into the formula and round the results up to the nearest trillion, we get:

$$\$10 \text{ trillion} = \$1.1 \text{ trillion} \times 9$$

Economists became quite excited upon discovering the velocity of money. (Who can blame them?) They quickly built on the concept to create *monetarism*.

EconoTalk

Monetarism is the school of economic thought that believes that economic stabilization and growth is best achieved by control of the money supply. Monetarists believe that central bank policies that influence interest rates and the availability of credit are the best tools for implementing economic policy.

The Equation of Exchange

As you know, GDP is the sum of the value of all goods and services produced and consumed in an economy, usually in a year. This means that GDP equals the price of all the goods and services produced in the economy multiplied by the quantity of all goods and services produced in the economy. Stated as a formula:

$$GDP = P \times Q$$

where P represents the average price level and Q represents the aggregate quantity of goods and services.

From this formula, the monetarists developed what is known as the equation of exchange. This equation relates the money supply and its velocity to the price level and the quantity of goods and services. Here's the equation of exchange:

$$M \times V = P \times Q$$

where M represents the money supply; V, the velocity of money; P, the average price level; and Q, the quantity of goods and services.

Economists point out that the equation of exchange is true by definition. In other words, the equation states that the number of times the money supply turns over *has* to equal GDP because the stock of money must change hands a certain number of times in order to produce GDP. It also states that GDP *has* to equal the price of the goods and services multiplied by the quantity of goods and services because the quantity of goods and services produced and purchased is valued by their total price. In other words, each side of the equation has to amount to GDP, even though they each get to the number by a different route.

With the equation of exchange in hand, the early monetarists developed the quantity theory of money, which states that the price level is determined by the money supply. If the money supply rises then prices will rise; if the money supply falls, then prices will fall.

The quantity theory of money comes from rearranging the equation of exchange so that you are solving it for velocity:

$$V = \frac{P \times Q}{M}$$

This equation—velocity equals price times quantity, divided by the money supply—led to the quantity theory of money.

Why?

Because if V and Q are constant and the money supply rises, then prices will rise. The early monetarists assumed that V is constant because personal and institutional behavior remains essentially the same over time. They assumed that Q is constant because the economy is at the output level of full employment when inflation occurs. For the early monetarists, the link between the money supply and prices worked both ways. If the money supply falls, then prices will fall—but inflation, that is, rising prices, is usually a monetarist's main concern.

Modern Monetarism

The quantity theory of money was developed by the American economist Irving Fisher (1867–1947) in the early 1900s. Later economists, in particular another American economist, Milton Friedman, recognized two problems in the quantity theory of money: First, velocity does not remain constant and, second, the economy is not always at full employment when inflation occurs.

Yet as these more modern monetarists updated the quantity theory of money, they came to the same basic conclusion as Irving Fisher: Changes in the money supply are the most important factor determining the level of GDP. This is the central belief of monetarists. They also believe that the Federal Reserve should more or less limit its activities to permitting slow and steady growth in the money supply. (The updated theory acknowledges that velocity changes very gradually and that price levels can change even without full employment.)

EconoTip

Milton Friedman, probably the best known practicing economist in the United States, was born in Brooklyn in 1912 and grew up in New Jersey. His ideas fostered the so-called Chicago School of Economics, which is characterized by an emphasis on math and, of course, monetarism.

Friedman's thinking revolved around the role of incomes and consumption on the one hand, and money and the banking system on the other. He believed that these factors were far more important to the economy than the government's role and that markets perform best when unfettered by regulation. Hence, he became identified as an anti-Keynesian as well as a monetarist. His books, such as *Capitalism and Freedom* and *Free to Choose*, both set forth his ideas and served as conservative credentials.

Although he worked at the U.S. Treasury from 1941 to 1943, Friedman spent his career in teaching, research, and writing on economics, based at the University of Chicago. He won the Nobel Prize in Economics in 1976 and retired from teaching in 1977. Since then, he has been associated with the Hoover Institution at Stanford University.

Monetarists generally don't believe in using monetary policy to try to alter the path of the economy. Most monetarists are economic conservatives who believe that the private sector will ensure steady economic growth and that this growth should be accommodated by steady, noninflationary growth in the money supply.

Some monetarists believe that the Federal Reserve and government efforts to fine-tune the economy generally do more harm than good. Some believe that the Fed touched off or worsened the Great Depression. All monetarists believe that the money supply, velocity, and interest rates exert the most important effects on economic growth and prices.

Monetarists and Keynesians have often found themselves at loggerheads. Keynesians believe that changes in taxes and spending by the federal government are the preferred tool for stabilizing the economy during cyclical swings and for ensuring steady growth with high employment and low inflation. Monetarists believe that the money supply has more impact—or at least more potentially positive impact—on the economy than taxes and government spending, which they generally want kept to low levels.

Today, however, most economists believe in employing the most useful tactics of both fiscal policy and monetary policy in a given situation. This is not to say that strict disciples of the Keynesian and monetarist schools—as well as truly outlandish schools—cannot be found. But today's economists, except those bound by ideology or political paymasters, consider every tool at their disposal when confronting complex economic issues.

Where We're Going

Despite the wish of strict monetarists for limited tinkering by the Federal Reserve, activist monetary policy has become an important tool in managing the economy. This has been particularly true during the reign (probably the right word) of Fed Chairman Alan Greenspan.

With an understanding of the money supply, the velocity of money, and their relationship to GDP, we're now prepared to learn how monetary policy works. Chapter 16 will show you how, but first Chapter 15 takes you into the Federal Reserve and the banking system, which is the key medium through which monetary policy is implemented.

The Least You Need to Know

- The key requirement for money is that everyone in an economy accept it in transactions.

- Demand for money consists of transaction demand and asset demand. The demand for money is driven mainly by price levels, income, and interest rates. Demand for money rises when prices or incomes rise, but it falls when interest rates rise.

- Economists define the money supply in various ways. M-1, the most commonly used measure, includes currency, demand deposits, NOW and ATS accounts, credit union share drafts, and traveler's checks.

- The velocity of money is the number of times that the money supply changes hands, or turns over, in an economy in a year. It is calculated by dividing GDP by the money supply.

- Monetarists believe that changes in the money supply are the most important factor determining the level of GDP, and that the Fed should permit steady, noninflationary growth in the money supply.

Chapter 5

The Banks' Bank: The Federal Reserve and the Banking System

In This Chapter

- ◆ The function of the Federal Reserve
- ◆ Key operating units of the Fed
- ◆ How the Fed influences the money supply
- ◆ How the Fed works with the banking system

You've probably heard of the Federal Reserve System before reading this book. You've almost certainly heard of Alan Greenspan, the current Chairman of the Federal Reserve. The business news regularly reports the pronouncements, and even the passing opinions, of the Fed chairman as well as the Fed's monetary policy moves.

The Federal Reserve is so important to the economy that there's a whole cottage industry of "Fed watchers" within the business community. They monitor the Fed's moves, try to fathom the chairman's thinking, and develop forecasts of interest rates, money supply aggregates (M1, M2, and so on), and the growth of the economy.

This chapter takes you into the Federal Reserve System and shows you what it is, how it operates, and why it is so important.

A Bank for All Reasons

The Federal Reserve System is the central bank of the United States. The Fed oversees and regulates the commercial banking system and formulates and implements monetary policy. The goal is to keep the economy on a path of steady growth with low inflation and low unemployment.

The Federal Reserve was created by Congress with the passage of the Federal Reserve Act in 1913. This established the United States' central bank as the lender of last resort for banks in need of liquidity unavailable elsewhere. Establishment of the Fed aimed to shore up the strength of the banking system and the public's faith in the system. Until then, there had been recurring financial problems in the U.S. banking system, notably a wave of bank failures after the Panic of 1907.

Over time the Fed's role expanded. Today the Fed has four main responsibilities:

♦ Formulate and implement the nation's monetary policy

♦ Supervise and regulate banking institutions and protect the rights of consumers who use credit

♦ Maintain the stability of the financial system

♦ Provide certain financial services to the U.S. government, the public, financial institutions, and foreign government institutions

Later in this chapter, I'll discuss how the Fed fulfills these responsibilities. First, let's look at the structure of the organization.

Structure of the Fed

The Federal Reserve System consists of a seven-member board of governors headquartered in Washington, D.C., and 12 regional Reserve Banks located in different U.S. cities.

The members of the Board of Governors are appointed by the president, confirmed by the Senate, and serve 14-year terms. Each member comes from a different Federal Reserve District, which are the regions overseen by the 12 Federal Reserve Banks.

The president appoints, and the Senate confirms, two of these seven members to be Chairman and Vice Chairman of the Board of Governors, which amounts to Chairman and Vice Chairman of the Fed.

The Real World

The current Fed Chairman Alan Greenspan was appointed by President Reagan in 1987 and reappointed every four years by every president since then. His current term ends in 2004. Prior to his appointment, Mr. Greenspan, who was born in New York City in 1926, founded the economic consulting firm of Townsend-Greenspan & Co. He had also served as chairman of President Gerald Ford's Council of Economic Advisors.

Mr. Greenspan received a B.S. in economics (summa cum laude) in 1948, an M.A. in economics in 1950, and a Ph.D. in economics in 1977 (conferred although he had not written a dissertation), all from New York University. He is an avid tennis player, an A-list member of Washington's social set, and reportedly writes his speeches in the bathtub.

He has been frequently described as the second most powerful person in Washington.

The main responsibility of the Board of Governors is to formulate monetary policy. The seven Board Members represent a majority on the 12-member Federal Open Market Committee (FOMC). This committee makes the key decisions affecting interest rates and the availability of credit in the United States. (You'll learn more about the FOMC later in this chapter.)

The board also regulates and supervises banks that are members of the Federal Reserve System, *bank holding companies*, and international banks in the United States. Of the nation's approximately 8,200 commercial banks, about 3,400 are members of the Federal Reserve System. Banks chartered by the federal government—called national banks—must belong to the system, while those chartered by state governments may choose to belong to the system and use the Fed's services. Although member banks are less than half of those in the country, they control three-fourths of the nation's bank deposits.

The board plays a key role in maintaining the nation's inter-bank payment systems, which include the Fedwire and the Fed's automated clearinghouse (ACH). The Fedwire provides electronic funds transfer and payment services. These enable banks to move money and settle accounts for their customers and among themselves. The automated clearinghouse also

 EconoTalk

Bank holding companies are corporations set up to own banks as well as other financial institutions such as finance companies and insurance companies.

processes electronic funds transfers, which enable banks to clear checks and settle accounts.

Finally, the Board of Governors, which meets several times a week, develops regulations governing consumer credit, such as the Truth in Lending Act and the Equal Opportunity Credit Act.

Federal Reserve Banks

The 12 Federal Reserve Banks are the operating arms of the Federal Reserve System. These are "banks for banks" set up and operated by the Federal Reserve System. They are located in Boston, New York, Philadelphia, Cleveland, Richmond, Atlanta, Chicago, St. Louis, Minneapolis, Kansas City, Dallas, and San Francisco. More Fed districts and banks are located east of the Mississippi due to the distribution of the population when the system was created.

Federal Reserve Banks influence the flow of money and credit in the U.S. economy. They hold the cash reserves of depository institutions and make loans to them. They move currency in and out of circulation, and collect and process millions of checks each day. They provide checking accounts for the U.S. Treasury, issue and redeem government securities, and provide other services to banks.

Think of the Federal Reserve Banks as 12 day-to-day operating centers of the Fed, each serving its own district and various government agencies. They operate check processing services as well as the automated clearinghouses (ACHs)—computerized facilities for electronic exchange of payments among banks—that constitute the ACH system. In addition, they operate through a total of 25 Reserve Bank Branches.

> **The Real World**
>
> As you probably know, very little money—as in currency—is actually moved from bank to bank. The vast majority of banking transactions occur through checks and electronic bookkeeping entries. This is probably the way your own personal financial transactions occur.

Each Federal Reserve Bank is supervised by a board of nine directors who review their bank's finances, supervise internal audits, and bring an independent, regional perspective to the Federal Reserve System. The directors also appoint the Reserve Bank president, subject to the approval of the Board of Governors.

The Federal Open Market Committee

The Federal Open Market Committee (FOMC) is the key policymaking body in the Federal Reserve System and makes the key decisions regarding the Fed's open market operations, hence the name of the committee. Open market operations are purchases and sales of U.S. government and federal agency securities. I'll describe how these purchases and sales affect the money supply later in this chapter, but they are critical in implementing monetary policy.

The FOMC has 12 members—the seven members of the Board of Governors and five Reserve Bank presidents. The president of the Federal Reserve Bank of New York is always on the FOMC. The other four seats on the committee are filled on a rotating basis by the presidents of the other Reserve Banks, who serve one-year terms.

By law the committee must meet at least four times a year in Washington. Since 1980, it has met eight times a year, or every five to eight weeks. At each meeting, the members vote on the monetary policy to be carried out until the next meeting. At least twice a year, the committee also votes on its long-run policy objective for growth in the money supply.

The financial and business communities monitor the outcomes of these meetings carefully. When you hear that "the Fed cut the fed funds rate yesterday" or "the Fed raised the discount rate" (I'll explain these rates in a moment), that decision was the result of a meeting of the FOMC. Of course, the Fed can choose not to change those rates, a move that holds its own significance.

A Bit of Background on Banking

The banking system makes it possible for the Fed to change the money supply. So before we look at how the Fed implements monetary policy, some background on the banking system is in order.

Banks in the United States, like banks everywhere, practice what is known as *fractional reserve banking*. Fractional reserve banking emerged when early bankers realized that only a small percentage of deposits would be withdrawn on a given day. For instance, if the bank had total deposits of $10 million dollars, perhaps the most they would see withdrawn on a given day would be $1 million.

This would leave the bank with $9 million available to lend to borrowers. (All banks take deposits and loan them out at a higher rate of interest.) Depositors know their money is being loaned out, and they're comfortable with that. After all, they borrow money when they need it.

Reserve requirements are funds—in the form of cash and other liquid assets—that a bank must, by law, keep in its vaults or on deposit with the nearest Federal Reserve Bank. The reserve requirement is a percentage of the bank's demand deposits and, occasionally, time deposits (that is, certificates of deposit). Currently the requirement is 10 percent of demand deposits.

If the Fed raises the reserve requirement, it will decrease the supply of loanable funds and slow the growth of the money supply. Why? Because funds in the vault or on deposit with a Federal Reserve Bank cannot be loaned out. Also, if the supply of loanable funds decreases, then their price—the interest rate—will increase. This is called tight monetary policy, and it is used to slow the economy down and combat inflation.

Conversely, if the Fed lowers the reserve requirement, banks have more money to lend. A lower reserve requirement increases the supply of loanable funds and speeds up the growth of the money supply. That's because having to keep less money in the vault or at the Federal Reserve Bank, means more money available for banks to lend. If the supply of loanable funds increases, then interest rates decrease, and demand for loans increases. This is called loose, or easy, monetary policy, and it is used to speed up the growth of the economy and combat unemployment.

EconoTip _____

The word "reserve" in Federal Reserve System refers to the fact that U.S. banks are required by law to keep funds—called reserves—in the form of cash or liquid assets either in the bank's own vaults or on deposit with the nearest Federal Reserve Bank.

Funds that banks have on deposit with the Fed or in their own vaults above the amount of the reserve requirement are called excess reserves. Banks are free to lend excess reserves to their customers as well as to one another.

Monetary Moves

The Fed rarely changes the reserve requirement, but it is one of three tools it can use to implement monetary policy. All three monetary policy tools affect the level of reserves in the banking system and the supply of loanable funds. We'll look at the process of money creation later in this chapter. First, let's get familiar with the Fed's main tools of monetary policy:

- Open market operations
- Changes in the discount rate
- Changes in reserve requirements

We'll take these tools one at a time, but first a word of caution: Although writers use the phrase "control the money supply," the Fed doesn't really "control" the money supply, let alone the economy. Instead, using these tools, the Fed *influences* the demand for and the supply of funds that banks must have on deposit at the Federal Reserve Banks (that is, the amount of required reserves). This, in turn, influences the *federal funds rate*, which in turn influences other interest rates, the availability of money and credit, and ultimately the economy. The Fed also uses these tools to influence the amount of excess reserves—that is, the amount of loanable funds—in the banking system.

EconoTip

Federal funds are funds deposited by commercial banks at Federal Reserve Banks. These include the required reserves and any funds beyond the required amount. Required reserves are amounts—expressed as a percentage of checking account deposits—that a bank must maintain in its vault and on deposit with the Fed.

Banks can lend excess reserves to each other on an overnight basis—at the fed funds rate—in order to meet their reserve requirements. The federal funds rate is the interest rate charged by banks for these loans. The federal funds rate is set daily by the market, not by the Fed. That makes it the most sensitive indicator of the direction of interest rates.

The Fed influences—it does not dictate or set—the federal funds rate. (We'll see how in a moment.) That's why an accurate news report will say that "the Fed is targeting a federal funds rate of 3 percent" or whatever. The Fed *targets* a fed funds rate. It does not set the rate.

Open Market Operations

Open market operations are purchases of U.S. government securities from financial institutions and sales of U.S. government securities to financial institutions by the Federal Reserve. Decisions about the purchase or sale of securities in the open market are based on a directive from the FOMC. The directive indicates the approach to monetary policy that the FOMC wants to pursue.

Open market operations enable the Fed to increase or decrease the supply of reserves in the banking system.

Sales of securities by the Fed *decrease* the supply of excess reserves. The *money moves from the banks to the Fed* when the banks pay for the securities. The banks get the securities, and the Fed gets the money. This takes money out of the banking system. Decreasing the supply of excess reserves decreases the supply of funds that banks have available to lend to one another to meet their reserve requirements. This raises the fed funds rate, and slows the growth of the money supply.

Purchases of securities by the Fed *increase* the supply of excess reserves. The money moves from the Fed to the banks when the Fed pays for the securities. The banks get the money and the Fed gets the securities, which puts money—in the form of excess reserves—into the banking system. Increasing the supply of excess reserves increases the supply of funds that banks can lend to one another. This decreases the fed funds rate, and speeds up the growth of the money supply.

The Manager of the System Open Market Account and the staff of the Trading Desk (known as "the Desk") conduct open market operations at the regional Federal Reserve Bank of New York. The actual transactions take three basic forms, depending on the Fed's objectives:

- Short-term repurchase agreements (RPs) are used when the Fed wants to *add* reserves to the banking system temporarily. RPs are the most common transactions at the Desk. In an RP, the Desk buys securities from the banks, which agree to repurchase them at a specific date and price. Upon repurchase, the reserves that were added to the system by the Fed's purchase are automatically subtracted.

- Matched sale-purchase transactions (MSPs) are used when the Fed wants to temporarily *subtract* reserves from the system. MSPs involve a contract for the Desk to sell Treasury bills to a bank, and a contract for the Desk to buy the bills back at a later date.

- Outright purchases or sales of securities by the Fed are used less often than RPs and MSPs. These transactions involve no agreement that reverses the transaction at a later date, so the effect on reserves is more permanent. (Again, the Fed's purchases of securities increase excess reserves, and sales of securities decrease excess reserves.) Outright purchases or sales are used to address a persistent need to increase or decrease reserves.

Open market operations occur every business day and give the Fed the most flexibility in implementing monetary policy. The Desk gathers information from securities dealers and large commercial banks, and data on bank reserves and on the Treasury's operations. With this information and through open market operations, the Fed keeps a finger on the pulse of the money supply and adjusts reserves accordingly.

Changes in the Discount Rate

Changes in the *discount rate* are used less often by the Fed. The discount rate is the interest rate that the Fed charges on loans to member banks. These loans are usually secured by government securities and other short-term paper and are used by the banks mainly to meet their reserve requirements.

These loans, which are made at the Fed's *discount window*, are a privilege rather than a right—one that the Fed discourages banks from using. To receive a discount window loan, the borrower must first use alternative sources of funds, such as the federal funds market. In a normal week, few banks borrow at the discount window. These loans provide a small fraction of the banking system's total reserves.

Therefore, although they affect the cost of funds borrowed at the discount window, changes in the discount rate are viewed in the business community more as indicators of monetary policy. Historically, the rate has changed infrequently, and often remains the same even when monetary policy changes. Incidentally, it is usually lower than the fed funds rate, but the Fed does not allow banks to borrow at the discount rate and loan the money out at higher market rates.

> **EconoTalk**
>
> The **discount rate** is the interest rate that the Fed charges on secured loans to banks that need to meet their reserve requirements. These loans are made at the Fed's **discount window,** and are generally discouraged. (Banks must first use alternative sources of funds.) However, the Fed remains the lender of last resort for the banking system, which is one reason for the discount window.

Changes in Reserve Requirements

The Monetary Control Act (MCA) of 1980 authorizes the Fed's Board of Governors to impose a reserve requirement of 8 percent to 14 percent on demand deposits, and of up to 9 percent on nonpersonal time deposits. There are other provisions of the act and other adjustments to the reserve requirements permitted, depending on a bank's level of deposits.

In practice, the relationship between reserve requirements and money creation is weak. The requirements apply mainly to demand deposits, leaving other accounts beyond the Fed's influence. Moreover, the Fed permits banks to acquire needed reserves from the money markets, as long as they are willing to pay the prevailing federal funds rate.

Therefore, the Fed rarely changes reserve requirements to implement monetary policy. The requirements impose a cost on banks in the form of foregone interest income, a cost that the Fed would rather not impose. Also,

> **EconoTip**
>
> Current reserve requirements are low by historical standards. For instance, from 1937 to 1958, the required reserve ratio on deposits was 20 percent for banks in New York and Chicago, which were "central reserve cities" (a term no longer in use). Today, the requirement is 10 percent, having been reduced from 12 percent in April 1992 in order to put banks, in the Fed's words, "in a better position to extend credit."

banks earn no interest on reserves at the Federal Reserve Bank. The Fed favors paying interest on these reserves, but that requires Congressional approval, which Congress has not given because the taxpayers would pay the interest. As it stands now, the Fed's revenue exceeds its expenses, and Congress and the Treasury like that state of affairs.

The Fed retains the right to raise and lower reserve requirements, whether or not it regularly exercises that right. If indeed the Fed ever needs to administer strong monetary medicine, it is best that it have some on hand.

How Money Is Created

Here's the part of the book I know you've been waiting for: how money is created. It's a beautiful thing to see. Unfortunately, banks are the only outfits legally allowed to create money, and they do it under the auspices of the Federal Reserve.

By "money" I mean deposits, not currency. Most money—most of M-1—exists in the form of deposits. When banks have reserves above the amount required by the Fed—excess reserves—they are allowed to create new deposits. These new deposits are created in the form of loans. So actually the term "money creation" in our economy means expansion of credit and debt.

No single bank can "create money." Some people believe that one bank can take in new deposits and somehow lend out a multiple of that amount. That's not the case. A single bank can only lend out money that it has on deposit. However, numerous banks and the banking system can together expand their loans at a multiple of the new reserves of cash, as you will see in a moment.

First, a few words about a bank's finances. When a bank accepts a deposit, it creates a liability for itself. In other words, the bank is liable for paying the depositor when he wants his money (in the case of demand deposits) or when the term of the deposit has expired (in the case of time deposits, such as six-month certificates of deposit, also referred to as CDs).

When a bank lends money, it creates an asset for itself. The bank is legally entitled to payments of interest and principal over the life of the loan. Indeed, that is how the bank earns its profit—by accepting deposits and making loans.

With that background in banking, let's look at money creation.

The Process in Action: First Round

Let's assume Mudpuddle National Bank has deposits totaling $10,000, a required reserve ratio of 10 percent, and $1,000 in reserves (which is 10 percent of $10,000).

The reserves are the total of the cash in the bank's vault plus its deposits with the regional Federal Reserve Bank. The bank also has loans totaling $9,000.

Here is how Mudpuddle National's accounts would appear.

Mudpuddle National

Assets	Liabilities and Net Worth
Reserves $1,000	
Loans 9,000	Demand Deposits $10,000

Let's also assume that the nation's money supply amounts to $1.2 million, which includes demand deposits of $1 million and currency of $200,000. Here's the composition of the money supply:

Nation's Money Supply

Demand Deposits	$1,000,000
Currency	200,000
M-1	$1,200,000

Now let's assume that Harry Hobstweedle deposits $1,000 in cash into his checking account at Mudpuddle National. Here is the effect on the bank's accounts and on the money supply.

Mudpuddle National

Assets	Liabilities and Net Worth
Reserves $2,000	
Loans 9,000	Demand Deposits $11,000

Nation's Money Supply

Demand Deposits	$1,001,000
Currency	199,000
M-1	$1,200,000

At this point, there is *no effect on the total money supply*, only in its composition: $1,000 moved from currency into demand deposits.

The bank's accounts show $1,000 more in deposits—the liability that it must pay when Harry writes checks against that account—and an additional $1,000 in reserves, or cash in the vault. Here's a key point: Some portion of those reserves are excess reserves, because the bank is only required to maintain reserves of 10 percent against the $11,000 in demand deposits.

If demand deposits are now $11,000 and the required reserve ratio is 10 percent, then the reserve requirement is now $1,100. That means that Mudpuddle National has excess reserves of $900 (which equals $2,000 in reserves, minus $1,100 in required reserves).

Excess reserves generate no interest income, so Mudpuddle National will loan that $900 to an eager borrower. Let's call her Samantha. To give Samantha the money she has borrowed, Mudpuddle National will create a demand deposit account for her (or give her a check drawn on Mudpuddle). The effect on the bank's accounts and on the nation's money supply will be as follows:

Mudpuddle National

Assets	Liabilities and Net Worth
Reserves $2,000	
Loans 9,900	Demand Deposits $11,900

Nation's Money Supply

Demand Deposits	$1,001,900
Currency	199,000
M-1	$1,200,900

At the bank, the cash is still in the vault, but a loan has been booked and a demand deposit has been created—both in the amount of $900, the amount of excess reserves (*not* a multiple of the excess reserves).

Yet, the nation's money supply has expanded! It has grown by $900 because of the demand deposit created to give Samantha her loan. As I pointed out, it is expanding credit—in this instance, extending the $900 loan—that creates money in our economy.

That completes the first round in the process of money creation. The money supply has grown by $900.

The Process in Action: Second Round

Samantha didn't borrow the $900 and agree to pay interest on it in order to let it sit in a checking account. Instead, she will quickly spend that money on the purpose for which she borrowed it. Suppose she uses it to buy an antique clock from Theo.

Theo will take from Samantha a $900 check drawn on Mudpuddle National and deposit it into his account at InterTrust BankCorp. After the check clears, the effect on Mudpuddle and InterTrust will be as follows:

Mudpuddle National

Assets	Liabilities and Net Worth
Reserves $1,100	
Loans 9,900	Demand Deposits $11,000

InterTrust BankCorp

Assets	Liabilities and Net Worth
Reserves +$900	Demand Deposts +$900

There is no additional effect on the money supply at this point.

At Mudpuddle National Bank, when the check clears, Mudpuddle pays the liability of the $900 demand deposit created for Samantha, and does so by using the $900 that was held in its reserves. Samantha's $900 loan remains on Mudpuddle's books until it is paid.

At InterTrust BankCorp, demand deposits rise by the $900 Theo deposited from the transaction with Samantha, and InterTrust's reserves rise by $900.

What happens to complete this second round in the money creation process?

InterTrust BankCorp will lend its excess reserves—in this case $810—to an eager borrower of its own. The $810 figure is the amount of InterTrust's excess reserves. (Multiplying the $900 increase in demand deposits at InterTrust by the 10 percent required reserve ratio yields $90. Taking the reserves of $900 and subtracting the required reserves of $90 yields $810.)

When InterTrust BankCorp lends that $810, it will create a demand deposit of $810 for the borrower. That will increase the money supply by $810, just as the first loan from Mudpuddle National increased the money supply by $900. And that completes the second round of money creation.

There will be a third round of money creation and a fourth round and a fifth round and so on until the banking system reaches a point of equilibrium. That point is reached when no bank in the banking system has excess reserves. The process of each bank lending its excess reserves will continue until that point is reached.

In our example that point will be reached when each dollar of reserves is supporting $10 of deposits. In other words, ultimately, with the 10 percent reserve requirement in our example, the system will make loans that create new deposits until the new deposits reach 10 times the amount of the original new reserves added to the system. The system would ultimately create $10,000 in new deposits, because the initial increase in reserves was $1,000—the amount deposited by Harry Hobstweedle.

The amount of monetary expansion can also be calculated by a simple formula:

$$\text{Change in Demand Deposits} = \frac{1}{R} \times \text{Change in Reserves}$$

Here R equals the required reserve ratio and $\frac{1}{R}$ is called the *deposit expansion multiplier*.

Plugging in the numbers and solving the formula, we get:

$$\text{Change in Demand Deposits} = \frac{1}{.10} \times \$1,000$$

$$\text{Change in Demand Deposits} = 10 \times \$1,000$$

$$\text{Change in Demand Deposits} = \$10,000$$

This is how the banking system creates money and how the money supply keeps expanding.

Now it should be clear how a change in reserves—no matter which tool the Fed uses to bring it about—will affect the money supply. If the Fed creates excess reserves, banks will loan them and that will increase the money supply. Conversely, if the Fed decreases excess reserves, banks will curtail their lending, which will decrease the growth of the money supply. If tight monetary policy were pursued long enough, the money supply would contract as loans were paid off and not fully replaced by new loans.

A Money Tree?

Central banking and a system of money creation gives modern capitalist nations a measure of control over their economies that would otherwise be impossible. Although the Federal Reserve System and the mechanisms of monetary policy are neither foolproof nor guaranteed to yield the intended results, they are dreams come true compared with the traditional alternatives. These alternatives were to have the health of banks depend mainly on the faith of depositors, and to have the money supply depend on the amount of gold being discovered and mined.

EconoTalk

The **deposit expansion multiplier** is the value obtained by dividing 1 by the required reserve ratio. This multiplier indicates the magnitude by which the money supply will expand if excess reserves expand. The dollar amount by which the money supply will expand equals the initial increase in reserves (in the "first round") times the deposit expansion multiplier.

As we will see in the next chapter, monetary policy has compiled a record that's as mixed as that of fiscal policy. Nonetheless, over the past 20 years, it has become increasingly effective as the Fed has become more skilled at formulating and implementing its policies.

The Least You Need to Know

- ◆ The Federal Reserve System (the Fed) formulates and implements monetary policy, regulates banks, maintains the stability of the financial system, and provides services to financial and government institutions.

- ◆ The Federal Reserve System consists of the Board of Governors in Washington and 12 regional Federal Reserve Banks. The Federal Open Market Committee plays a key role in formulating monetary policy.

- ◆ The three main tools for implementing monetary policy are open market operations, changes in the discount rate, and changes in reserve requirements. Open market operations are by far the most important today.

- ◆ Sales of securities in open market operations decrease the supply of excess reserves. Purchases of securities by the Fed increase the supply of excess reserves.

- ◆ Changes in the discount rate are relatively rare and mainly signal the direction of monetary policy. The Fed discourages banks from borrowing at the discount window.

◆ Money creation occurs by means of credit expansion as the banking system responds to changes in the level of excess reserves. Increased excess reserves mean increased lending activity and growth in the money supply. Decreased excess reserves mean decreased lending and slower growth in the money supply.

Chapter 16

Monetary Policy: Stepping on the Gas, Hitting the Brakes

In This Chapter

- ◆ How monetary policy is applied in practice
- ◆ How to become a skilled "Fed watcher"
- ◆ A look at the Fed's record

With a clear understanding of money and how it fuels the economy and of the Federal Reserve System and how it influences the growth of the money supply, you are prepared to see monetary policy in action. As I've mentioned, the Fed can implement monetary policy far more quickly than the president and Congress can agree on the budgetary provisions that constitute fiscal policy. So it's an extremely useful tool. In addition, the financial markets monitor every move the Fed makes (or chooses not to make), and they often respond even more rapidly to monetary policy than the banking system.

In this chapter, we complete our study of monetary policy by examining how it works in practice. You'll learn when monetary policy changes, and what good those changes have done in the past. And you'll learn about the unique role that the Chairman of the Federal Reserve System plays in the economy.

Monetary Policy in Action

In general, a policy acts as a framework for the appropriate action to take in a given situation. The government's economic policy aims to maintain a stable, growing economy with low inflation and unemployment. We've examined the fiscal policy actions that work toward those ends. In a sluggish economy, fiscal policy calls for a decrease in taxes or an increase in spending, or both. In an overheated economy, fiscal policy calls for an increase in taxes or a decrease in spending, or both.

In a sluggish economy, monetary policy calls for an increase in the growth of the money supply, which occurs when the Fed targets a lower federal funds rate, buys securities through its open market operations, lowers the discount rate, or lowers reserve requirements. In an overheated economy, monetary policy calls for a decrease in the growth of the money supply (or even a contraction in the money supply). This occurs when the Fed targets a higher fed funds rate, sells securities, raises the discount rate, or raises reserve requirements.

Ideally, monetary policy stabilizes the economy by cushioning the effects of the ups and downs of the business cycle. People in the financial and business communities often express it in the following ways (with well-mixed metaphors):

- When an expansion is underway and the economy and inflation begin to heat up, the Fed should apply the brakes. It should target higher interest rates and slower growth in the money supply. Thus the Fed is often accused of "taking away the punch bowl, just as the party gets going."

- When a recession is on the way and the economy is cooling, the Fed should step on the gas—gently. In this way, the Fed can engineer what is known as a soft landing. Rather than aiming to reverse the downward cycle, the Fed lowers rates and increases the growth of the money supply enough so the economy does not sink deeply into recession.

In this way, monetary policy tries to work with the business cycle instead of fighting it. The goal is to minimize inflation on the upswings in the cycle and to moderate rising unemployment on the downswings. If the Fed tried to keep the economy constantly expanding, it would be fighting the natural ebb and flow of demand in the economy. As a result, monetary policy would stimulate the economy to grow beyond its natural long-run growth rate, which would generate inflation.

The Real World

Central bankers are often characterized as "inflation hawks," that is, as officials who prefer to keep inflation low, even at the cost of higher unemployment. There is some truth to this characterization. Central bankers tend to be both financially and politically conservative. Financial conservatism calls for a strong currency and a business environment in which companies can plan and banks can lend with some certainty about the future value of the currency. The idea that everyone who wants a job should be able to get one is associated more with the liberal side of the political spectrum.

Factors Affecting Monetary Policy

Formulating monetary policy is complicated mainly by lags between the implementation and the effects of policy and by the influence of other factors on the economy.

Although markets respond quickly to changes in monetary policy, there's a lag between the time policy is set and the time it affects the economy. In addition, the effect of a measure is by no means certain. For example, in May, 2000, the fed funds rate stood at 6.50 percent. By November, 2002, the Fed had lowered it to 1.25 percent—the lowest level in four decades! Yet economic sluggishness persisted throughout the 12 rate cuts over that timeframe. (It is, however, quite reasonable to believe that the economy would have been worse off without the rate cuts.)

This lag and uncertainty mean that the Fed must try to anticipate the path of the economy and the future effects of its actions. For example, if the Fed waited for an increase in inflation before raising rates, the inflationary momentum would already be underway. This would make it harder to diffuse the inflationary pressures, and might cost more in lost jobs and output. This is why the Fed is accused of taking away the punch bowl as soon as the party—that is, an expansion—starts. Expansions often bring inflation, and the Fed wants to head it off before it starts.

Demand, output, inflation, and employment are also affected by forces outside the Fed's control. These include taxes and government spending at all levels, developments overseas, conditions in the financial markets (such as the late-1990s stock market bubble), and new technologies (such as the Internet). In 1997 and 1998, the economies of several East Asian nations slowed down significantly, which reduced their demand for U.S. products. This could have slowed the growth of the U.S. economy, which exports huge amounts of goods. In the 1990s, heavy investment in personal computers, computer networks, and Internet-related technology began to pay off in terms of increased productivity. An increase in productivity enables the economy to grow at a higher rate without higher inflation. The Fed has to factor developments like these into its policies.

Adding to these difficulties is the ever-changing composition of the money supply. So, while the Fed still exerts a very real influence in the economy, a good portion of that influence is psychological rather than purely financial.

The Real World

Stabilizing the financial system during times of stress stands among the Fed's key responsibilities. It does a good job of doing this. Such stress occurred after the stock market crashed in October, 1987; during the international debt crisis in autumn, 1998; and after the terrorist attacks on September 11, 2001.

In such instances, the Federal Reserve promoted the stability of the financial system by providing ample liquidity (balances at the Federal Reserve) through large open market purchases of securities (using short-term repurchase agreements) and by extending discount window loans to banks. Although it has never done so, the Fed even has the authority to lend to corporations, partnerships, and individuals.

How the Fed Gets the Word Out

The financial and business community closely monitors the Federal Reserve's view of the economy as well as its actions. The Fed employs several means of communicating with its various constituencies, the most important being the Monetary Policy Report to the Congress, the Commentary on Current Economic Conditions (the "Beige Book"), and a statement that follows each meeting of the Federal Open Market Committee (FOMC):

- ◆ **Monetary Policy Report to the Congress:** By law the Board of Governors of the Federal Reserve must deliver a report to Congress two times a year on economic and financial developments and the nation's monetary policy. This testimony is delivered by the Chairman of the Fed, usually in February and July. It includes a report on key economic variables, a review of the monetary policy measures taken since the previous testimony, and a forecast of economic growth. Highlights of this testimony are widely reported in the business news.

EconoTip

Check out the Fed's website—www.federalreserve.gov—for the most up-to-date versions of these reports.

- ◆ **Commentary on Current Economic Conditions:** Eight times a year, the Fed publishes an informal survey by the 12 Federal Reserve Banks on current economic conditions in their districts. This report is commonly known as "the Beige Book" because of the color of its cover. The commentary gathers anecdotal information from the Bank presidents and branch directors. Other sources include interviews with key business executives, economists, and market experts.

The Beige Book summarizes this information by district and industrial sector (agriculture, manufacturing, and so on).

♦ **Statements after FOMC Meetings:** At 2:15 P.M. on the last day of each FOMC meeting, the committee releases a statement announcing the targeted fed funds rate (or the lack of a new target, if there has been no change). The statement also describes the balance of the risks to economic growth and, since March 2002, the vote of each member of the FOMC on monetary policy decisions.

The comments about the risks to economic growth are followed closely by the financial community and economists. The comment generally characterizes the risks to the economy as positive, negative, or balanced. For instance, after the December 11, 2001 meeting, the press release stated that "the risks are weighted mainly toward conditions that may generate economic weakness in the foreseeable future." After the November 6, 2002 meeting, the release stated that "the risks are balanced with respect to the prospects for both goals in the foreseeable future" (meaning both price stability and sustained economic growth).

If that language seems less that bold, it is meant to be. The Fed and its chairman are very conscious of the fact that any statement they make may be viewed as prophecy, and the last thing they want to do is upset the markets. Instead, they want the markets to function as freely from direction by the Fed as possible. Sometimes this desire has motivated the Fed to be downright secretive, but in recent years the Fed has become more open.

> **The Real World**
>
> The Fed now operates with far more transparency than it did in the past. Indeed, in a Joint Economic Committee Study in 1997, members of Congress specifically called for greater transparency and less secrecy in the Federal Reserve's conduct of monetary policy.

Leadership and Moral Suasion

In a country where Henry Kissinger was viewed (by some) as a sex symbol, it was only a matter of time before the Chairman of the Federal Reserve became a cult figure. That certainly occurred in the case of Alan Greenspan, who in the 1990s was given ample credit for the lengthy expansion and rising stock market. Editorial cartoons often portrayed him as a king, seer, wizard, and in one cartoon I recall, someone whose burp in a restaurant attracts all ears.

All of this belies the very real leadership role that the Chairman of the Federal Reserve plays in the U.S. economy. Mr. Greenspan hasn't held his post for four terms under four presidents because he's good at tennis. He projects intelligence, expertise, and a bankerly bedside manner, and he clearly knows his business.

As part of the leadership role of the position, the Fed Chairman uses *moral suasion* as a policy tool—or rather he used to use it. In the 1960s and before, it was fairly common for the Chairman of the Federal Reserve to urge banks to ease or tighten their lending policies, depending on the Fed's desires. Students of economics were taught that moral suasion was among the tools for implementing monetary policy, although a less powerful one than changes to interest rates or reserve requirements.

EconoTalk

Moral suasion refers to the central bank or the president urging the banking system, the markets, or other players in the economy to take a certain course of action "voluntarily." At times, moral suasion is backed up with the implied threat that strong official action will be taken if the (per)suasion doesn't work.

Today, however, the role of moral suasion appears to be diminished, perhaps because large companies rely far less heavily on banks for short-term funds. (The commercial paper market emerged in the 1970s.) Or perhaps in this age of hyper-coverage of business and economics by the media, the Fed would rather not put itself on the line in that manner. All of this said, the Fed Chairman can move the markets—sometimes.

The Real World

Some people feel that the Fed contributed to the stock market bubble of the late 1990s by leaving interest rates too low during that decade's expansion. However, the Fed Chairman attempted mild moral suasion at the beginning of the bubble. In December 1996, Mr. Greenspan implied that stock prices could become "unduly escalated" by investors' "irrational exuberance."

The following March, the fed funds rate was increased by a quarter point to 5.50 percent. But three rate cuts over the next 20 months brought the rate down to 4.75 percent by November 1998, where it remained until June 1999. During this period, both the Dow Jones Industrial Average and the NASDAQ continued to rise.

In August 2002, Mr. Greenspan told his critics (who mostly held their criticism until after the bubble burst) that the Fed did not want to "substitute its judgment for the actions of millions of investors." He added that "it would be very hard for the central bank to curb stock market euphoria." He then cited three previous instances when the Fed raised interest rates by more than 3 percentage points in the 1980s and mid-1990s and stock prices retreated briefly, and then continued to advance.

Let's Look at the Record

When the Federal Reserve was established in 1913, its main purpose was to prevent financial panics and runs on banks by acting as lender of last resort to the banking system. The Fed served this function by making loans to banks through the discount windows of the Reserve Banks. The Fed's limited charter, along with the gold standard, minimized the central bank's role in economic policy.

The Great Depression and the fiscal policy ideas of John Maynard Keynes prompted the government to take a more active role in managing the economy. After World War II, the Employment Act of 1946 required the federal government to "promote maximum employment, production, and purchasing power." This act didn't explicitly mention the Fed's role in this endeavor, and again, the Fed was somewhat constrained—relative to the leeway it has today—in influencing economic growth.

During the 1950s, annual inflation averaged about 2 percent as the economy expanded by an average of almost 3 percent a year and unemployment averaged 4.5 percent. The Federal Reserve was doing something right. For one thing, it established the overnight market in federal funds in the mid-1950s, which provided another, more flexible way to influence the money supply. In addition, the central bank deliberately focused on keeping inflation in check by raising rates in anticipation of increases in prices.

Inflationary pressures increased in the late 1960s due largely to budget deficits generated by spending on the Vietnam War and the Great Society social programs. As measured by the *consumer price index*, inflation averaged 3.9 percent from 1966 through 1969 versus 1.3 percent from 1960 through 1965. Unemployment averaged 4.8 percent for the decade, a modest increase over the 4.5 average of the 1950s. The prevailing view, especially among monetarists, is that the Fed failed to fight inflation vigorously as this decade of economic growth and deficit spending progressed.

Whether or not that is so, inflation rose to unprecedented levels in the 1970s due to continuing budget deficits and the tripling of oil prices. During this period, the Fed definitely didn't fight inflation actively enough. Both the *real* discount rate and the *real* fed funds rate were negative for most of the second half of the decade as inflation rose from 5.8 percent in

EconoTalk

The **consumer price index** measures the increase or decrease in the price of a "market basket" of goods and services that a typical consumer purchases in the course of a month. A **real** interest rate is the rate under consideration—the discount rate, fed funds rate, or prime rate—minus the rate of inflation.

1976 to 11.35 in 1979. Meanwhile, the unemployment rate rose to an average of 6.2 percent for the decade.

Beating inflation became the priority in the 1980s. The consumer price index rose by 13.5 percent in 1980 and by 10.3 percent in 1981. But the real fed funds rate was cranked up to the 7 to 9 percent range in those years, and inflation dropped to 6.2 percent in 1982 and to 3.2 in 1983. From 1984 through 1989, inflation averaged 3.7 percent. This occurred in an environment of vigorous deficit spending, showing that aggressive management of the money supply can indeed combat inflation. However, there may have been a price to pay in unemployment, which rose to an average of 7.3 percent for the decade (and exceeded 9.5 percent in 1982 and 1983).

Under Alan Greenspan the Fed has continued to keep inflation at bay. In the 1990s, the consumer price index rose by an average of 3.0 percent for the entire decade, and by 2.5 percent from 1993 through 1999. In the early 2000s, it hovered around 2 percent. Unemployment averaged 5.5 percent from 1990 through 2001.

Over the past 50 years, judged by its goal of helping to maintain a growing economy with low inflation and low unemployment, the Fed succeeded in the 1950s and early 1960s. It failed in the late 1960s and the 1970s, succeeded on inflation but failed on unemployment in the 1980s, and succeeded in the 1990s—all to the extent that the Fed can indeed be blamed or credited.

EconoTip

One major difficulty in judging the effectiveness of economic policy is that increases or decreases in output, unemployment, inflation, and other measures may or may not be directly attributable to the policy in question.

For instance, was it monetary policy that created the expansions of the 1980s and 1990s? Or was it fiscal policy? Probably both. Would the Fed have worsened matters by raising short-term rates in the 1970s to try to curb inflation? Maybe, maybe not. The prime rate and mortgage rates reached historic highs without curing inflation, so perhaps it wouldn't have helped. On the other hand, the Fed didn't inspire enough confidence in the 1970s, so action might have helped. People seem happy with the activist Fed of today.

Fed Watching

Fed watching is the name given to the pastime of anticipating and understanding changes in monetary policy. Serious Fed watchers pour through the Fed Chairman's testimony before Congress and the Beige Book at the Fed's website. Anyone with any interest in the direction of the economy will watch for changes in the targeted fed funds rate after a meeting of the FOMC. The schedule of meetings is posted at the Fed's website, as are the press releases of the statement issued after each meeting.

Most Fed watchers believe that the Fed knows what it is doing, particularly because the Board of Governors and the FOMC have access to the best economic and financial data and information. Moreover, whether or not the Fed gauges the condition or future path of the economy correctly, monetary policy can amount to a self-fulfilling prophecy. If the Fed believes that inflationary pressures are rising, and as a result increases the targeted fed funds rate, the effect will be to slow the growth of the money supply and perhaps the growth of the economy. Conversely, if the Fed believes that the economy needs a boost, and as a result adopts a policy of easy money, the effect will be to increase the growth of the money supply and perhaps economic growth.

In the previous paragraph, the word "perhaps" is important. While people often speak of the "levers" of monetary policy—rates, reserves, and so on—there isn't a mechanical relationship between lower rates and higher growth or vice versa. The latest evidence of this occurred during the economic sluggishness of 2002, when the Fed reduced the fed funds rate 12 times, to its lowest level in three decades: 1.25 percent. Despite record low interest rates, the economy remained lackluster.

Of course, the uncertainty emanating from 9/11 and the possibility of war with Iraq contributed to the soft economy. But some economists believe that the United States could face a problem similar to that in Japan, where sustained low interest rates failed to spark growth, due to huge amounts of bad debt in the banking system and a deterioration of stock and real estate values.

So as you watch the Fed, watch with the knowledge that whatever the Fed does may or may not work as intended.

> **The Real World**
>
> Believe it or not, Fed watching reached the point where people tried to anticipate whether or not the FOMC would announce a rate increase based on the thickness of Chairman Greenspan's briefcase as he headed into the meeting. The theory was that a rate increase would require more justification and, therefore, more background information, which would bulk up the briefcase.

The Least You Need to Know

- ◆ Monetary policy tries to work with the business cycle instead of fighting it. The goal is to fight inflation during expansions and to moderate rising unemployment during contractions.

◆ The Fed communicates by means of its Monetary Policy Report to the Congress, Commentary on Current Economic Conditions (the Beige Book), and statements following each meeting of the Federal Open Market Committee—and through its website at www.federalreserve.com.

◆ The Fed helped to maintain a growing economy with low inflation and low unemployment in the 1950s and early 1960s, failed in the late 1960s and the 1970s, and succeeded on inflation in the 1980s, and on both in the 1990s.

◆ Fed watchers believe that the Fed has superior economic and financial information and that monetary policy affects the economy. Therefore, they try to anticipate, or at least understand, the Fed's thinking and decisions.

Part 5

The Global Economy

Like any economy, the global economy is a system in which transactions—exchanges of goods and services for money—take place, in this case in the form of foreign trade and international finance. Several factors make these transactions more complicated than transactions in a national economy. These factors center on the many differences—in currencies, laws, languages, customs, and cultures—among nations.

In this part, we look at the workings of foreign trade, international finance, the global marketplace, and developing economies. We also touch upon such timely topics as globalization, trade blocs, and the capitalist impulses that have emerged in China. Our goal in this part is to understand why nations do business—and refuse to do business—with one another, and the transformative power of economics in the world today.

Chapter 17

International Trade: Made in USA, Japan, Mexico, Italy ...

In This Chapter

- ◆ Why nations import and export goods
- ◆ International trade agreements
- ◆ Protectionism and other trade policies

Up to now, we have left exports and imports—the final component of GDP—out of our analysis. Now it's time to bring them in. It's a potentially complex area, but this chapter will first show why nations export and import goods, and then examine barriers to trade and various steps that have been taken to lower barriers to trade.

While foreign trade isn't as emotionally loaded as say, taxes and government spending, like most topics in economics it stirs the blood of certain people—those whose livelihoods and lifestyles are most affected by exports and imports. These people have very real concerns, but those concerns are specific to their individual lives. Economists almost universally believe that foreign trade in a free global marketplace will create the greatest good for the greatest number of people.

Let's start with why they would believe this.

Exports, Imports—Why Bother?

The fundamental reason for foreign trade is quite simple: Some nations are better at producing certain things than others. This means that they will all be economically better off if they specialize in what they do best and exchange a portion of what they produce for the goods of other nations who also specialize in what they do best.

In a way, the rationale for international trade follows the same line of logic that caused a worker in a medieval village to specialize in butchering or baking or candlestick making, and then exchange her goods with other specialists. International trade works the same way, only on a larger scale.

To illustrate this, let's suppose that there are only two countries on the planet—the United States and Japan—and they make only two products: food and personal computers. The following two tables show the production possibilities, per week, for each nation.

Table 17.1   U.S. Production Possibilities (in thousands per week)

Possibility	Bushels of Food	Personal Computers
A	0	12
B	3	9
C	6	6
D	9	3
E	12	0

Table 17.2   Japan's Production Possibilities (in thousands per week)

Possibility	Bushels of Food	Personal Computers
A	0	12
B	1	9
C	2	6
D	3	3
E	4	0

Figure 17.1 shows the production possibility functions of each nation. It is simply the graphic representation of the values in Tables 17.1 and 17.2.

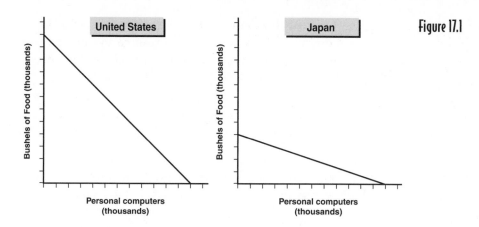

Figure 17.1

Each nation can produce the same number of personal computers in a week. But the United States can produce three times as much food as Japan. In other words, if each nation chose to produce only computers, they would each produce 12,000, but if each chose to produce only food, the United States would produce 12,000 bushels and Japan would produce only 4,000.

At first glance, it may seem as if the two nations—particularly the United States—have no reason to engage in foreign trade. After all, the United States is just as efficient at producing computers and three times as efficient at producing food. Why would the United States be interested in trade?

Here's where the notion of *comparative advantage* comes in. The United States can produce either food or computers at a one-to-one trade off. In other words, if the United States chooses to produce another personal computer, it must give up one bushel of food. That bushel of food is the United States' opportunity cost of producing another computer.

However, if Japan gives up one bushel of food, it can produce three personal computers. The opportunity cost of producing personal computers in Japan is only one-third what it is in the United States. Japan sacrifices less food than the United States would in order to increase its production of personal computers.

The nation with the lower opportunity cost in producing a good has a comparative advantage in the production of that product. In this case, Japan has a lower opportunity cost than the United States in producing computers. The U.S. has what economists call an *absolute advantage* in producing food. The U.S. can produce 12,000 bushels of food per week while Japan can produce only 4,000. But absolute advantage doesn't necessarily indicate that a nation should export that product. That's because the nation might have to give up producing some of a product in which it has an even greater absolute advantage.

EconoTalk

Comparative advantage arises for a nation when its opportunity cost of producing a good is lower than that of another nation. **Absolute advantage** arises when a nation can produce a good more cheaply than another nation. Comparative advantage, not absolute advantage, indicates which good a nation should export or import.

The British economist David Ricardo (1772–1823) developed the concept of comparative advantage to answer the question, "Which nation should specialize in producing which good?" He found that the nation having a lower opportunity cost than other nations in producing a product should specialize in that product, and called that the principle of comparative advantage.

So in this example, even though the United States has the absolute advantage in producing food, and is equally efficient at producing personal computers, Japan has a comparative advantage in producing personal computers. However, the United States also has a comparative advantage relative to Japan—in food.

Why? Because the United States only has to give up one personal computer to produce an additional bushel of food, while Japan must give up three computers. The United States faces a lower opportunity cost than Japan when it chooses to produce food instead of computers. That means that the United States should produce food, and exchange it with Japan for computers.

So, in our example and in theory, the United States would produce only food, Japan would produce only personal computers, and they would each exchange some of their production with one another.

The Argument for Free Trade

Obviously, the example here is incredibly oversimplified. In the real world, there are hundreds of nations producing thousands of products, most with different cost structures and at different levels of efficiency. However, in this simple example is the fundamental argument for free trade, which most economists support both in theory and in practice.

Economists support free trade because in general they want an economy, including the global economy, to deliver the greatest good to the greatest number of people. A look back at the example of U.S. and Japanese food and computer production will reveal the benefits of specialization and exchange.

If you pick any possibility from the range of production possibilities in Tables 17.1 and 17.2, you will see that the greatest total production of food and computers occurs when the United States produces only food and Japan produces only personal computers. The following table below shows one example:

Table 17.3

	Food	Computers	
Possibility C:			
United States	6,000	6,000	
Japan	2,000	6,000	
Total	8,000	12,000	Total production = 20,000 units
With Specialization:			
United States	12,000	0	
Japan	0	12,000	
Total	12,000	12,000	Total production = 24,000 units

Specialization generates the highest level of production of the two goods. Then, through trade, each nation can consume the amount of the good that it wants to consume. In this way, production is maximized because each nation is doing what it does most efficiently.

Again, this is an oversimplification. A range of issues, including transportation costs, quality, differences in domestic demand, and national security considerations, are all left out of the analysis. Yet the very real principle of comparative advantage and the equally real benefits of trade form the basic argument in favor of free trade.

Unfortunately, numerous arguments—and measures—against free international trade have taken hold in the world.

Arguments Against Free Trade

Today, most arguments against free international trade are mounted by special interest groups. Both labor unions and management oppose free trade when they believe—sometimes correctly, sometimes incorrectly—that it will make them worse off. What they conveniently ignore is that free trade will make everyone else better off.

It is true that if the U.S. auto industry loses 5,000 jobs to foreign competitors, those 5,000 workers and their households are worse off. However, the millions of other households that can purchase less expensive, more efficient vehicles from a wider range of choices, are better off. The pain endured by one of those 5,000 households may well be greater than the benefit enjoyed by any given car-buying household. That is why labor unions fight so hard to keep their members' jobs. But an economist would argue that if another nation can make cars more efficiently, those autoworkers should move into another U.S. industry and let the whole population enjoy the benefits of free trade with the more efficient auto industry of another nation.

Special interest groups put forth various arguments to support their view. Some of these arguments make a certain amount of economic sense, and others are incorrect or at least suspect. The truth, however, is that those asking for protection from free trade usually stand to benefit the most.

The arguments most often heard are …

- It's important to keep jobs in the United States.
- We don't want money leaving the country.
- National security is at stake.
- Other nations don't treat their workers fairly.
- Other nations are "dumping" and don't open their market to us.

Let's look at these positions one at a time.

Keeping jobs in the United States is important, but it's more important to keep jobs in industries in which we operate efficiently. Otherwise, we are subsidizing inefficiency, which hurts national productivity as well as consumers. If, indeed, another nation is more efficient—has a comparative advantage—in producing a product, it's in our interests to buy it from them.

As to the idea that we are "exporting jobs" when, say, U.S. auto manufacturers set up assembly plants in Mexico, the autoworkers' union has a point. But the same counter-argument applies. If Mexico is the least expensive place to assemble the vehicles, from the economic standpoint, that is where it should be done—as long as it can be done with the same level of quality.

The quality argument is often put forth as a reason to keep jobs in the United States. In reality, however, imported goods of inferior quality sell at lower prices, which reflects their quality and gives the consumer another choice. (Some people *like* cheap shoes.) Also, foreign producers have a good record of improving the quality of their goods to meet U.S. standards. The Japanese auto industry of the 1970s provides an outstanding example of this. American producers in certain industries have done the same thing. For instance, over the past 20 years the California wine industry has improved the quality of its wines to compete with imports from France in the States. That created jobs in the United States' wine industry—and in trucking, warehousing, advertising, retailing, and restaurants (thereby employing otherwise unemployable wine stewards)—while combating imports of burgundy and Bordeaux.

> **EconoTip**
>
> The argument that "cheap foreign wages" will destroy a U.S. industry is bogus. What matters is not the level of wages, but the level of wages relative to the productivity of the workers. If a U.S. industry has high wages—say, quadruple the level of the foreign wage—but is six times more productive, that industry is still quite competitive with the foreign one.
>
> Also, labor is only one component of the cost of a product. If a low-wage industry threatens a U.S. industry, it basically means that the foreign nation has a comparative advantage in that industry.

We don't want money leaving the country may sound like a sensible argument when you look at the GDP formula. If we import more than we export, GDP is lowered. Doesn't that mean we are worse off? In a way, yes, but in a way, no.

The money-leaving-the-country argument goes all the way back to mercantilism, the economic theory that international trade generates wealth for a nation. The mercantilists believed that exports should be encouraged, imports should be discouraged, and gold should be hoarded. Mercantilism flourished in the 1600s and 1700s and fueled the worldwide exploration and imperialism of Western European nations in those centuries. However, as economic theory, mercantilism is dead.

Keeping money in the country is not a priority. We don't want exports to be high because they keep money in the country but because they fuel domestic production and incomes. If those incomes are spent on imports, that can be a very good thing for consumers. From the economists' point of view, the way to promote exports is not by limiting imports. Other nations will retaliate against protectionist policies anyway. The way to promote exports is to be as innovative, productive, and efficient as we can be.

National security is at stake with regard to some industries. Defense is the best example of an industry that requires protection on the basis of national security. Steel may be another, but the steel industry has been only partly successful with this argument. Oil is another industry on which national security can depend, although U.S. consumption of and dependence on foreign oil has been virtually encouraged by the phase out of fuel efficiency standards for passenger vehicles and low gasoline taxes (relative to those in Europe).

Although economists disagree about various ways to protect industries on which national security depends, most agree that some industries warrant such protection. They also agree that some industries that have claimed this status, such as the American watch industry (I'm serious), probably do not warrant it.

Other nations' unfair treatment of their workers is a relatively new argument against imports, and it can be a tough argument both to document and deflect. It's hard to document because, as we've learned, everything is relative. The awful truth is that jobs in sweatshops may enable people in poor nations to feed and cloth themselves. Limiting imports from these nations may hurt the very people we would be trying to help. These arguments are hard to deflect because the truth is that low cost foreign production sites often don't meet reasonable health and safety standards.

Then there is the issue of child labor and forced labor, which virtually everyone sees as highly exploitative. The U.S. Congress estimates that at least 250 million child laborers between the ages of 5 and 14 are now working worldwide, about half of them full time. The United States has funded and contributed to a number of efforts to prevent child labor, and is the world's largest contributor to the International Program for the Elimination of Child Labor.

Several efforts to have other nations voluntarily comply with guidelines for eliminating child labor are underway. In fact, the United States devotes some $30 million a year to international programs to end abusive child labor. In 1999, the United States ratified a new international initiative to eliminate child slavery, debt bondage, and forced labor. In addition, the Child Labor Deterrence Act was introduced as a bill to the U.S. Congress in 1999, but it has yet to pass. If it became law, the act would prohibit the importation of manufactured or mined products produced by children under the age of 15.

Other nations "dumping" goods in the United States and keeping our imports out do give protectionists ammunition in their battle against free trade. Dumping occurs when a nation sells its goods in a foreign market at a price that is lower than its price in the domestic market or lower than it cost to produce. The objective is to drive the domestic producer out of the market—and out of business—and then to raise the price when the domestic competition has gone out of business. Both dumping and protectionism by other nations can put the United States at a disadvantage.

Under current laws and trade agreements, dumping is illegal. If U.S. producers can prove that dumping is occurring, special duties can be added to the price of the goods being dumped. One reason that dumping occurs is that many foreign industries are subsidized by their government in ways that ours are not (although U.S. agriculture is highly subsidized, as is agriculture in most industrial nations). The steel industry is a good example of an industry that recently won protection, and in March, 2001, President Bush levied tariffs of up to 40 percent on certain types of steel imports.

When other countries practice protectionism, the preferred method is to work toward free—or at least fair—trade through a process of negotiation. These processes have been quite useful in recent years and have brought the world into an age of much freer international trade.

Barriers to International Trade

Free trade refers to the elimination of barriers to international trade. The most common barriers to trade are *tariffs*, *quotas*, and *nontariff barriers*.

A tariff is a tax on imports, which is collected by the federal government and which raises the price of the good to the consumer. Also known as duties or import duties, tariffs usually aim first to limit imports and second to raise revenue.

A quota is a limit on the amount of a certain type of good that may be imported into the country. A quota can be either voluntary or legally enforced.

The effect of tariffs and quotas is the same: to limit imports and protect domestic producers from foreign competition. A tariff raises the price of the foreign good beyond the market equilibrium price, which decreases the demand for and, eventually, the supply of the foreign good. A quota limits the supply to a certain quantity, which raises the price beyond the market equilibrium level and thus decreases demand.

Tariffs come in different forms, mostly depending on the motivation, or rather the stated motivation. (The actual motivation is always to limit imports.) For instance, a tariff may be levied in order to bring the price of the imported good up to the level of the domestically produced good. This so-called scientific tariff—which to an economist is anything but—has the stated goal of equalizing the price and, therefore, "leveling the playing field," between foreign and domestic producers. In this game, the consumer loses.

A peril-point tariff is levied in order to save a domestic industry that has deteriorated to the point where its very existence is in peril. An economist would argue that the industry should be allowed to expire. That way, factors of

EconoTalk

A **tariff** is a tax on imported goods, while a **quota** is a limit on the amount of goods that may be imported. Both tariffs and quotas raise the price of and lower the demand for the goods to which they apply. **Nontariff barriers,** such as regulations calling for a certain percentage of locally produced content in the product, also have the same effect, but not as directly.

EconoTip

You may wonder why a nation would ever choose to use a quota when a tariff has the added advantage of raising revenue. The major reason is that quotas allow the nation that uses them to decide the quantity to be imported and let the price go where it will. A tariff adjusts the price, but leaves the post-tariff quantity to market forces. Therefore, it is less predictable and precise than a quota.

production used by that inefficient industry could move into a new one where they would be better employed.

A retaliatory tariff is one that is levied in response to a tariff levied by a trading partner. In the eyes of an economist, retaliatory tariffs make no sense because they just start tariff wars in which no one—least of all the consumer—wins.

Nontariff barriers include quotas, regulations regarding product content or quality, and other conditions that hinder imports. One of the most commonly used nontariff barriers are product standards, which may aim to serve as "barriers to trade." For instance, when the United States prohibits the importation of unpasteurized cheese from France, is it protecting the health of the American consumer or protecting the revenue of the American cheese producer?

Other nontariff barriers include packing and shipping regulations, harbor and airport permits, and onerous customs procedures, all of which can have either legitimate or purely anti-import agendas, or both.

The Real World

It took several years for U.S. business people to realize it, but one of the toughest barriers to trade in Japan is its system of distribution for goods. A complex array of middlemen and regulations stands between a foreign exporter and the customer in Japan. It requires knowledge of local customs and relationships with local business people to bring a product to market though this maze.

In contrast, foreign exporters of most goods find it relatively easy to bring their products to market in the United States. The network of wholesalers, common carriers, and sales channels (such as retail stores and specialty distributors) is transparent and open in the United States, which represents a huge market for many types of products.

International Trade Agreements

Trade agreements regulate international trade between two or more nations. An agreement may cover all imports and exports, certain categories of goods, or a single category. The United States is currently engaged in some 320 trade agreements with various nations. (These are listed at www.tcc.mac.doc.gov.) However, several general trade agreements have shaped trade policy on broad levels.

The most important general trade agreement is called, simply enough, the General Agreement on Tariffs and Trade (GATT). GATT was signed in October 1947 to liberalize trade, to create an organization to administer more liberal trade agreements, and to establish a mechanism for resolving trade disputes. The GATT organization is small and located in Geneva. More than 110 nations have signed the general agreement, which originally was signed by 24 nations, including the United States. To a large degree, the role of GATT as an organization has been superceded by the World Trade Organization, which I discuss later in this section.

Since GATT was signed, several "rounds" of talks to liberalize trade have occurred. The most significant of these were the Kennedy rounds, which eventually led to a one-third reduction in tariffs and, more recently, the Uruguay rounds. The Uruguay rounds dealt with general barriers to trade and the relatively new issues of intellectual property rights, fishing practices, and environmental concerns.

A major trend of the past 25 years has been the creation and growth of free trade zones among nations agreeing to form regional trade blocs. The agreements that create free trade zones all share the same aims: to liberalize trade, promote economic growth, and provide equal access to markets among the member nations.

The most significant free trade zones are the European Union (EU), the North American Free Trade Agreement (NAFTA), and the Association of Southeast Asian Nations (ASEAN).

In addition, the World Trade Organization (WTO) is a global organization, headquartered in Geneva, for dealing with trade between nations. Established in January 1995 by the Uruguay round negotiations under GATT, the WTO included 144 nations as of January 2002. The WTO administers trade agreements, provides a forum for trade negotiations and resolving trade disputes, monitors trade policies, and provides technical assistance and training for developing countries.

Let's Trade

Despite calls for protectionism from those who stand to lose from free trade, the world has clearly been liberalizing trade policy, lowering barriers to trade, and forming regional trade blocs. As a result, international trade is freer than it has ever been. We can all thank economists for this. They are without a doubt the steadiest, strongest, clearest voices in favor of free trade.

U.S. tariffs stand at their lowest level in history. Before World War II they ranged up to 40 percent on some imports. Today, tariff revenues amount to less than 5 percent of import dollar volume, and many imports are exempt from tariffs and quotas. Nontariff barriers to trade have also been largely—but not completely—eliminated.

This does not mean that all is rosy in the world of foreign trade, nor does it mean that the United States always plays fair in the global marketplace. U.S. agricultural subsidies and textile tariffs, for example, hinder imports of food, cloth, and clothing from poor nations in order to protect these domestic industries. Nevertheless, the

United States and the world in general are expected to continue on the path toward freer international trade.

> **EconoTip**
>
> From time to time you will hear about so-called fast track trade legislation, in which Congress would give the president the authority to negotiate trade agreements. This legislation has not been passed, and it remains controversial.
>
> Supporters of the legislation believe that the present method of negotiating trade agreements, which requires Congressional approval, is too slow and cumbersome for today's world. Opponents point out that trade agreements are treaties with other nations and that the Constitution invests Congress with the authority to enter these agreements. They also point out that the fast track legislation would limit public debate on trade policy. That debate, of course, is one of the reasons that the present method is slow and cumbersome.

The Least You Need to Know

◆ A nation has a comparative advantage in producing a good when its opportunity cost of producing it is lower than that of another nation. A nation has an absolute advantage when it can produce a good more cheaply than another nation can.

◆ Comparative advantage, not absolute advantage, determines which goods a nation should export and import. A nation should export goods in which it has a comparative advantage and export those in which it has a comparative disadvantage, vis-à-vis another nation.

◆ While some arguments against free trade are sound, others are mere excuses for protectionism put forth by those who would benefit most by limiting imports.

◆ The most significant trade agreements have been the General Agreement on Tariffs and Trade (GATT) and those that have produced the free trade zones of the European Union, NAFTA, and ASEAN.

◆ Over the past 25 years, trade policy has become more liberal across the world, and economists expect this trend to continue.

Chapter 18

International Finance: Pesos, Euros, and Yen

In This Chapter

- ◆ Foreign exchange rates and how they work
- ◆ Trade deficits and their importance
- ◆ The international monetary system
- ◆ Why a strong dollar can be good or bad

In our discussion of foreign trade in Chapter 17, we left out one crucial element: How do buyers and sellers in different countries do business when they all use different currencies? When a giant bluefin tuna is packed in ice and flown from Cape Cod to Tokyo, the fishing boat captain wants to be paid in dollars. But the Japanese fishmonger has nothing but yen. That doesn't help the Cape Cod captain, who has to pay his crew and his bills in dollars. So the Japanese fishmonger must somehow pay for the tuna in dollars.

How are these problems resolved? What determines how many yen a dollar is worth? In other words, how does the foreign exchange system work?

This chapter answers these questions and explains the foreign exchange markets, balance of payments, International Monetary Fund, and what is meant by a "strong" and "weak" dollar.

About Foreign Exchange

As you know, money is anything that is accepted as a medium of exchange. In most of the world, people accept pieces of paper imprinted with pictures of national heroes or local wonders of nature as money. But in each nation, they accept different pieces of paper.

EconoTalk

Currency conversion is the procedure of changing one currency into another currency. The **exchange rate** is the ratio by which one currency is converted into another. It is the price of one currency expressed in another currency. Exchange rates are necessary because currencies have different values relative to one another.

EconoTalk

The **foreign exchange market** includes the importers, exporters, banks, brokers, traders, and organizations involved in currency conversion. The FX or FOREX market, as it is called, is not a physical place—though many participants work in offices and on trading floors—but rather the entire network of participants in the market.

This means that if someone in the United States wants to buy something from someone in, say, Mexico, she must first exchange her local currency—dollars—for the currency accepted in Mexico—pesos. This *currency conversion* occurs at an *exchange rate*.

The exchange rate—the price of one nation's currency in terms of another nation's—is a central concept in international finance. Virtually any nation's currency can be converted into the currency of any other nation, thanks to exchange rates and the *foreign exchange market*. For instance, let's say the current exchange rate between the U.S. dollar and the Mexican peso is $1 to 10 pesos. This means that $1 will buy 10 pesos and that 10 pesos will buy $1. (I am ignoring transaction costs, such as the commission charged by the bank or foreign exchange broker who does the currency conversion.)

Importers and exporters need foreign currency in order to complete transactions. Banks and brokers maintain inventories of foreign exchange, that is, various currencies, and convert currencies as a service to customers. Traders and speculators make (or lose) money on the movement of foreign exchange rates (which I'll describe later). As you will see, central banks also play a role in the foreign exchange market.

Types of Exchange Rates

Foreign currency exchange rates have historically been determined in three different ways:

- ◆ Fixed rates

- ◆ Floating (or flexible) rates

- ◆ Managed rates

With a fixed exchange rate, the value of the currency is determined by the nation's central bank and held in place by central bank actions, mainly the purchase and sale of the currency. Another way to fix exchange rates, which has been used by the United States and other nations in the past, is to tie currencies to the gold standard. If all the currencies in the exchange rate system have a value pegged to gold, it is a simple matter to convert the currencies to one another according to their value in gold.

Floating exchange rates are determined by the market forces of supply and demand. We will examine these forces in this chapter. Essentially, if demand for a currency increases, the value of that currency in terms of other currencies increases. If demand for the currency decreases, then the value of the currency decreases.

Managed exchange rates are influenced by nations' central banks, but are not targeted to a fixed rate. In practice, the system of managed rates that we have today operates through the forces of supply and demand *and* are influenced by central banks. So we now have a mix of floating and managed rates, which is called managed float.

Foreign Currency Supply and Demand

The economic forces that determine foreign exchange rates are rooted in supply and demand, both of which are determined mainly by foreign trade activity. For instance, if Americans increase their demand for products from Mexico, Americans will need to buy more pesos in order to buy those Mexican products. Thus an increase in U.S. demand for Mexican imports will increase the demand for pesos. The dynamics are illustrated in Figure 18.1.

An increase in the demand for any item, including currency, will increase its price. As we see in Figure 18.1, that is the case when Americans demand more pesos. The increase in the demand for pesos from $10 billion worth to $12 billion worth increased the price of pesos. Where $1.00 used to buy 10 pesos, after the increase in U.S. demand for Mexican imports—from $10 billion worth to $12 billion of Mexican goods—it takes $1.20 to buy 10 pesos. Put another way, a peso that used to cost 10¢ costs 12¢ after the increase in demand.

Figure 18.1

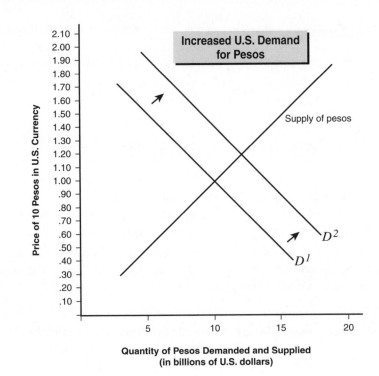

Quantity of Pesos Demanded and Supplied
(in billions of U.S. dollars)

In this situation, the dollar is said to have depreciated against the peso. Other ways of stating this are to say that the dollar lost value, lost ground, or weakened against the peso. This sounds worse than it is. All it means is that the United States demanded more imports from Mexico. But this kind of language is used for a simple reason: The dollar buys less than it used to in Mexico. After the increase in the peso to dollar exchange rate, it takes $1.20 to buy what $1.00 used to buy in Mexico.

EconoTip _____

Business news reporters often employ colorful turns of phrase to describe economic events, but the terminology can be confusing. When a reporter states that the "dollar rallied" in that day's trading, it means that the dollar (or whatever currency is being discussed) strengthened against most currencies. When a reporter says there was a "sell off" of the dollar or that the dollar "was attacked," it means that the dollar weakened against most currencies.

Given the law of supply and demand, this only makes sense. When Americans demand more Mexican products, they bid up the price of those products. When that occurs, the exchange rate mechanism adjusts itself to reflect that price increase. Therefore, the price of the peso, and thus of Mexican goods, rises.

Let's look at this from Mexico's point of view. If the dollar has depreciated—lost value, lost ground, and weakened—against the peso, then the peso has appreciated—gained value, gained ground, and strengthened—against the dollar. While this makes Mexico's products more expensive for Americans, it also makes U.S. products cheaper for Mexicans. The effects of the changes in two currencies mirror one another.

Effect on Imports, Exports, and GDP

Recall the formula for gross domestic product, C + I + G + (Ex – Im). The expression (Ex – Im) equals net exports, which may be either positive or negative. If net exports are positive, the nation's GDP increases. If they are negative, GDP decreases. All nations want their GDP to be higher rather than lower, so all nations want their net exports to be positive. (Of course it is not possible for all nations to have positive net exports because one or more nations must import more than they export if the others export more than they import.)

Returning to our example of the United States and Mexico, here is the sequence of events I just described and the impact on trade and GDP:

- U.S. demand for Mexican imports increased.

- This increased U.S. demand for pesos.

- The increased U.S. demand for pesos raised the price of the peso in dollars.

- When Americans purchase more imports from Mexico—holding all else equal—U.S. net exports (and GDP and employment) will decrease.

- *However*, the change in the exchange rate will automatically correct this situation, because a) as the price, in dollars, of Mexican imports rises, U.S. demand for Mexican imports will fall, and b) as the price, in pesos, of U.S. exports to Mexico falls, Mexican demand for U.S. products will rise.

- When U.S. exports to Mexico rise (because they are cheaper), it will reverse the trend that began when U.S. demand for Mexican products increased. It will also reverse the effect on U.S. net exports, which will increase when exports to Mexico increase.

The price of the peso in dollars—the dollar-peso exchange rate—is determined by U.S. demand for Mexican goods and Mexican demand for U.S. goods. However, when the exchange rate changes, that affects the price of each country's goods. That price change affects each country's demand for the other's goods in ways that tend to reverse the initial trend.

This mechanism depends on floating exchange rates. If exchange rates are not permitted to respond to the forces of supply and demand, these automatic adjustments cannot occur. Given the high levels of international trade in the world today, and the "managed float" nature of exchange rates, the economies of most nations are intertwined in various ways. Let's examine some of those ways.

The Balance of Payments

The balance of international payments, commonly known as the balance of payments, is the overall accounting of a nation's international economic activity. It is a statement summarizing the transactions that took place between a nation and the rest of the world, usually over a calendar quarter or year. It shows the sum of all the transactions between the individuals, businesses, and government agencies of the nation and those of the rest of the world.

Transactions are recorded as debits and credits in the balance of payments. Transactions that cause money to flow into the country (inflows) are credits, and those that cause money to leave the country (outflows) are debits.

EconoTip

The U.S. balance of payments includes a current account, which summarizes imports and exports and a capital account, which summarizes forgiveness of debts, transfers of goods or financial assets accompanying migrants, and other transfers of assets. It also includes a financial account, which summarizes U.S. and foreign investment in fixed assets, securities, and other financial assets, and intangible assets. The current account should balance out to zero against the sum of the capital and the financial accounts.

For example, if the U.S. exports a cement mixer to Brazil, the transaction is a credit to the U.S. balance of payments and a debit to Brazil's balance of payments. If Malaysia borrows $1.5 billion from the U.S. government, the transaction is a debit to the U.S. balance of payments and a credit to Malaysia's. However, when Malaysia makes its first payment on the principal and interest on the loan, it is a credit to the U.S. balance of payments and a debit to Malaysia's.

The balance of payments statement divides international transactions into three accounts: the current account, capital account, and financial account, as follows:

- **The current account** includes trade in goods and services; income receipts, such as dividends and interest; and unilateral transfers of assets, such as foreign aid.

♦ **The capital account** includes forgiveness of international debt, migrant transfers (goods or financial assets accompanying migrants into or out of the country), transfers of funds arising from gift and inheritance taxes, and uninsured damage to fixed assets.

♦ **The financial account** records trade in fixed assets such as companies and real estate; in financial assets such as stocks and bonds; in government-owned assets and foreign-owned assets in the United States; and in rights and intangible assets, such as mineral rights, copyrights, patents, trademarks, franchises, and leases.

Each of these three accounts—the current account, the capital account, and the financial account—is summed separately. The sum of the current account should balance with the sum of the capital account plus the financial account. Thus, the current account should balance out to zero against the capital and financial accounts. In practice, the balance is close to zero relative to the sums involved, but is rarely exactly zero. This is due to statistical discrepancies, accounting conventions, and exchange rate movements that change the recorded value of transactions.

Why should the current account balance out to zero against the capital and financial accounts?

Because when the United States imports more goods and services than it exports, the result is a current account deficit. The United States must finance that current account deficit, either by international borrowing or by selling more capital assets than it buys internationally. Conversely, when the United States exports more that it imports, its trading partners must finance their current account deficits, either by borrowing or by selling more capital assets than they purchased.

Table 18.2 shows the U.S. balance of payments for 2001.

Table 18.2   U.S. Balance of Payments, December 31, 2001 (billions of dollars)

	Inflows	Outflows	Net
Current Account			
Merchandise Account (Exports/Imports)			
Goods	$719	–$1,146	
Services	279	–210	
Total Merchandise Account	$998	–$1,356	–$358

continues

Table 18.2 U.S. Balance of Payments, December 31, 2001 (billions of dollars) (continued)

	Inflows	Outflows	Net
Income Account	284	–269	15
Transfers			–50
Balance on Current Account			–$393
Capital Account			1
Financial Account			
Foreign Investment in the United States	753		
U.S. Investment Abroad		–371	
Balance on Financial Account			$382
Statistical Discrepancy			10
Balance on Capital and Financial Accounts			$393

Source: Bureau of Economic Analysis, International Accounts Data

The deficit on the merchandise account, commonly known as the *trade deficit,* accounts for almost all of the deficit on the capital account. It is a deficit in exports of goods that causes the U.S. trade deficit. In 2001, the United States imported almost 60 percent more goods than it exported (because $1,146 – $719 = $427 and $427 ÷ $719 = .59). However, the United States runs a surplus in services, exporting $279 billion and importing $210 billion of services in 2001.

EconoTip

Although economists used to point out that services generally were not exported—haircuts were the favorite example—that has changed. The vast majority of international trade is still in goods, but trade in services has grown considerably over the past two decades. Categories of services exported and imported include transportation, financial, consulting, engineering, and telecommunications services.

As the financial account shows, the current account deficit is offset by the amount of foreign investment in the United States, which exceeds U.S. foreign investment. While America does a lot of foreign investment—placing $371 billion abroad in 2001—the rest of the world invests very heavily in the United States, to the tune of $753 billion in that year. So America's ability to attract foreign investment helps to finance its appetite for imports.

The United States has run a merchandise trade deficit since 1976, although it typically runs a surplus in services. The merchandise trade deficit rose from $36 billion in 1982 to a peak of $160 billion in 1987. In the recession year of 1991, the trade deficit stood at $71 billion, but the run-up during the 1990s was particularly strong. During that period, the United States enjoyed a vigorous economic expansion while the economies of Europe and Asia languished. By 2000, the merchandise trade deficit had grown to $434 billion. In 2001, which included three quarters of contraction, the trade deficit still reached $358 billion.

EconoTalk

A **trade deficit** occurs when, during a certain period, a nation imports more goods and services than it exports. A **trade surplus** occurs when a nation exports more goods and services than it imports.

Trade Deficits: Bad or Good?

As usual in economics, there are several different views of trade deficits. Depending on who you talk to, they are bad, good, both (depending on the situation), or immaterial. However, few economists argue that trade deficits are always good.

Economists who consider trade deficits to be bad believe that a nation that consistently runs a current account deficit is borrowing from abroad or selling off capital assets—long-term assets—to finance current purchases of goods and services. They believe that continual borrowing is not a viable long-term strategy, and that selling long-term assets to finance current consumption undermines future production. (If this reminds you of the discussion about federal budget deficits and the national debt, that's no accident. The mechanisms at work are similar.)

Labor unions oppose trade deficits because they believe that when imports exceed exports, jobs are being lost to overseas workers, or soon will be. On the surface, it seems a reasonable argument, but the data on trade deficits and unemployment don't support it. In the late 1990s, when the trade deficit reached record highs, unemployment dropped to its lowest level in three decades.

Some economists who oppose trade deficits see them as a symptom, rather than a cause, of trouble, specifically bad central bank policy. They believe that trade deficits arise from loose monetary policy. A rapidly growing money supply boosts demand, including demand for imports. This has two effects: First, it generates inflationary pressure, some of which is "exported" to other nations, in the form of higher prices over there. Second, it directs too much investment in other nations into export industries. These nations' economies then suffer when America hits a recession and imports less.

Economists who consider trade deficits good associate them with positive economic developments, specifically, higher levels of income, consumer confidence, and investment. They argue that trade deficits enable the United States to import capital to finance investment in productive capacity. Far from hurting employment, they believe that trade deficits financed by foreign investment in the United States help to boost U.S. employment.

Some economists see trade deficits as mere expressions of consumer preferences and as immaterial. These economists typically equate economic well being with rising consumption. If consumers want imported food, clothing, and cars, why shouldn't they buy them? That range of choices is part of a successful economy.

The Real World

You will occasionally hear the term petrodollars used in discussions of world trade. Petrodollars are U.S. dollars earned by oil exporting nations, particularly those in the Mideast, from oil exports. Petrodollar surpluses are U.S. dollars earned from the sale of oil that are in excess of the exporting nation's development needs. Most petrodollars are invested in U.S. government securities and short-term paper of U.S. and European banks. (Some economists define petrodollars as funds from oil exports deposited in any currency in Western banks.)

Serious economic and political questions surround the issue of petrodollars. Among these are fears on both sides of the transaction. Some people in the West fear that the Mideast could disrupt the financial markets by pulling money out of those markets. Some people in the Arab world feel vulnerable to changes in the value of the U.S. dollar, which is affected by U.S. economic policy, and even to potential seizure of bank accounts by the U.S. government.

Another issue is the recycling of petrodollars. Where does all that money go? Some petrodollars are used by oil exporting nations to buy imports from oil importing nations. But they can't import enough to use all of the petrodollars. Therefore a large portion of petrodollars in Western banks are loaned to governments that need to finance balance of payments deficits. These nations use some of that borrowed money to buy oil and other imports. If petrodollars are not recycled, that money—billions of dollars—is taken out of circulation, which can slow the growth of the world economy.

Perhaps the best view of trade deficits is the balanced view. If a trade deficit represents borrowing to finance current consumption rather than long-term investment, or results from inflationary pressure, or erodes U.S. employment, then it's bad. If a trade deficit fosters borrowing to finance long-term investment or reflects rising incomes, confidence, and investment—and doesn't hurt employment—then it's good. If a trade deficit merely expresses consumer preferences rather than these phenomena, it is immaterial.

But what about the effect on GDP? Shouldn't Americans worry when net exports are negative and GDP is smaller than it otherwise would be?

Most mainstream economists believe that because the current account deficit is offset by foreign investment in the United States, the effect on GDP is negligible. The security of the U.S. economy and the U.S. dollar make investments in U.S. productive capacity and in U.S. corporate and government securities quite attractive. So as long as the trade deficits are financed by foreign investment and the dollar is not overly weakened by them, then GDP will be fine.

So, given the size of the U.S. economy and the benefits of foreign investment in the United States, the effect of trade deficits on GDP is minimal. This is particularly true when compared with the effect of other, more easily influenced factors, such as U.S. monetary policy. It's best to view trade deficits in the context of growth, unemployment, inflation, and other measures of economic performance. The size of the trade deficit itself, and even its trend, reveals very little about the condition of the U.S. economy.

EconoTip

The U.S. dollar is among the world's most stable currencies, backed by a strong economy with low inflation. Therefore many foreigners hold their savings in U.S. dollars. Sometimes, entire countries adopt U.S. currency as their own currency. These officially "dollarized" nations include Panama, Ecuador, El Salvador, and Guatemala. The dollar is also widely used in the Bahamas, Cambodia, and Haiti.

The International Monetary System

The rules and procedures for exchanging national currencies are collectively known as the international monetary system. This system doesn't have a physical presence, like the Federal Reserve System, nor is it as codified as the Social Security system. Instead, it consists of interlocking rules and procedures and is subject to the foreign exchange market, and therefore to the judgments of currency traders about a currency.

Yet there are rules and procedures—exchange rate policies—which public finance officials of various nations have developed and from time to time modify. There are also physical institutions that oversee the international monetary system, the most important of these being the International Monetary Fund.

Exchange Rate Policies

In July 1944, representatives from 45 nations met in Bretton Woods, New Hampshire to discuss the recovery of Europe from World War II and to resolve international trade and monetary issues. The resulting Bretton Woods Agreement established the International Bank for Reconstruction and Development (the World Bank) to provide long-term loans to assist Europe's recovery. It also established the International Monetary Fund (IMF) to manage the international monetary system of fixed exchange rates, which was also developed at the conference.

The new monetary system established more stable exchange rates than those of the 1930s, a decade characterized by restrictive trade policies. Under the Bretton Woods Agreement, IMF member nations agreed to a system of exchange rates that pegged the value of the dollar to the price of gold and pegged other currencies to the dollar. This system remained in place until 1972. In 1972, the Bretton Woods system of pegged exchange rates broke down forever and was replaced by the system of managed floating exchange rates that we have today.

The Bretton Woods system broke down because the dynamics of supply, demand, and prices in a nation affect the true value of its currency, regardless of fixed rate schemes or pegging policies. When those dynamics are not reflected in the foreign exchange value of the currency, the currency becomes overvalued or undervalued in terms of other currencies. Its price—fixed or otherwise—becomes too high or too low, given the economic fundamentals of the nation and the dynamics of supply, demand, and prices. When this occurs, the flows of international trade and payments are distorted.

In the 1960s, rising costs in the United States made U.S. exports uncompetitive. At the same time, western Europe and Japan emerged from the wreckage of World War II to become productive economies that could compete with the United States. As a result, the U.S. dollar became overvalued under the fixed exchange rate system. This caused a drain on the U.S. gold supply, because foreigners preferred to hold gold rather than overvalued dollars. By 1970, U.S. gold reserves decreased to about $10 billion, a drop of more than 50 percent from the peak of $24 billion in 1949.

In 1971, the U.S. decided to let the dollar float against other currencies so it could find its proper value and imbalances in trade and international funds flows could be corrected. This indeed occurred and evolved into the managed float system of today.

A nation manages the value of its currency by buying or selling it on the foreign exchange market. If a nation's central bank buys its currency, the supply of that currency decreases and the supply of other currencies increases relative to it. This increases the value of its currency.

On the other hand, if a nation's central bank sells its currency, the supply of that currency on the market increases, and the supply of other currencies decreases relative to it. This decreases the value of its currency.

The Real World

Private sector foreign currency traders buy and sell currencies with the goal of making money on foreign exchange rate movements. They make their judgments based on the economic fundamentals of the nation behind the currency. They also look at trends in the supply and demand of the currency. They want to buy currencies that will appreciate and avoid those that will depreciate. Like stock investors, they want to buy low and sell high. But these folks are not investors. They are traders with "investment horizons" often measured in hours or even minutes.

Many FX traders engage in arbitrage, the practice of profiting from the differences in price when the same currency (or security or commodity) is traded in more than one market. For instance, if an arbitrageur can buy yen with dollars more cheaply in the Tokyo than in London, and then sell the yen for dollars in London, she can make money on the transaction (with minimal risk). Currency traders also use sophisticated devices, such as futures contracts, to minimize their risk and make money.

The International Monetary Fund plays a key role in operations that help a nation manage the value of its currency.

The International Monetary Fund

The International Monetary Fund (www.imf.org) is like a central bank for the world's central banks. It is headquartered in Washington, D.C., has 184 member nations, and cooperates closely with the World Bank, which we discuss in Chapter 19. The IMF has a board of governors consisting of one representative from each member nation. The board of governors elects a 20-member executive board to conduct regular operations.

The goals of the IMF are to promote world trade, stable exchange rates, and orderly correction of balance of payments problems. One important part of this is preventing situations in which a nation devalues its currency purely to promote its exports. That kind of devaluation is often considered unfairly competitive if underlying issues, such as poor fiscal and monetary policies, are not addressed by the nation.

Member nations maintain funds in the form of currency reserve units called Special Drawing Rights (SDRs) on deposit with the IMF. (This is a bit like the federal funds that U.S. commercial banks keep on deposit with the Federal Reserve.) From 1974 to 1980, the value of SDRs was based on the currencies of 16 leading trading nations. Since 1980, it has been based on the currencies of the five largest exporting nations. From 1990 to 2000, these were the United States, Japan, Great Britain, Germany, and France. The value of SDRs is reassigned every five years.

SDRs are held in the accounts of IMF nations in proportion to their contribution to the fund. (The United States is the largest contributor, accounting for about 25 percent of the fund.) Participating nations agree to accept SDRs in exchange for reserve currencies—that is, foreign exchange currencies—in settling international accounts. All IMF accounting is done in SDRs, and commercial banks accept SDR-denominated deposits. By using SDRs as the unit of value, the IMF simplifies its own and its member nations' payment and accounting procedures.

In addition to maintaining the system of SDRs and promoting international liquidity, the IMF monitors worldwide economic developments, and provides policy advice, loans, and technical assistance in situations like the following:

♦ After the collapse of the Soviet Union, the IMF helped Russia, the Baltic states, and other former Soviet countries set up treasury systems to assist them in moving from planned to market-based economies.

♦ During the Asian financial crisis of 1997 and 1998, the IMF helped Korea to bolster its reserves. The IMF pledged $21 billion to help Korea reform its economy, restructure its financial and corporate sectors, and recover from recession.

♦ In 2000, the IMF Executive Board urged the Japanese government to stimulate growth by keeping interest rates low, encouraging bank restructuring, and promoting deregulation.

♦ In October 2000, the IMF approved a $52 million loan for Kenya to help it deal with severe drought. This was part of a three-year $193 million loan under an IMF lending program for low-income nations.

Most economists judge the current international monetary system a success. It permits market forces and national economic performance to determine the value of foreign currencies, yet enables nations to maintain orderly foreign exchange markets by cooperating through the IMF.

The Real World

The euro was officially adopted in January 1999 and introduced as the single currency in 2002. The euro was designed to be equivalent in value to the dollar. Since 2002, the value of the euro has fluctuated from a high of about $1.17 in its early days to a low of about 82 cents.

The EU and the Euro

The biggest news on the foreign currency front over the past few years is the adoption of the euro by the European Union (EU). Twelve member states of the EU use the euro instead of their old local currencies: Austria, Belgium, Finland, France, Germany, Greece, Ireland, Italy, Luxembourg, Netherlands, Portugal, and Spain.

Nations that adopt the euro participate in a single EU monetary policy and are subject to fiscal guidelines requiring them to keep deficits to a certain level and to balance their federal budgets by 2006. Although it will reconsider the matter again, Britain has refused to adopt the euro and has stuck with the pound sterling. This reflects England's traditional sense of "apartness" from continental Europe and its reluctance to give up sovereignty over its economic policies.

The Dollar and the U.S. Economy

A strong dollar—one that can purchase more foreign currency relative to a weak dollar—means that U.S. consumers pay less for imports. It also means that foreign consumers must pay more for U.S. exports.

A weak dollar—one that can purchase less foreign currency relative to a strong dollar—means that U.S. consumers must pay more for imports from foreign nations. However, foreign consumers will pay less for U.S. goods and services, which will help increase production and employment in America.

So the strong dollar and the weak dollar each have positive and negative effects. Think about it: A strong dollar helps U.S. consumers because it makes foreign goods, which American consumers clearly enjoy buying, cheaper. Yet it hurts U.S. exports and therefore U.S. production and employment. It also makes the United States a less affordable travel destination for foreign visitors.

Meanwhile, a weak dollar makes U.S. exports and travel in the United States more affordable for foreigners. That helps U.S. production and employment. However, it also raises the price of imports for Americans. This, in a sense, limits U.S. consumers' choices (and can contribute to inflation), but it shifts buying behavior in favor of U.S. products, which also helps U.S. employment.

The best "dollar policy" is, therefore, one that balances the pros and cons of a strong and weak dollar, and that takes the economies of our trading partners into account. That last point can be important: A dollar that is strong against the euro, for example, will weaken the euro. EU products will become more affordable to Americans, and Americans will be encouraged to travel to Europe. That can help EU nations struggling with recession and unemployment.

Indeed, much of Europe and Asia correctly view the United States as the engine of growth for the global economy. The U.S. market is so large, strong, driven by consumption, and partial to imports that it can boost production in European and Asian nations. That's a large responsibility and one that Americans, by virtue of their free spending ways, unwittingly but willingly take on. Likewise, when the U.S. business cycle turns down and demand decreases, no one in Europe or Asia is happy about it. Of course, economic policies and behavior in Europe and Asia are larger determinants of their economic fate. So it would be going too far to say, "When the U.S. sneezes, Europe catches cold," but there is a grain of truth in it.

The Least You Need to Know

- Fixed exchange rates are set by the nation's central bank or international agreement. Floating exchange rates are determined by market forces. Managed exchange rates are influenced by central banks, but are not targeted to a fixed exchange rate. The "managed float" that we have today mixes elements of floating and managed rates.

- The balance of payments summarizes all the international transactions of a nation.

- Some people worry about the balance of trade, yet most economists believe that a trade deficit or a trade surplus can be good or bad, depending on the situation.

- The International Monetary Fund functions as the central bank for the world's central banks. The major goals of the IMF are to promote world trade and stable exchange rates.

- A strong dollar and a weak dollar each have their positive and negative effects.

Chapter 19

The Global Market and Developing Nations

In This Chapter

◆ The international distribution of income

◆ Key developments in the global economy

◆ The role of multinational corporations

◆ Pros and cons of "globalization"

In this world of extremes, many of the world's extremes stem from economics. So the term global economy covers a lot of ground. It includes the mansions of Beverly Hills on the one hand and, on the other, the favelas (shantytowns) in the hills of Rio de Janeiro. Its inhabitants range from multibillionaire oil sheiks to people so poor that they eat rats in order to survive. Its markets operate with all the sophistication of the Goldman Sachs trading floor in Manhattan and all the simplicity of the barter society of the Huli tribe in Papau New Guinea.

It's not going too far to say that it's impossible to understand the world we live in without understanding its economics. In this chapter, we take a tour of the world economy and get to know the key players on a national level.

We also look at the major economic developments going on in the world today, and the stakes in these issues for various parties.

A Three Part World?

In the past, people classified nations into three different "worlds": The "first world" of nations aligned with the United States and capitalism, the "second world" of nations aligned with the now-defunct Soviet Union and communism, and the "third world" of nonaligned (and generally poor) nations. People use the term "third world" to refer to poor nations in general, but many people are not certain of its origin. (Some think that it means that one-third of the world is poor.) In any event, the classifications of nations according to their wealth and poverty and stage of economic development has become more sophisticated over the past two decades.

This is just as well and not just because more precise language is generally better. With the end of the Soviet Union in 1989, the "three world" scheme became obsolete. The United States, standard-bearer of capitalism, and the Soviet Union, the star of socialism, served as polar opposites and organizing principles for the world economy. However, the Soviet economy collapsed due to its inefficiency and its attempts to compete with the U.S. defense industry.

Without the countervailing force of the Soviet Union and the alternative economic system of socialism—as ineffectual as that force ultimately proved to be—the United States stands out as an economic superpower even more, for better and worse. On the one hand, it stands as a shining example of the standard of living industrious people can achieve in a free market economy. On the other hand, it stands as a symbol of acquisitiveness, consumption, and even economic and cultural imperialism. It is easy and comfortable for many Americans to ignore or dismiss the negative characterization, but that doesn't make in any less real for people around the world who agree with it.

Let's take a look at that world, with the goal of understanding it.

The World's Economies

Rather than take the three-world view, economists classify the world's economies as:

- Industrial or developed nations
- Newly industrialized nations
- Developing nations

Each of these types of countries has fairly specific characteristics, and economic issues, which we examine in this section. The countries also are classified by their level of income, which we'll look at after we examine their economic characteristics and issues.

Industrialized Nations: Growing and Growing Old

An industrialized economy has a large base of productive capital, sophisticated banking systems and financial markets, a variety of industries producing a broad range of products, and vigorous and varied international trade. Industrialized nations also have well established systems of government and law, and provide educational opportunities for their people.

The countries in the Group of Seven (G-7) have the most industrialized economies. The G-7 are the United States, Canada, Japan, Germany, France, the United Kingdom, and Italy (with Germany, France, the United Kingdom, and Italy comprising Europe's so-called Big Four). However, the entire EU—which also includes Austria, Belgium, Finland, Greece, Ireland, Luxembourg, the Netherlands, Portugal, and Spain—and some European nations outside the EU, such as Switzerland, Sweden, and Denmark, are also industrialized. So are Australia, New Zealand, and Taiwan.

EconoTip

The G-8 includes the G-7 plus Russia, which may best be described as an economy in transition. The transition will take Russia from a planned economy to a free-market, capitalist economy. The central planning structure has been dismantled, but the transition to a successful market economy is still in progress. In that sense, Russia is also a developing economy.

Less than 20 percent of the world's population lives in industrial nations, and they account for about 70 percent of world output. That fact—and the income inequality that it generates—creates some of the questions these countries face, such as: What is the realistic and responsible role for developed nations to play in the economies of less developed nations? What are the moral and ecological implications of using such a large share of the earth's resources (relative to the share other nations use) to sustain the levels of production and growth that industrial nations have achieved? What, in fact, constitutes *sustainable growth*, and is it achievable?

EconoTalk

The term **sustainable growth** refers to economic growth based on renewable resources (and efforts to renew them) and minimal environmental degradation. You will often hear about efforts to achieve sustainable growth in an economy or in the global economy.

Industrialized economies also face the problems of maintaining low unemployment and inflation, choosing the optimal mix of public and private goods, and coping with domestic poverty, crime, and disease. Also, the United States, Japan, and Western Europe are experiencing record low birth rates coupled with longer life expectancies. This translates to a "graying" of the population, in which older people will come to outnumber younger people. This holds serious implications for funding their retirement and health care, as we saw in our look at the U.S. Social Security system in Chapter 12.

On top of all this, the threat of terrorism, mainly from Islamic extremists from less developed countries, may well represent the most difficult and dangerous problem for industrialized nations, particularly the United States.

Newly Industrialized Nations: Getting Going

Newly industrialized nations (NICs) have a rapidly growing base of productive capital and rising incomes. Most of these nations have sound governments and banking and financial systems, although they may occasionally be subject to financial or political dislocation. For instance, Brazil is weighed down with international debt and must work hard to control inflation. Pakistan may face political instability and a shaky relationship with neighboring India.

Newly industrialized nations include Hong Kong, Singapore, Taiwan, and South Korea—which are known as Asia's "Four Tigers"—Pakistan, Malaysia, Indonesia, Thailand, Mexico, Brazil, Chile, Venezuela, Israel, South Africa, and Hungary.

Less than 5 percent of the world's population lives in NICs, and they earn less than 5 percent of the world's income.

The Four Tigers followed a strategy of export-oriented industrialization, in which they moved from the status of developing country to that of NIC in the 1970s and 1980s. These nations ambitiously took Japan as a role model, but concentrated on light manufacturing. The Tigers have been held up by the World Bank and the International Monetary Fund as models for other developing and underdeveloped nations. However, export-oriented growth isn't possible for every nation, especially when other nations, including China and some industrialized nations, still engage in protectionism.

NICs face a variety of problems, depending on their specific situations. One common issue is financing growth. How much can and should they rely on foreign borrowing? How much money for capital investment can they reasonably expect to generate themselves? A number of newly industrialized countries need more sophisticated banking and financial systems, and more stable governments.

The Real World

The U.S. textile industry is protected by the Multi-Fibre Agreement, a set of quotas imposed by industrialized nations on imports of textiles from less developed nations. This was signed in 1973 and remains in effect today. Economists point out that this agreement is counter to the aims of GATT and protects the jobs of workers in the textile trade in industrialized nations at the expense of those in less developed countries.

Some NICs are moving from economies based on producing and exporting natural resources to producing and exporting manufactured goods. Diversity of exports is both the mark of an industrial economy and a stabilizer of any economy. But this transition can be difficult, especially for nations such as Venezuela and Mexico, which export oil and have come to depend on the large revenues that oil exports produce.

Developing Nations

Developing nations range from the poorest in the world to those that have begun to build an industrial base, but have yet to achieve stable growth in production and income. These economies are also called underdeveloped, undeveloped, and, most commonly, less developed countries (LDCs). A number of these nations have large, growing urban populations and serious difficulties with unemployment, crime, and poverty in the cities.

The Organization for Economic Cooperation and Development, which I'll discuss later in this chapter, includes the following nations in its official list of less developed countries:

- All countries of Africa except the Republic of South Africa

- All countries of Asia except Cambodia, China, Japan, Laos, North Korea, and Vietnam

- All countries in Latin America, except Cuba

- All countries in the Middle East

- Malta, Portugal, Spain, Greece, and Turkey

The People's Republic of China could be considered an LDC. However, most economists view the PRC as a special case because it is beginning to industrialize but still relies heavily on small farms.

This list literally covers a lot of ground, and includes some nations that some economists would classify elsewhere. For example, Cuba is by many measures a less developed country, and while Portugal, Spain, and Greece are poor by European standards, they are wealthy compared with most nations of Africa. Regarding the Middle East, many economists think of Israel as an industrialized nation, albeit one that uses significant amounts of foreign aid.

Most economists also place the oil producing nations of the Middle East in a separate category. OPEC nations suffer serious internal income equality and have not diversified their industrial base significantly beyond oil production. But it's difficult to think of Saudi Arabia, with per capita income of about $7,000 as being in the same category as Ghana, with per capita income of $400.

Many less developed nations experience intense periodic political upheaval, including war, as well as natural disasters, such as drought and hurricanes. Most of them depend on small scale commercial farming, which produces exports such as coffee, bananas, and timber, and on subsistence farming, in which people grow their own food.

The staggering array of economic problems in truly less developed nations includes lack of skills, productive capital, organized financial markets, commercial diversification, transportation and communication infrastructure, technological infrastructure, capital formation, stable currency, and stable government. The poverty in many of these nations results in lack of food, clothing, housing, health care, education, and even drinkable water and basic sanitation.

Virtually all less developed nations receive some forms of economic aid and assistance. Yet the extent and persistence of their internal economic and political problems render this help almost symbolic.

Production and Income Classifications

Another quantitative method of classifying national economies is by per capita GDP or per capita income. In 2000, the approximate average per capita GDP for the three levels of nations broke out as follows:

Table 19.1   Per Capita GDP for National Economies

Type of Nation	Per Capita GDP
Developed Nations	$19,000
Newly Industrialized Nations	11,500
Less Developed Nations	3,400

As the table shows, developed nations enjoy five and a half times the per capita GDP of developing nations. Newly industrialized nations have over three times the per capita GDP of less developed nations.

You may recall that in the United States, households in the top 20 percent, the highest income quintile, earn almost 50 percent of the nation's income. The other 80 percent of the population divide up the other 50 percent. I presented this as an indicator of income inequality in the United States.

Income inequality on a worldwide level is even more pronounced. The top 20 percent of the world's population earns about 80 percent of its income. While this may be yet another instance of the *80-20 Rule*, it also means that 80 percent of the population is getting by on 20 percent of the world's income.

EconoTalk

The **80-20 Rule** states that 80 percent of an effect is attributable to 20 percent of the cause. For instance, 80 percent of a company's sales come from 20 percent of its sales force, or 80 percent of its profits come from 20 percent of its products.

The formal name for this rule is the Pareto Principle, named for the Italian economist Vilfredo Pareto (1848–1923), who realized that 20 percent of his country's population owned 80 percent of its wealth. The Pareto Principle is not really a statistically proven "rule." It's really a rule of thumb (because your thumbs account for 20 percent of your fingers, but do 80 percent of their work).

The World Bank classifies countries into high income, upper middle income, lower middle income, and low income groups. The average incomes for each group, in 1995 U.S. dollars, and examples of nations in each group, are as follows:

Table 19.2   World Bank Income Classifications

World Bank Classification	Average Income	
High Income	$22,818	(United States, Western Europe, Japan)
Upper Middle Income	5,175	(Argentina, Mexico, Poland, Hungary)
Lower Middle Income	1,808	(Costa Rica, Philippines, Romania, Jordan)
Low Income	388	(Sub-Saharan Africa, India)

Here are the numbers and percentages of the world's population in each of these groups:

Table 19.3 Population and Percentage of World's Population in World Bank Income Classifications

	Population (thousands)	Percentage
High Income	955,000	15.6
Upper Middle Income	503,700	8.2
Lower Middle Income	2,163,500	35.3
Low Income	2,511,400	40.9
Total	6,133,600	100.0

Here are selected characteristics I've chosen from those compiled by the World Bank on the four groups of economies. (You can find more of these data, which are called competitiveness factors, at worldbank.org/psd/compete.nsf.)

Table 19.4 Characteristics of World Bank Classifications

	Upper Income	Upper Middle	Lower Middle	Low Income
Average per capita income	22,818	5,175	1,808	388
Percent of world pop.	15.6	8.2	35.3	40.9
Life expectancy (years at birth)	76.8	70.1	68.1	54.6
Manufactered Exports as % of Total Exports	73.8	52.6	43.2	28.0
Phone lines per 1,000 people	487	180	113	17
Waiting time for phone line (years)	0.03	1.85	4.51	5.31
Televisions per 1,000 people	490	293	205	65.1
Personal Computers per 1,000 people	170	35	11	2
Literacy Rate (percent of adult pop.)	97	86	81	54
Scientists & technicians per 1,000 people	3.3	1.0	1.3	0.4
Patent Applications	76,507	18,801	10,008	336

These data speak for themselves. They show the correlation between technological and communications infrastructure (telephones and so on) and economic success. They also show the importance of investment in human capital in terms of literacy and scientific and technical education. The low life expectancy in low income countries indicates the lack of adequate nutrition and health care, and a high infant mortality rate.

A Worldwide Market?

The degree and extent of poverty in the world holds many implications. When over a billion people are living on $1 a day or less and more than another billion are living on $1 to $2 a day, and while one fifth of the world garners 80 percent of its income, the situation can only be described as income inequality.

Here are the quintile averages for income across the world's population. In other words, these quintile classifications cut across all nations: The highest quintile includes the wealthiest people from all nations. (Note that these values, which are from the World Bank, are not quintile breaks, but rather the average income within each quintile.)

Table 19.5   Average Income per Quintile

	Average Income
Highest Quintile	$25,000
Fourth Quintile	7,000
Third Quintile	3,000
Second Quintile	730
Lowest Quintile	365

The degree and extent of poverty in the world holds many implications. But rather than dwell on the moral aspects, which are as controversial as they are obvious, I want to point out the implications for the global market.

Quite bluntly, the industrialized nations of the world cannot sell goods and services to people who are living on less than $2 a day—those in the lowest and second quintiles. Many of these people go through their entire lives without riding in a car or using a telephone. How do you mass market merchandise to a population that has only 65 televisions per 1,000 people? How to you sell goods to people who don't have a home? How do you sell to people who spend all day trying to get enough food to live on? You cannot. The only goods that can be sold to people in the lowest two quintiles are those that can be distributed through relief agencies.

Even in the third quintile, where income takes a big jump over the lowest two, many people are doing without a refrigerator, let alone a car. Their average annual income of $3,000 is about $8.20 a day, which is what most working people in the highest quintile spend on commuting and lunch each day.

So the three lowest quintiles, by definition, account for about 3.7 billion of the world's 6.2 billion people. That is an immense potential market—if they had a decent level of income.

The fourth quintile is the first one where people normally have decent housing, refrigerators, and maybe even a car. They earn about $19 per day per person, so they have disposable income beyond that needed for the bare necessities. Yet they possess less than one-third the purchasing power of people in the top quintile.

By virtue of the fact that you're reading this book, you are probably in the top income quintile. Most marketing efforts, as companies in industrialized nations normally define them, are directed to this segment of the world's population. This means that when people talk about "the global market," they are generally omitting 60 to 80 percent of the world's population from their definition of "global."

Indeed, the goal of a multinational corporation dealing with an LDC may not be developing the local market, but rather developing an inexpensive production site. You might think that would lead to the LDC becoming a viable market—after all, production means jobs, jobs mean income, and income means consumption—but sometimes that isn't the case.

Multinational Corporations and Globalization: The Pros and Cons

First, let's define these two terms. A multinational corporation (MNC) is a large company engaged in international production and, usually, sales. The largest MNCs—also known as MNEs, for multinational enterprises—have production sites in several or even dozens of nations. An MNC typically scans the whole world, or at least substantial regions of the world, for markets, production sites, and sources of raw materials.

Globalization essentially means free movement of goods, services, people, and capital across national borders. This creates global markets for goods, services, labor, and capital. However, the term globalization has also come to mean something more: economic and cultural hegemony on the part of industrial enterprises, such as MNCs, and industrialized nations, particularly the United States. Those who oppose globalization use the term to describe these negative phenomena and to raise the specter of a world controlled by a handful of MNCs.

I'm discussing MNCs and globalization together because they are related. An MNC benefits from free movement of goods, services, people, and capital across national borders, just as U.S. companies have benefited from that situation in North America. As a corporation, an MNC has one main objective—to make a profit—and the free movement of goods, services, workers, and capital enhances profitability. It does that by giving management freer access to the factors of production and the ability to make decisions based more purely on cost and revenue considerations.

Also, MNCs promote globalization by their very existence and business practices. When McDonald's introduces its "customer experience" and its menu, even in modified form, to another culture, it begins to change that culture. When Ford sets up an assembly plant in Brazil, it attracts workers from the countryside and changes their economic aspirations, for better or worse. Similarly, the agenda of the World Bank and the IMF generally favor freer trade—a force for globalization—but many developing nations find free trade to be a mixed blessing.

The key problem in talking about MNCs and globalization, aside from the emotions they stir up, is that they are both creatures of the industrialized world. That is an undeniable fact, whether you oppose or support MNCs and globalization. The poorest nations in the world are not launching MNCs. Given that economically powerful entities rarely aim to benefit the poor, those who oppose MNCs and globalization—regardless of how emotionally they state their case—do have a case.

The Real World

Various nongovernmental organizations (NGOs) organize protests against globalization. NGOs typically state that they represent the interests of poor, working, oppressed, and economically disadvantaged people. Critics view them as uninformed elitists, while supporters see them as fighting exploitation and economic injustice. In truth, some NGOs, such as Amnesty International, Oxfam, and the Red Cross, do much to alleviate misery and aid the suffering. Others indeed amount to radical fringe groups.

People from each type of NGO, as well as unaffiliated protesters, have targeted globalization as evil. They have mounted protests in Washington (against the International Monetary Fund and the World Bank), Seattle (against the World Trade Organization), Barcelona (against the European Union), Genoa (against the G-7), and Davos, Switzerland (against the World Economic Forum, which is sponsored by some 1,000 major corporations from across the industrialized world), to name a few.

The major points in the case against MNCs are …

◆ They don't alleviate local poverty.

◆ They give economic and political power to external, commercial interests.

◆ They create economic instability when they become a major employer and then cut production or shut down operations.

◆ They substitute local customs, values, and traditions with Western style materialism, consumer customs, values, and traditions.

◆ They extract more economic benefit from local economies than they contribute.

On the other hand, supporters of MNCs argue that …

◆ They provide employment that usually pays better than other available opportunities.

◆ They stabilize and stimulate local economies, and raise standards of living. (Remember the multiplier effect?)

◆ They promote positive values, such as nonviolent conflict resolution, diversity, and equality for women.

◆ They promote efficient production and bring a broader range of products to the widest possible market.

◆ They create an environment of nonviolence and international peace and economic cooperation.

As usual, each side has valid points. Moreover, each side can cite statistical and anecdotal evidence to support its case.

In any event, globalization has been a fact of international business life. However, the United States is now the world's sole "superpower" and its major producer and consumer of goods and services. America draws criticism (and sometimes violent responses) for its real and perceived economic power. From France's complaints about Euro Disney to radical Islam's characterization of the United States as "the Great Satan," from lack of U.S. cooperation on international environmental agreements to its role in often negatively perceived, pro-growth institutions like the World Bank and the IMF, there are forces working against the United States and globalization.

Thus, the story of globalization and the role of MNCs in the world is still being written. MNCs and globalization can be forces for good or ill. Both could clearly help the world economy produce the greatest good for the greatest number of people. However, in practice, MNCs may have to go about their business a bit differently and globalization may need to be less imperialistic for that to occur.

Overcoming Barriers to Development

Regardless of how it happens or what form it takes, economic development and only economic development will alleviate poverty and raise standards of living. But there are many barriers to development that must be overcome. The success of the United States, Canada, Western Europe, Japan, and Australia has been difficult for other nations to duplicate.

Many observers in these democracies argue that establishing democratic governments and reducing corruption would set the LDCs on the path to economic achievement. Others believe that the right kind of foreign aid would do the trick. Still others believe that if these nations engaged in free trade and "took a seat at the table" with industrialized nations, they would prosper. While some of these measures would help, none of them alone would generate development.

Democracy and reduced corruption might help in some cases, but movement to democratically elected governments (for instance, in South America) has not eliminated economic chaos. Western democracy means more than free elections. It means a free press to ensure greater governmental accountability and sound fiscal and monetary policies. A sound central bank is as important as an elected government.

Foreign aid can do wonders. It was the *Marshall Plan*, one of the largest foreign aid programs in history, that rebuilt Europe after World War II and helped Germany become an economic giant. Many people who denounce foreign aid forget this, yet it is often difficult to assess the benefits of foreign aid in LDCs. Some of the money almost certainly finds its way into the wrong pockets. That said, many economists believe that the wealthy creditor nations that have lent billions to developing nations should forgive much or even all of that debt in order to give these nations a fresh start.

EconoTalk

The **Marshall Plan,** named for Secretary of State George C. Marshall, who proposed it in 1947, provided up to $20 billion in aid (in late-1940s dollars) for relief and rebuilding. The condition was that European nations had to act together and cooperate economically. By 1953, the United States had contributed $13 billion and Europe was on its way to recovery.

The U.S. economy also benefited from the plan, because the money was used to buy productive capital and other goods from America. These were to be shipped to Europe on American merchant vessels. Without a doubt, the Marshall Plan was a success for all parties involved.

Free trade doesn't necessarily help a country join the ranks of developed nations. Argentina tried it, and it failed badly. Most economists believe that developed nations should end protectionist practices that limit imports from developing nations. Textiles, as noted, are one area, and farm products are another.

Thus a mix of economic and political measures—ideally, tailored to the specific nation—is the recipe for economic development.

What Does the Future Hold?

Economic trends and forecasts bear out the old saying, "The rich get richer and the poor get poorer." Well, not exactly. The poor are slowly earning more money in real terms. However, as is the case in the United States, the rich are earning even more. So in relative terms the gap between the wealthy—meaning the developed nations—and the poor—meaning the less developed countries—is widening, and it is expected to continue to widen unless international policies change in significant ways.

The Least You Need to Know

- Economists classify the world's economies as industrialized or developed nations, newly industrialized nations, and developing or less developed nations.

- The top 20 percent of the world's population earns about 80 percent of its income.

- Multinational corporations have production sites in several or even dozens of nations. An MNC typically scans the whole world, or at least substantial regions of the world, for markets, production sites, and sources of raw materials.

- Globalization means free movement of goods, services, people, and capital across national borders, which creates global markets for goods, services, labor, and capital.

- Barriers to economic development include lack of sound financial markets and central banking systems, lack of education and skills, and lack of stable, accountable government.

- China has grown its economy by adopting some features of a capitalist, market economy. However, China has not moved toward democracy and has kept many aspects of its totalitarian government in place.

Part 6

Everyday Economics

Does economics have any practical application to those of us who are not trading currencies or attempting to influence the money supply? Can this stuff help you make money, save money, or manage your business or career?

Yes! But first you have to spend a little time monitoring the economy. And I do mean a little. If you simply glance at the business pages of your newspaper, listen with one ear to the business news on the radio or TV, and, once a month, check in at three or four websites you will be "monitoring the economy" enough to get something out of it.

So in the first chapter in this final part of the book, I'll show you how to monitor the economy so you know where you are in relation to it. Then, in the last chapter, I'll show you what to do about it.

Chapter 20

It's Down! It's Up! Monitoring the Economy's Pulse

In This Chapter

- ◆ Sources of economic data and information
- ◆ Economic indicators and what they mean
- ◆ Characteristics of recent business cycles

For the businessperson, professional, employee, or consumer, the key questions about the economy center on the business cycle: Is the economy in an expansion or a recession? If it is expanding, how strong is the expansion and how long is it likely to continue? If it is contracting, how long will it continue to do so? Also, if the economy is sluggish, are there any areas of strength? Finally, what fiscal and monetary policies are being implemented, and what will be their likely effects?

In this chapter, you'll learn how to read the signposts that signal the condition and likely direction of the economy. Unfortunately, these signposts are not always clear. But if you see enough of them and you can read between the signs, so to speak, you will have a good idea of what's going on in the economy.

The Value of Economic News and Information

The economy is the environment in which we make our professional and financial plans and decisions, and it's best to understand the environment in which you are planning and deciding. I am not saying that you should base a decision on the nation's economic situation. Rather you should understand that situation and the potential effect on your decision.

For example, suppose you wanted to move to a booming economic area, such as Silicon Valley or Las Vegas in the late 1990s, after those booms had been in progress for a few years. You should understand that booms don't last forever. Thus, there's a real possibility that the price of the house that you would buy at that time could go down, or at least not rise at the rate that housing prices had been rising.

Does this mean that you shouldn't move to one of these areas? Hardly. It means that you should understand the nature of booms, and what happens to housing prices when they end. (Housing prices usually either fall or level off after a regional or local economic boom and then return to normal growth rates.)

It's equally important to understand the overall business environment and "the mood of the country." The expansions of the 1980s and 1990s were social as well as economic phenomena. In the 1980s, conspicuous consumption and a fascination with wealth took hold in the United States. This was reflected in television shows such as *Dallas*, *Dynasty*, and *Lifestyles of the Rich and Famous*. This trend continued in the 1990s, a period when consumption grew even more conspicuous and people in all walks of life became enthralled with the stock market. Magazine cover stories—in the newsweeklies, not just business magazines—featured articles on stock trading and portfolio management.

Understanding the economy of America and the economic drives of Americans helps you understand not only the business environment but also the culture of America and its place in the world.

So much for generalities. Let's look at the economic news and at specific indicators and at what they mean.

Key Economic Indicators and Their Importance

Official economic data are compiled and released by a number of sources, and reported by the media, which gets them from the same sources. The most prominent sources include the Federal Reserve, Bureau of Economic Analysis, and Bureau of Labor Statistics. Data is released by these sources according to a schedule that's usually published at the source's website and in many newspapers.

For example, the Bureau of Economic Analysis (BEA) publishes its data release dates for the current and the coming years at its website (www.bea.gov/bea/newsrel). The BEA data include GDP, personal income and outlays, gross state product by industry, corporate profits, U.S. international trade in goods and services, and state personal income, among many others.

Certain data are called economic indicators because they point to the condition of the economy. While the numerical value of an indicator is important, the trend—that is, the direction and magnitude of movement in the value of the indicator—is even more important. A trend can be upward, downward, or flat. Some data occasionally follow a saw-tooth trend (up, down, up, down). Whatever the recent trend is, you want to be aware of it.

Of course, whether a particular value and trend of an indicator is favorable or not depends on the indicator. The key things to watch for are peaks and troughs. New highs and new lows can indicate either a particularly strong trend or a possible turning point ahead in the trend. For instance, the national annual unemployment rate approached 10 percent in 1988 and 1989, but didn't break the 10 percent mark. A 10 percent unemployment rate for the year would indeed be widely reported news, and bode very poorly for the presidential administration. (In fact, given the rates that did occur, President George H.W. Bush soon found himself unemployed.)

More recently, the fed funds rate hit a three-decade low of 1.25. Now the Fed could take the rate lower, but it was safe to assume that it couldn't go much lower. Therefore, there would probably be a turning point for interest rates in the near future.

Let's look at some specific indicators, and at how to look at them.

GDP Growth

This is the major indicator to watch. GDP growth is reported on a monthly basis, but the BEA's quarterly readings—reported as a seasonally adjusted, annualized rate of growth in real GDP—are the ones to watch. That's because three months provides a more accurate measure of economic growth than one month. In other words, monthly fluctuations in GDP growth don't mean all that much.

Seasonally adjusted data have been subjected to statistical calculations that correct for variances in the data caused by seasonal differences—meaning fluctuations caused by factors such as climate and patterns of business activity. An example would be the decrease in home construction during the winter months.

Annualized data are data for a part of the year which have been extended by statistical techniques (and, usually, seasonally adjusted) so that they represent the annual value that would occur if that rate continued for the whole year.

The BEA reports the GDP growth rate in advance, preliminary, and final forms. This reflects the fact that the BEA releases the GDP growth rate before all the nationwide data that feeds into that value has been reported and analyzed. The final form incorporates all of the available data, and the variance can be as high as 1 or 2 percentage points—or more.

The trend in GDP growth is determined by 1) comparing the recent growth rate to that of the same period in the previous year—year-over-year comparisons and 2) comparing it to the rate for the previous period. Year-over-year comparisons are indicated with words such as, "GDP grew at an annual rate of X percent in the first quarter compared with Y percent in the first quarter of last year." Comparisons to the rate for the previous period are usually reported with words such as, "GDP grew at X percent for the second quarter, which is down (up) compared with the Y percent rate for the first quarter."

As you know, the long-term trend for GDP growth is about 3 percent. So look for deviations from that figure. Sustained reports of growth above 3 percent indicate a strong expansion or perhaps a shift in underlying fundamentals that may prove to be temporary. Sustained growth of less than 2 percent indicates a sluggish economy. Of course, negative growth indicates an economic contraction. Two consecutive quarters of contraction are the official definition of a recession.

The growth rate of the economy should be viewed in the context of the unemployment rate and the inflation rate.

Unemployment Rate and Related Data

The unemployment rate is widely reported, and tends to change gradually. Rising unemployment accompanies decreasing economic growth—but the magnitude of the increase in the unemployment rate can be surprisingly low. Sometimes this occurs because management cuts back overtime or moves workers from full-time to part-time status, rather than lay people off.

Economists disagree about the *full-employment rate of unemployment* in the United States. Some believe it is as low as four percent, while others peg it as high as six percent. Unemployment over six percent, however, is considered too high by most economists and public officials.

A wealth of interesting data on unemployment and employment, including duration of unemployment and reasons for unemployment, are available at the Bureau of Labor Statistics (BLS) website (www.bls.com). Among the most interesting are data on job loss and growth:

◆ **Jobs lost:** Jobs are typically lost to the economy during a recession due to lay-offs and companies going out of business. The number of jobs lost is often reported in the general business news.

◆ **New jobs created:** A growing economy usually creates new jobs, and the number of new jobs created is tracked and reported by the BLS.

◆ **Net jobs lost or net new jobs:** This is the most useful single figure because the net figure tells you whether more jobs were lost than created (net loss) or more were created than lost (net gain). The economy is usually both losing and creating jobs and the net figure tells you which occurred in greater quantity.

EconoTalk

The **full-employment rate of unemployment** is the rate of unemployment at which everyone in the workforce who wants a job, has a job. At that rate, the unemployed are between jobs or, even though they could get jobs, are taking a short break from work or holding out for better pay. Economists call this frictional unemployment, and there is always some of it in an economy. So the full-employment unemployment rate is the lowest possible rate of unemployment.

The Real World

A "jobless recovery" is one that has yet to produce a net job gain. The first year of the expansion that officially began in 1991 and lasted until early 2001 produced no net gain in the number of jobs. Critics usually cite management's unwillingness to hire new workers as the reason for a jobless recovery. However, that unwillingness is usually related to a lag between the official beginning of a recovery and renewed hiring.

Companies are a bit more conservative than they used to be about rehiring workers when an expansion begins, and they may forestall hiring to save money. But this is hardly either malevolent or bad decision-making. It is conservative management to make sure that the recovery is materializing—and demand for the company's products is picking up—before rehiring workers.

Inflation

Although inflation has been under control over the past several years, make sure it stays that way. Any notable increase in inflation will probably cause the Fed to tighten monetary policy at least a bit. Also, an inflationary trend might affect some of your business decisions. We'll discuss them in the next chapter.

Two measures of inflation are worth noting: the consumer price index (CPI), which you learned about in Chapter 10, and the producer price index (PPI). The CPI measures the increase (or decrease), over a month, quarter, or year in the prices that consumers pay for a "market basket" of popular goods and services. The PPI measures the increase (or decrease) in the general price that producers pay for raw materials, labor, and other inputs. Both are reported each month at the BLS website.

The "rate of inflation" generally means the CPI or, more accurately, changes in the CPI. The CPI is an index similar to others you've learned about in which changes to the index are measured in relation to a base year, which is given the value of 100. Therefore it is changes in the index, not the value of the index that is important—and the changes are what is reported. For instance, when you hear that prices rose at an annual rate of 2.5 percent over the past quarter, it means that the *value of the CPI* rose 2.5 percent. It is not saying that the CPI itself is 2.5 percent.

Table 20.1 shows the overall rate of inflation (on the line labeled "All items") and the rates of inflation in specific expenditure categories for the three months ending October 2002.

Table 20.1 August–October 2002 Rates of Inflation

	Compound Annual Rate for 3 Months Ending 10/02
All items	3.1
Food and beverages	0.9
Housing	2.9
Apparel	4.7
Transportation	5.1
Medical care	4.7
Recreation	1.5
Education and Communication	2.2
Other goods and services	1.2

	Compound Annual Rate for 3 Months Ending 10/02
Special indexes	
Energy	13.4
Food	0.9
All items less energy and food	2.3

The 3.1 percent value for "all items" represents a weighted average of all the items in the "market basket." Food and recreation remained two of the best deals in America during this period. Areas seeing relatively sharp increases in prices included clothing, transportation, health care, and especially energy (reflecting a rise in oil prices due to the uncertainty surrounding the planned invasion of Iraq). This listing of inflation rates—available every month at the BLS website—can keep you in closer touch with price trends than the overall inflation rate.

EconoTip

The producer price index, also available at the BLS website, is often an indicator of future trends in the consumer price index. That's because if producers get hit with price increases, they pass them on to consumers, to the extent that they can.

Interest Rate Movements

Interest rates are key indicators of the business outlook, because borrowing costs are among the most important considerations in investment decisions. High borrowing costs curtail investment and consumption, while low borrowing costs encourage investment and consumption.

The key interest rates to watch are the fed funds rate, the prime rate, and the *fixed rate* for a 30-year mortgage for a house. Changes in the fed funds rate signal the direction of monetary policy. The prime rate indicates the general affordability of money for business because many business loans are tied to the prime rate. Increases in the prime signal higher borrowing costs for business, while decreases signal lower borrowing costs. While many households now have *adjustable rate* mortgages or mortgages

EconoTalk

On a **fixed rate** loan of any kind, the borrower is charged one interest rate that does not change over the life of the loan. On **adjustable rate** loans, the interest rate fluctuates over the life of the loan to reflect variations in prevailing interest rates. Variable rate loans are usually tied to a standard interest rate, plus one or more percentage points.

with a term shorter than 30 years, the rate for the standard, fixed rate, 30-year mortgage is still a good indicator of long-term interest rates for consumers.

It's also useful to track the interest rates on federal government securities of various maturities. The yield on a range of these securities—called Treasury securities or, simply, Treasuries—is used to define the yield curve, and it's useful to know the general shape of the yield curve. In fact, it's one of the best tools available for the serious Fed watcher.

A yield curve is a graph that shows the interest rates of bonds of the same quality but various maturities, arranged from the lowest to the highest maturity. When economists and financial professionals talk about *the* yield curve, they are generally referring to the yield curve defined by Treasury securities ranging from three-month T-bills to the 30-year bond. Usually, the yield curve slopes upward, because short-term rates are typically lower than long-term rates.

Figure 20.1 shows the yield curve prevailing at around the start of 2003.

Figure 20.1

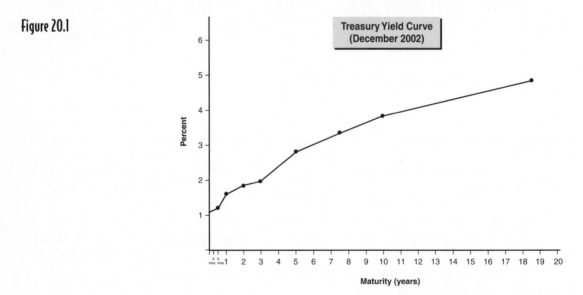

Figure 20.1 shows a positive yield curve. This means that short-term interest rates are lower than long-term rates. Economists normally expect a positive yield curve because investors demand a higher interest rate over the long-term to compensate them for having their money tied up for years.

A positive yield curve signals an expanding economy. Why? Because investors demand a high long-term rate when they expect rates to rise. And they expect rates to rise in an expansion when the demand for money rises. When future rates rise, they want a long-term rate that compensates them for being locked into that long-term bond. Also, investors demand a high long-term rate when they expect the increased inflation associated with economic growth. In other words, expectations about the future determine the shape of the yield curve.

Sometimes there is little difference between short- and long-term rates. This is called a narrow *spread* between short- and long-term rates. When the interest rate spread is narrow, a flat yield curve prevails because short-term and long-term rates are almost the same.

EconoTalk

Here, the interest-rate **spread** is the difference between short-term and long-term rates on securities of similar quality. People in the financial markets will talk about the spread between short-term and long-term rates narrowing or widening. The word spread has other meanings in finance as well. For instance, the spread is also the difference between the rate a bank pays on deposits and earns on loans. The spread is also the difference in the exchange rate of a currency in two different markets. In the context of the yield curve, however, it means the difference between short- and long-term rates.

A flat yield curve typically occurs after all interest rates have been rising and investors sense that rates are reaching a cyclical peak. When they feel that interest rates are peaking, investors shift from short-term to long-term securities in order to lock in the higher long-term rates. This flattens the yield curve because when money shifts from short-term to long-term investments, long-term rates decline. They decline because people bid up bond prices and when the price of a bond rises, its interest rate falls.

After the yield curve flattens, the movement of money from short-term into long-term securities increases short-term yields. They increase because the price of short-term securities falls, and when the price of a security that pays interest falls, the yield on it rises. Eventually, this creates an inverted yield curve, in which short-term rates are higher than long-term rates.

What does an inverted yield curve indicate?

It means that a recession is probably around the corner. How far around the corner and how bad it will be are hard to predict. But an inverted yield curve—in which short-term rates are higher than long-term rates—means that investors have moved to long-term bonds. Their expectations of the future are relatively pessimistic. They see demand for borrowings drying up because businesses are going to be investing less and consumers will be spending less. Businesses and consumers are going to be holding cash, which they tend to do in a recession.

The Interest Rate Cycle

Interest rates change with the business cycle. They are low at the beginning of a recovery and rise as the economy expands. Rates are high at the peak of an expansion, and then fall as the economy contracts. In a contraction, people and businesses want to hold cash rather than invest it in an uncertain future. In an expansion, they spend their cash and then start borrowing, which pushes up interest rates and starts the interest rate cycle all over again.

So, a positive yield curve means an expansion lies ahead. This is particularly so in the case of steep positive curves because the Fed has cut short-term rates (the only ones that it can directly influence) quite low in order to stimulate the economy. Again, how far ahead the expansion lies or how strong it will be are hard to predict, but an expansion should be on the way.

During the expansion, the yield curve will gradually flatten and eventually (but not always) become inverted. This flattening or inversion signals a coming recession.

Then, when recession hits, the Fed will lower short-term rates in order to stimulate growth. The lowering of short-term rates will cause the yield curve to become positive again. People will hold cash, but only until they have to start spending it again (when their cars and clothing and appliances wear out again) and demand revives.

EconoTip

The Treasury yield curve is published daily in the *Wall Street Journal*, which also shows the curve for a month earlier and a year earlier. This enables you to see whether it is flattening, inverting, or getting steeper. Several websites for investors, including www.wealth.bloomberg.com and www.bondsonline.com, publish a daily yield curve.

The U.S. Treasury Department site, www.ustreas.gov publishes current and historical yield curve rates. Scanning the list of historical rates at this site, which shows monthly values for a range of maturities, clearly shows how the curve flattens, inverts (or almost inverts), and then gets steeper with the business cycle. (Keep in mind that recessions occurred in 1990/91 and 2001.)

Consumer and Business Confidence

I discussed the two most widely followed indicators of consumer confidence—the Conference Board's Consumer Confidence Index and University of Michigan

Consumer Confidence Index—in Chapter 10, so we need not cover them again here. Keep tabs on them every month or two. They are somewhat "soft" as indicators go—meaning not based on market activity or dollars allocated—but they are measures of the consumer's "mood."

Housing Starts and Auto Sales

Housing starts and auto sales may be even better measures of the consumer's mood. Rising housing starts indicate an economic expansion is in progress or on the way, because those houses will be purchased and then filled with furniture, appliances, and, usually, another mouth to feed. Note, however, that housing starts can be a very local phenomenon, so the data for your state may tell you more than data for the nation.

You can find data on housing starts at the website of the National Association of Homebuilders (www.nahb.org). Look for a rising or falling trend over two or more months. The reported figure is an annualized, seasonally adjusted number, that is, the annual total if housing starts were to continue at the current pace. If the report states that housing starts increased this month by 8 percent, to an annual rate of 1.7 million units, it means that the annual rate last month was about 1.6 million (because 1.6 million times 1.08 equals 1.7 million). It also means that if starts continue at their current pace, the total for the year will be 1.7 million.

The record for housing starts was set in 1986 at 1.8 million. Total housing starts—the reported number—includes both single-family homes and multifamily dwellings. However, the report from the NAHB breaks out the two classifications. It also discusses regional patterns and forecasts for the months and year ahead.

Retail Sales and Auto Sales

With consumer spending accounting for two-thirds of GDP, retail sales trends are a useful economic indicator. The U.S. Department of Commerce issues a report on monthly sales for retail and food services at www.census.gov. Look at both the month-to-month trends and the year-over-year comparisons. This report breaks spending out into major categories, including motor vehicles, furniture, electronics, building materials, clothing, and so on. Retail sales trends are also widely reported in the business news, particularly before, during, and after the Christmas season.

Auto sales are a good gauge of the consumer's willingness to spend. You can find more detail on vehicle sales at the website www.carmetrics.com in their monthly reports of vehicle sales. Be aware that passenger cars and light trucks (where SUVs are counted) are reported separately.

Financial Market Indicators

A few financial market indicators, in addition to interest rates, are widely reported and worth noting. These include the major stock market averages, the price of gold, and the price of oil.

Market Averages

The widely reported stock market averages may be best viewed as another indicator of mood. Yes, stock prices rise during expansions and fall during contractions, and the long-term market averages have grown as the economy has grown. However, by the time a market trend becomes established, most people are aware of what the economy is doing. Also, market averages are heavily influenced by investor psychology. In addition, moves by large institutional investors who have their own financial motives for buying and selling also affect the short-term movement of market averages.

EconoTip

The main U.S. market averages are the Dow Jones industrial average, the S&P Composite Index of 500 Stocks, and the NASDAQ-OTC Price Index, each of which have shorter nicknames. "The Dow," a weighted average of 30 large-company stocks, is the most widely reported market average. The S&P 500, based on 500 stocks selected by the financial information company Standard & Poor's, obviously represents a broader measure of the market's performance. The NASDAQ (National Association of Securities Dealers Automatic Quotations) is a broad average of stocks of smaller companies traded "over the counter." These OTC stocks are not listed on a major exchange, but are nonetheless bought and sold through brokers.

Nevertheless, many people believe that the market accurately reflects investors' expectations about six months out and that stock prices are driven by corporate profits and economic fundamentals. They believe that stock prices are a good economic indicator because they reflect the buy-and-sell decisions of millions of investors operating with the best information they can get. Also, as you will see later in this chapter, the S&P 500 does have predictive value as a leading indicator.

The problem is that most people don't take a very analytical view of the market averages, which are widely reported on a daily basis. So people tend to be overly affected by the market's performance on a given day or week. It's best to look at the trend in the market averages over several weeks rather than to get hung up on the daily closing value of the S&P 500 (let alone the Dow, which is based on only 30 stocks). Viewed in that light, the market averages can give you another indication of where the economy is headed.

The Price of Gold

Gold has long been viewed as a *hedge against inflation* and as the ultimate in safe investments. However, with inflation under control for the past decade and with many stocks and most real estate (that is, residential real estate in populous areas) serving as safe long-term investments, gold may have lost some of its luster for the average investor. Yet the worldwide market for gold is alive and well, and gold still stirs the emotions of many investors.

The price of gold and the direction of price movements are widely reported. In general, rising gold prices indicate worries over the economy and a flight from securities such as stocks and bonds. Falling gold prices indicate optimism over the economy and movement of money into securities.

EconoTalk

A **hedge against infla-tion** is an investment that rises in value as prices rise due to inflation. Stocks have often been viewed as a hedge against inflation, but perhaps the best hedge against inflation is real estate, particularly housing. Housing prices have risen at the rate of inflation, and faster in many areas of the United States, over the past 25 years.

Oil Prices

Commodity trading is a highly specialized area of the financial community, so the price of soybeans and hog bellies won't tell us average folks much about the economy. The one exception among commodity prices would be that of oil. We can cut back on soy sauce and bacon, but it's harder to cut back on gasoline. Thus the price of crude oil, which is widely reported, can seriously affect the U.S. economy.

Oil prices are expressed as the price per barrel. In recent years, a price of around $18 to $22 has been considered normal, but lately the price has hovered around $25 per barrel. A sustained price above $30 per barrel would be bad news for the U.S. economy in the eyes of most economists. You can find oil prices at several websites, with www.bloomberg.com/energy one of the most accessible.

The Composite Index of Leading Indicators

The Composite Index of Leading Indicators is generated by the Conference Board and released around the twentieth of each month. It is widely reported in the media, and is available at the Conference Board's website www.globalindicators.org/us/latestreleases. The press release at the website discusses which of the 10 individual indicators increased or decreased.

As is the case for most indexes, this one is tied to a base year (1996 in this case) in which the value of the index is pegged at 100. These are called leading indicators because movement in them—and in the index itself—occurs *before* movement in the economy as measured by GDP growth.

The 10 indicators in the composite index along with the statistical standardization factors—which indicate the weight that each indicator has in the index—are the following:

Factor

1. Average weekly hours worked, manufacturing   .1812

2. Average weekly initial claims for unemployment insurance   .0262

3. Manufacturers' new orders, consumer goods and materials   .0496

4. Vendor performance, slower deliveries index   .0276

5. Manufacturers' new orders, nondefense capital goods   .0130

6. Building permits, new private housing units   .0191

7. Stock prices, 500 common stocks   .0308

8. Money supply, M2   .3038

9. Interest rate spread, 10-year Treasury bonds less federal funds rate   .3305

10. Index of consumer expectations   .0183

These 10 indicators are those that the Conference Board has determined, by means of statistical analysis, best indicate the future direction of the economy. The factor assigned to the indicator represents the weight that the indicator has in the index. The higher the factor, the greater that indicator's weight in the index. In other words, the higher the factor, the higher the predictive value of the indicator. (The 10 factors add up to 1.)

According to this analysis, the two indicators with the greatest weight are the interest rate spread (with a weight of .3305) and the money supply (at .3038). In fact, these two indicators of monetary policy account for 63 percent of the predictive value of the composite index (because .3305 + .3038 = .6338, or 63 percent).

The next most important indicator is employment, as measured by average weekly hours worked in manufacturing industries (with a factor of .1812). That means that about 82 percent of the predictive value of the composite index is explained by the two monetary policy indicators and the employment indicator (calculated by adding the factors for the three indicators).

Thus, the other seven indicators account for less than 20 percent of the composite's predictive value. The most important two are manufacturers' new orders for consumer goods and materials and stock prices as measured by the S&P 500. Note that the index gives much greater weight to manufacturers' new orders for consumer goods (indicator #3) than to new orders for capital goods (indicator #5). Also, the composite uses an index of 500 stocks as opposed to the much narrower Dow Jones Industrial Average, which is based on only 30 stocks.

Because we are dealing with an index here, changes in the index are more widely reported than the value of the index (which in late 2002 was about 111). It's worth knowing whether the index has been rising or falling in recent months.

Economic Forecasting: Fact or Folly?

Essentially, the Composite Index of Leading Indicators attempts to do what so many economists in the investment, banking, and business community try to do: forecast the future of the economy. Economic forecasters have a very mixed record. This applies to forecasters as a group and to individual economists, who may nail three quarterly GDP growth rates in a row only to find themselves humbled by the fourth quarter.

There's a saying that applies here: Whether you think stocks will go up or down, you're right. The same applies to the economy. It will go up or down, sooner or later. Economists don't have much trouble knowing whether the economy is expanding or contracting. It's what it will do next that keeps them guessing.

Smart business people understand the proper uses of forecasts: first, forecasts present a range of alternative economic scenarios to consider, and second, forecasts are useful for sensitivity analysis.

A forecast that presents a range of potential economic outcomes, and assigns a probability to each one, helps you think about the future more precisely and creatively. For instance, the forecaster might say, "Our optimistic scenario (probability = 20 percent) calls for GDP growth of 3.5 percent next year with minimal inflation and unemployment. Our pessimistic scenario (probability = 30 percent) calls for a negative first quarter and flat growth for the year. Our best estimate (probability = 50 percent) calls for a flat first quarter and growth of 2.3 percent for the year."

Forecasts like these, which a number of economists prepare, give you parameters to think within. In this example, the economist doesn't expect a sharply negative year, although the first quarter will be flat or perhaps negative. But because she assigns a higher probability to the pessimistic scenario than to the optimistic one, the risks are weighted toward the negative side.

Sensitivity analysis can be even more useful. In sensitivity analysis, an economist uses a mathematical model to construct a baseline forecast, and then changes the economic variable that's being considered. The variable might be a tax cut, a sharp rise in oil prices, or an increase in imports due to lower tariffs. Changing the variable and then examining the effect on the baseline forecast can give the economist a good idea of the effect of the tax cut, rise in oil prices, or increase in imports on growth and, usually, on measures such as employment, interest rates, and tax revenues.

So, economic forecasts can be quite useful, if properly used. No one can accurately forecast the future with consistency. But good forecasters can help you think about the future more clearly and plan for it more carefully.

The Least You Need to Know

◆ Economic data are compiled and released by a number of sources, including the Federal Reserve, Bureau of Economic Analysis, and Bureau of Labor Statistics. The Conference Board and private firms provide economic analysis and forecasts.

◆ The growth of real GDP is the key economic indicator. The growth rate will rise and fall with the business cycle, but over the long term GDP growth will average about 3 percent.

◆ Economic growth should be viewed in light of the unemployment rate and the rate of inflation.

◆ The yield curve is among the best indicators of where we are in the business cycle. A normal, positively sloped curve means that the economy is expanding. An inverted curve signals a likely recession.

◆ Several measures of consumption, particularly housing starts, retail sales, and auto sales can be useful economic indicators. Mixed indicators typically mean that a change of direction in the economy lies ahead.

◆ The Composite Index of Leading Indicators is worth checking out, particularly if an expansion or recession has been going on for a while. It may help you anticipate the next turning point.

Chapter 21

Applied Economics in Business and Personal Life

In This Chapter

- The effects of the business cycle
- Applying principles of economics in your business
- Economics and investing

You are now positioned to nod knowingly when someone starts moaning about the inverted yield curve. You can argue intelligently for a tax cut or a tax increase—or both, if you really want to confuse people. To confuse them further, you can lecture on the need to spend money to boost consumption *and* to save money to build the nation's pool of investable funds. You can hold forth on trade policy and can explain why the Social Security system will be a mess by the year 2014.

As an anonymous economist once said, that and 15¢ cents will get you on the subway. (He said it in 1957, when the subway fare was 15¢.) What about applying economics to your everyday life?

Let's find out.

All Economics Is Local

Speaker of the House Tip O'Neil used to remind his colleagues that, "All politics is local." Well, all economics is local, too. By that, I mean that the broad economic policies and indicators that we've discussed have an impact on your region, state, city, industry, profession, and organization.

For instance, in fiscal year 2002, the federal government ran a budget deficit. This was mainly due to the recession of 2001 and the sluggish economy of 2002, both of which produced lower incomes and thus lower tax receipts. In fiscal year 2002, about two-thirds of the 50 states were also running deficits. As I noted previously, states have a more difficult time financing deficits than the federal government, because they must run balanced budgets. When states are running deficits, raising taxes will usually not make up the difference, so they must reduce some services. Moreover, higher state taxes discourage economic growth and anger voters. So service cuts are a more popular solution.

A number of states target higher education as an area for reduced spending when times get tough. Courses may be cut, even entire departments may be eliminated. Classes become larger, services are reduced, and salaries are frozen. Under these circumstances, might it make more sense for a student to work for a year or two, amass some savings, and start school after the budget crisis is over? If the quality of state schools will suffer, should the savings (along with some borrowings) be put into a private university education instead?

EconoTip

Over the past 20 years, media coverage of the economy and the business world has dramatically improved. Today, the Financial News Network on cable television carries nothing but business news. Coverage of the economic and business news on the networks has also expanded. As noted, scores of websites carry economic data, news, and analysis. All of this reflects growth in demand for this information.

Or suppose you were heavily invested in stocks when the market tanked in 2000. Suppose you planned to retire or reduce your working hours soon. Can you still do that? Can you shift your investments into, say, an apartment building in a growing city, so you can still reduce your working hours? Or must you wait until the market returns to a new high before you retire? If so, when might that high arrive?

Economic events impact everyone. They aren't just the stuff of magazine articles and presidential speeches. This means that everyone must understand how the national and even international economy affects his or her local and personal situations.

Rules of Thumb

The following sections introduce a few guidelines to help you think productively about economic trends and their effect on you.

The Laws of Economics Cannot Be Repealed

Among the more bizarre ideas floated during the 1990s boom was that a "new economy" had emerged, fueled by digital technologies. In this new economy, people worked with their brains instead of their hands, innovation trumped mass production, and concepts were more important than productive capital. People who believed this valued the stock of Yahoo and AOL more highly than that of IBM and General Motors.

I am not dismissing the value of innovation and ideas. But in any business, the economic realities—supply and demand, cyclicality, and the need to make and sell something profitably—inevitably assert themselves. In the 1990s, CEO and future New York mayor Michael Bloomberg, among others, wrote pieces pointing out these economic realities. (Economist Alan Greenspan issued his warning of "irrational exuberance" way back in December 1996.) Yet the herd mentality—sustained by the media and the public relations industry that feeds it—persisted until the laws of economics prevailed.

How did they prevail? Companies that had been investing in technology realized that they did not have unlimited funds to invest in technology. Soon thereafter, the tech stock bubble burst. The "I" in the prosaic C + I + G formula stopped growing, and the business cycle came to an end—as does every business cycle.

Expansions and Recessions Always End

The business cycle persists because human behavior in a market economy generates mismatches between supply and demand and savings and investment. While technological developments, population trends, and social phenomena can affect business cycles, they cannot eliminate them. They are embedded in the structure of market economies.

Fortunately, expansions generally last far longer than recessions. There were only two periods of extended economic malaise in the United States in the past century: the Great Depression of the 1930s and the Great Inflation of the 1970s. From 1929 through 2002, there were 12 recessions. The longest, by far, was the one that started in August 1929 and lasted through March 1933. This 43-month whopper kicked off the Great Depression, which included another severe 13-month contraction in 1937 and 1938. The rest of the 1930s featured periods of lackluster growth.

The other 10 recessions between 1929 and 2002 ranged from a mere six months to 16 months and averaged 11 months. That leaves a lot of room for expansion. In fact, in the years from 1939 through 2002, after the United States absorbed the lessons of the Great Depression, the nation experienced economic growth 86 percent of the time. Granted, some recoveries were stronger than others, but some of the recessions were mild as well.

The Real World

The Great Depression was so devastating that people, including those in government, actually learned from the experience. The major lessons were that the banking system and the financial markets cannot be left to themselves, and that the government should work to keep the economy stable and growing.

New regulation of the investment community and agencies such as the Securities and Exchange Commission helped to ensure more orderly securities markets. Federally insured bank deposits ended the periodic runs on banks that had often disrupted the economy. The government's use of fiscal and monetary policy to cushion the effects of the business cycle greatly improved the economic health of the nation in the past century—and the data prove it.

What does this pattern of business cycles mean to your wallet, purse, or piggy bank? It means that if you understand that a recession is cyclical and you believe the economic fundamentals are sound enough to support a renewed growth cycle, you can make moves that benefit you. I am not talking about trying to time the business cycle or the stock market's peaks and troughs. That is a fool's labor. I am saying that if the average recession lasts only 11 months, you can wait until the expansion is underway before making your move rather than trying to time it—but you shouldn't wait too long.

For example, if you buy a house, stock, or mutual fund two quarters into an economic expansion, you will still do pretty well. You'll certainly do better than you would by waiting two years to make sure that the expansion was underway. Similarly, if you understand that a recession will probably last no more than three to five quarters, you can make plans to ride it out in a clearer frame of mind than if you believe the next Great Depression has arrived.

Many Industries Have a Cyclical Element

Some businesses—financial services, advertising, real estate, construction, retail, restaurants, travel, and magazine publishing—are sensitive to recessions. Yet these businesses tend to do quite well in expansions, particularly in vigorous expansions.

Industries less affected by recessions, such as consumer packaged goods, food, beverages, tobacco, and gas, electric, and other utilities, are also less affected by expansions.

It is essential that you understand the relationship between your industry and the business cycle.

Separate Emotions from Economics

As you learned in Part 3, issues of economics can become emotionally charged. This often occurs by design. For instance, by playing on voters' emotions, politicians with economic agendas—on the right and the left—manipulate people who don't understand the economics of a situation. This lack of understanding extends to the voters' own stake in many issues, and politicians know it. So they appeal to voters' emotions when the economics don't argue for their policies.

This happens in business situations as well. We sometimes allow ourselves to be fooled—or fool ourselves—into ignoring economic realities in favor of emotions such as hope, pride, or trust. For example, when losses start to mount up, many investors cannot admit they invested incorrectly and simply sell the stock. Worse, many employees fail to understand that the employer-employee relationship is ruled by economics. It's easy for some employees to become emotionally attached to employers. These people find themselves shocked when they are permanently laid off or have their health insurance benefits reduced after "years of loyal service." I realize that some companies protect their employees, but they are in the minority.

> **The Real World**
>
> The people who emphasize the emotional aspects of a business arrangement—the people who say, "Trust me," instead of signing a contract—are usually the people who have the upper hand economically. In such situations, always insist on securing your economic interests, and on conducting business in a businesslike manner.

Impact of Economics on Business Decisions

In general, consider the following moves, particularly when your industry has a cyclical element:

◆ Expand your business during an economic expansion, but avoid buying or building based on the assumption that the recovery will last forever. Ask yourself, "What if a recession arrives in 12 months?" If you can finance the expansion through a downturn, proceed (with caution). If not, pull back a bit on your plans. Many companies could have avoided bankruptcy by basing their plans on conservative, rather than optimistic, assumptions.

◆ When a recession hits, don't wait too long before cutting your costs. Trying to keep people on board when you can't afford them may endanger the entire business.

◆ Borrow when interest rates are low, and, unless it's short-term, try to lock in the rate for the life of the loan.

EconoTip

Smart business people carefully monitor their customers' sales, changes in expenses, issues with employees, and areas such as debt levels and age of plant and equipment. Really smart business people also monitor their customers' customers in the same way. That's because if your customers are serving growing, financially sound customers, then you probably are, too. If they aren't, watch out.

◆ If you're an employee, realize that you may be vulnerable to layoffs and carefully manage your personal finances. Most people in advertising, for instance, understand the cyclical nature of the industry. They try to make themselves as valuable as they can so they minimize the chance of being laid off, but if it occurs, they don't take it (too) personally and they are prepared financially.

◆ If you want to enter a cyclical industry as an entrepreneur or employee, don't let its cyclical nature keep you out, even if you are trying to enter during a downturn. If the industry or company is a solid one, it will be around when the next expansion arrives.

Personal Business and Economics

Several concepts central to economics can enrich your life if you apply them to major personal decisions. I am not saying that every decision should be ruled by economic considerations. In fact, often the best way to generate a great financial outcome is to make the decision based on nonfinancial considerations. Choice of career is a good example. But often economic considerations don't receive the weight they deserve in a decision.

Education and Skills Training

Education is often called "an investment in yourself," and two concepts from economics clearly bear this out.

The first is the concept of human capital. Human capital enables an economy—or an individual—to produce more goods and services, and higher value goods and services. People increase their own human capital—their ability to produce more and higher value goods and services—by increasing their knowledge and skills through education and training.

The second concept is returns to education. As we discussed in Chapter 11, the returns to education are extremely high and, over an entire career, they really add up. Recent estimates state that high school graduates can expect to earn an average of $1.2 million over their working lives, but graduates of a four-year college will earn 75 percent more, an average of $2.1 million. That $900,000 difference represents a healthy return on the four years and $60,000 to $120,000 spent on tuition, books, room, and board.

Training also enables a person to make more money. The technical skills provided by training enable high school graduates to add more value and earn more income. They also give college graduates greater flexibility in the job market, particularly as emerging technologies demand new skills even of established workers.

Starting a Business

The option of starting a business as a career move appeals to more people than ever. This is partly a result of the demise of the social contract that existed between large companies and their employees from the 1940s through the 1970s. That contract stated that if an employee did his or her job well, the company would keep them on board and provide retirement benefits. That state of affairs unraveled in the 1980s and 1990s. Today, every employee is in a sense a freelancer who can be let go at any time. (In fairness to the companies, most employees will now readily leave for a better deal, too.)

Therefore, many people have set up shop for themselves. Women and minorities are starting businesses at a higher rate than white men. And more white men are starting businesses than ever, partly as a result of the *white collar recession* of 1992 and the continuing trend in management and professional layoffs.

From the economic standpoint, the individual starting a business must understand that being an entrepreneur differs from being an employee. Remember the role of the entrepreneur? It is to organize the factors of production, to take risks and develop new products and services to serve new needs (or old needs in new ways), and to make a profit. An entrepreneur needs a business plan, and needs to think like an owner, not an employee. This is true even for an entrepreneur in a one-person business.

Think in terms of supply and demand. Think about the market dynamics that affect your product or service. Think about ways of adding value to inputs, pricing of outputs, fixed versus variable costs, costs per unit, marginal cost per unit, and sources of profits above and beyond your salary. Few entrepreneurs think deeply about the economics of going into business, which is one reason that 90 percent of all businesses fail within five years.

EconoTalk

The term **white collar recession** arose in 1990 and 1991 to describe the lay-offs in the managerial and professional ranks that occurred in that downturn. Up to then, during recessions companies laid off hourly employees but kept managers and professionals on board. Hourly employees worked in production, and therefore were considered a variable expense. Managers as well as professionals in staff functions, such as planning, finance, and accounting, were considered a fixed expense.

But the white collar ranks swelled in the 1980s, as the baby boomers graduated and companies hired hordes of them in managerial and analytical jobs. When downturns hit or pressures to cut costs increased, they concluded that these workers were a variable expense.

Home Buying

I personally wouldn't move to an area just because it was growing rapidly or had good economic prospects, but I would avoid one with poor long-term economic prospects. A home is an investment, and a home in an area with poor long-term economic prospects will generally appreciate at a lower rate than one in a growing area.

Infrastructure is another important economic consideration in home buying. For instance, a home in a community known for superior schools is almost always a good investment. Other factors worth considering include business and job opportunities, accessible transportation, nearby universities, cultural and recreational opportunities, and, perhaps most important, the socioeconomic profile of the population.

I know a family who bought one of cheapest homes in one of the nicest communities on the north shore of Long Island (known as "the gold coast"). It cost a lot more than a larger home in a less prestigious community. However, they had an investment horizon of about seven to ten years on the house. They also wanted to enjoy life in the meantime, and felt that living in a higher-end community would enable them to do that. The husband also felt it would be better for his business.

"When I tell people I live in this town," he said, "they don't know whether I live in a $2 million mansion or over the pizza parlor."

Call him a geography snob, but he certainly made more on the house when he sold it than he would have had he purchased and then sold one in a lower-end community.

Quite simply, homes in "desirable" communities will usually appreciate faster and hold their value better when the real estate market softens.

Why?

Supply and demand is one reason. In any given region there are fewer "desirable" communities than there are average or lower-end communities. Another reason is that the demand for certain products actually increases as their price increases.

This phenomenon is called the *Veblen Effect*, for Thorsten Veblen, the American economist who identified it. The Veblen Effect states that demand for some products doesn't fall if the price rises. This runs counter to basic price theory and the law of supply and demand. On contemplating the situation, Veblen realized that high prices can create the perception of value.

I am not a real estate professional, so I am not dispensing professional advice here. But I am saying that before going to open houses and making an offer on a condo or house, consider the larger economic aspects of the decision.

EconoTalk

The **Veblen Effect** explains the fact that demand for some products doesn't fall, and may even rise, if the price is increased. In such cases, the buyer associates the higher price with higher quality and is willing to pay more for that level of quality in that product category. Luxury goods, such as Louis Vuitton luggage made of vinyl (okay, heavy vinyl), are priced with the Veblen Effect in mind.

Borrowing and Investing

In many ways, the United States truly is a "culture of debt." I say this not just because consumers and the government are carrying so much debt relative to their incomes and revenues, but because of what the debt is financing. In general, businesses use debt more wisely than consumers and the government.

What is debt financing in the United States? Mortgage debt is financing the purchase of homes. That's a good use of debt. A home is a long-term asset, and thus it should be financed with long-term debt. Even an auto loan makes sense because the loan is paid off over the life of the car. You use the home or the car as you pay it off.

Consider the difference when you finance a vacation, a lavish restaurant meal, or tickets to a Broadway play on a credit card. If you pay the total amount of the debt off when the credit card statement arrives, that's wonderful. Your interest expense will be minimal, even zero on some cards. But if you take months or years to pay off that vacation, meal, or play, you are not matching the term of the debt to the life of the "asset" being financed. You are paying for an asset (to use the term loosely) that you have long since consumed.

Here's the worst part: You're paying an interest rate of two to three times the rate for a mortgage or auto loan. Consider the cruel irony of paying a higher rate for what is supposed to be a short-term loan. The economics are so unfavorable that credit card debt is to consumers' financial health as cigarette smoking is to their physical health—it's deadly.

The Real World
The interest paid on a home mortgage is tax deductible, so is interest paid on a home equity loan. Until the Tax Reform Act of 1986, those who itemized their deductions could deduct interest on credit card debt and other consumer loans from a household's income. Ending the tax deductibility of interest payments on these borrowings raised their cost considerably, but that has done little to deter consumers from using them.

So rule number one is to match the term of a loan to the life of the asset being financed—and understand that a restaurant meal is not an asset. Pay for services with cash and checks (or pay off the monthly credit-card balance) and borrow only to finance long-term assets. These include houses and autos, and items such as major appliances and computers.

Rule number two is to obtain the best interest rate possible. The interest a household pays on a loan tends to be largely unrelated to its creditworthiness. If you qualify for a loan at a given lender, you will pay a rate very similar to that which other borrowers pay that lender, even if you have a better credit record. Consumer credit is a numbers game, and the lenders have limited time and operational resources for considering subtle differences among their borrowers, particularly if they'll earn a lower interest rate on the loan as a result.

That's why timing and the type of loan are the keys to getting a low rate. Timing means making major purchases during a recession if possible. Interest rates will be low and, as an added bonus, you may be able to negotiate a better price because the general demand for the product you are buying—house, car, or washing machine—is relatively low.

If you buy and borrow at the height of the market for *anything*, you will pay more than you would if you were to buy when demand is low. This is most dramatically evident when it comes to investing in financial assets.

Investing Economically

The legendary fund manager Peter Lynch said, "If you spend 13 minutes a year on economics, you've wasted 10 minutes." That's easy for him to say. He was a full-time money manager who focused intensely on the management, business, and financials of the companies he invested in. Average investors, however, might do well to apply a bit of economics to their buy-and-sell decisions. All the Wall Street investment banks and large commercial banks employ economists, and they have all heard Mr. Lynch's comment.

Even if Peter Lynch is right, I want you to get the most you can out of the three minutes that he feels weren't wasted. (I am not offering investment advice here, but rather perspectives on investing with some principles of economics in mind.)

First, watch out for companies with heavy debt loads, especially if the debt was used to finance assets, such as acquisitions, that have not proven to be profitable. If the debt payments are not being financed by the assets that were acquired—with some left over for profits—then the company's profits may erode. (I say "may" because other divisions of the company may be profitable enough to offset the effects of the bad acquisition.)

EconoTip

For information on companies that you may want to invest in, access the company's website. Also be sure to check out their financial statements, specifically the annual report issued by the company, which you can usually request from the company by telephone or e-mail. The 10-k report, filed with the SEC by publicly traded companies, provides similar information, but in greater depth.

Second, if you invest in bonds, you *must* understand the yield curve and the workings of the bond markets in relation to both the stock market and the interest rate environment. In general, bond prices fall as stock prices rise, and vice versa. This occurs because money moves out of stocks and into bonds, or out of bonds and into stocks, depending on the relative strength of each market.

Also, when bond prices rise, interest rates fall, and when bond prices fall, interest rates rise. In that way, the selling price of the bond is adjusted by the market to reflect the yield that the bond should be earning in the prevailing interest rate environment. For instance, if a $10,000 bond pays interest at 5 percent, that means that the holder of the bond is paid $500 a year. If the price of the bond rises to $11,000, the yield falls to about 4.5 percent, which equals $500 divided by $11,000. Similarly, if the price of the bond falls to $9,000, then the yield rises to about 5.6 percent, which equals $500 divided by $9,000. The company that issued the bond always pays the same amount. The yield that the amount represents, however, depends on the price the holder paid for the bond.

Third, for any investment, you must understand your investment horizon and the risks to the economy and to the financial markets over that horizon. For example, one scary thought is the potential effect on stock prices if millions of baby boomers liquidate their portfolios from 2015 to 2025. Baby-boomer money pouring into mutual funds did a lot to fuel the 1990s bull market. Could withdrawal of those funds fuel a bear market in the 2020s?

Finally, while it's good to understand where you are in the business cycle and to buy during stock market troughs and economic recessions, I emphasize that trying to time the peaks and troughs is generally judged to be a waste of time, or worse. Even professional money managers have a very poor record at it.

EconoTip

Dollar cost averaging is a sensible alternative to trying to time stock market peaks and troughs. Dollar cost averaging calls for picking several stocks or mutual funds that you believe in as long-term investments, and investing a fixed amount of money in them regularly, say every month or every quarter, regardless of where the market or the securities are in their cycle.

This way, you buy more shares when the price of the stock or fund is low than when it is high. The average cost of the stock or fund will be lower than if you purchased a fixed number of shares every month or quarter. This technique is also called the constant dollar plan.

The best long-term investment strategy is to understand the amount of risk that you can accept, and then to choose securities or mutual funds that reflect that risk and that will perform at least as well as the economy as it continues its long-term growth trajectory. (This doesn't mean that you can't set 10 percent of your portfolio aside for "flyers" on riskier investments.)

Economics and Citizenship: Understanding the Issues

Economics may come in handiest when trying to understand what politicians are saying—and not saying. The awful truth, which almost no politician will utter, is that goods, services, or transfer payments from the government must be paid for with tax revenues, and that individual taxpayers are the major source of those revenues.

So when a candidate or an official says that she can improve education without increasing taxes or reducing other government services, you will know that it can't be done. If he says that there should be a tax cut because there's a budget surplus, and that surplus is "the people's money," you will know that the $6 trillion national debt is also "the people's debt." Lack of knowledge of economics is arguably causing as much difficulty for the American electorate as lack of knowledge of history, and the two are extremely intertwined.

The Real World

Partisan economists, almost all of whom are paid for their "objective analysis," can always find an argument in favor of their party's program. They simply omit or distort the downside of that program.

On the other hand, academic economists who have no ideology or political paymasters are often unsure of what to do. They understand that every economic policy decision will create winners and losers. They understand that value judgments and power plays often dictate who will be the winners and losers. Therefore they often limit themselves to pointing out the effects—both positive and negative—of policy decisions (as I have tried to do in this book).

Most issues in government today revolve around economic realities, and the more in touch with those realities we are, the better we can decide where we want to go as a nation and what we are willing to pay to get there.

The Least You Need to Know

◆ The business cycle is a permanent fixture of a market economy because people are free to make their own production and purchasing decisions. Sooner or later those decisions create a mismatch between supply and demand and savings and investment.

◆ Attempting to time the peak or trough of the business cycle or the stock market consistently is impossible. Sophisticated economists in government and the investment community, armed with the best analytical tools, cannot do it.

◆ In any situation involving money, keep emotional considerations separate from economic considerations.

◆ When borrowing money, match the term of the loan to the life of the asset being purchased and obtain the best possible interest rate. This means not using credit cards, unless you pay the full balance each month, and always paying for services with cash or a check.

◆ Bond prices fall as stock prices rise, and vice versa, because money moves out of stocks and into bonds, or out of bonds and into stocks, depending on the relative strength of each market.

◆ Education and training builds human capital, for individuals as well as for nations. They also yield high returns in dollars, as well as in the quality of life for an individual or a nation.

Resources for the Economically Inclined

Associations

American Agricultural Economics Association
www.aaea.org

American Economic Association
www.vanderbilt.edu/AEA/org/htm

The American Real Estate & Urban Economics Association
www.areuea.org

Canadian Association for Business Economics
www.cabe.ca

International Health Economics Association
www.healtheconomics.org

National Association for Business Economics
www.nabe.com

Government Agencies

Bureau of Economic Analysis
www.bea.gov

Bureau of Labor Statistics
www.bls.gov

European Union
www.europa.eu.int

Federal Reserve System
www.federalreserve.gov

U.S. Agency for International Development (Information Center)
www.usaid.gov

U.S. Census Bureau
www.census.gov

U.S. Department of Commerce
www.commerce.gov

U.S. Department of Labor
www.dol.gov

U.S. Department of the Treasury
www.ustreas.gov

World Bank
www.worldbank.org

World Trade Organization
www.wto.org

Economic Information Companies

The Conference Board
www.conference-board.org

Economy.com, Inc.
www.economy.com (or www.freelunch.com)

Global Insight, Inc.
www.globalinsight.com

Books

Capitalism and Freedom by Milton Friedman (University of Chicago Press; 40th Anniversary edition, 2002).

Economics by Paul A. Samuelson & William D. Nordhaus (McGraw-Hill, 16th ed., 1998).

Economics by Michael Parkin (Addison-Wesley, 2nd ed., 1993).

Economics: A Self-Teaching Guide by Stephen L. Slavin (Wiley & Sons, 1988).

Cliffs Quick Review: Economics by John Duffy (Cliffs Notes, 1993).

Economics Explained by Robert L. Heilbroner and Lester C. Thurow (Touchstone Books/Simon & Schuster; revised edition, 1998).

Economics in One Lesson by Henry Hazlitt (University of Chicago Press, 40th Anniversary edition, 2002).

The Economist Guide to Economic Indicators by the staff of *The Economist* magazine (Wiley & Sons, 1998).

Naked Economics: Undressing the Dismal Science by Charles J. Wheelan (W.W. Norton & Company, 2002).

The Worldly Philosophers: The Lives, Times, and Ideas of the Great Economic Thinkers by Robert L. Heilbroner (Touchstone/Simon & Schuster, 7th ed., 1999).

Index

P

packing and shipping regulations (nontariff barrier to
international trade), 258
Pareto Principle. *See* 80-20
Rule
partisan economists, 321
Patent and Trademark Office,
191
payroll taxes, as government
revenue, 185
People's Republic of China,
281
percentages
  as pitfall to interpreting
  financial data, 44-45
  percentage of income, determining degree of elasticity
  of demand, 76-77
perfect inelasticity, 74
peril-point tariffs, as barrier to
international trade, 257
periods of negative growth
(business cycle), 150
personal business and economics, 314-321
  borrowing and investing,
  317-318
  citizenship, 320-321
  economical investing,
  318-320
  education and skills training,
  314-315
  home buying, 316-317
  starting a business, 315-316
petrodollars, 270
policies, exchange rates,
271-273
population growth
  as factor driving consumer
  spending, 21-22
  changing demand, 50-51
positive net exports, 28
positive relationships (chart
curve functions), 38
positive yield curves, 302

poverty, 166
  consumer debt, 176-177
  government's role, 174-175
  income inequality, 166-171
  inflation, 177
  quality of life, 177-178
  social systems, 166-167
  spending patterns, 175-176
  threshold, 81
PPI (producer price index),
154, 298
predictions of behavior, 5-6
President's Council of
Economic Advisors, 192
prices
  as driver of demand for
  money, 215
  demand schedule, 49-50
  elasticity of demand, 68-77
  gold, as financial market
  indicator, 305
  goods and services, changing
  demand, 51-52
  interventions, 77-83
  perception of future prices,
  53, 59
  price ceiling, 80
  price floor, 80
  price mechanism, 8
  price wars, 127
  price-fixing, 132
  utility, 92-93
pricing strategies of businesses,
126-127
producer price index. *See* PPI
product standards (nontariff
barrier to international trade),
258
production
  classifications, global economy, 282-285
  complements in production,
  changing supply, 59
  factors of production, 104
  substitutes in production,
  changing supply, 58
profit, 104

progressive income tax, government's role in addressing
poverty, 174
propensity to spend and save,
fiscal policy, 201
protectionism, 28
protective service workers, 138
public assistance programs,
government's role in addressing poverty, 174
public goods, 11
  government's role in economy, 180-181
purchase agreements. *See* RPs
purchasing a home, personal
business and economics,
316-317

Q–R

quality of life, examining
wealth and poverty, 177-178
quantities, demand schedule,
49-50
quintile classifications, global
economy, 285-286
  measuring income inequality, 167-170
quotas, as barrier to international trade, 257

rallied dollars, 264
rate of return on investments,
business investments, 25
reading charts (economic data),
36-43
reading tables (economic data),
32-36
real dollars versus nominal dollars, 33-35
real interest rates, 243
recessions (business cycle),
150-151
  initiation of recessions,
  155-157
  white collar recession, 316
record, Federal Reserve,
243-244